LIVING ENGLISH

Thinking Speaking Writing

Contemporary Issues and Essay Writing

D0682506

... other language books from ELM ...

Enjeux, Débats, Expression:
Contemporay issues and essay writing in French
Madeleine Le Cunff-Renouard and Dolorès Ditner
A *unique* combination of information on current issues in
French society with learning strategies
at first year degree level.

isbn 1 94613 912 1

Japanese for business communication:
beginner's level
Nakagawa and Takako Takekoshi
Workbook and accompanying two-sided audio cassette.
Familiar business and social situations develop a knowledge of
the language and culture. Fifteen graded lessons.

isbn 1 85450 010 4

Tutor's Manual of exercises, notes and materials
to accompany the above book

isbn 1 85450 030 9

LIVING ENGLISH

Thinking Speaking Writing

Contemporary Issues and Essay Writing

Madeleine Le Cunff-Renouard
Dolorès Ditner
Bronwen Martin

ELM Publications

© Copyright Madeleine Le Cunff-Renouard, Dolorès Ditner and Bronwen Martin - March, 1993

This first edition of **Living English** is published October, 1993 by ELM Publications, Seaton House, Kings Ripton, Huntingdon, PE17 2NJ. (Tel.04873-254 or 04873-238 Fax 04873-359).

All rights are reserved. No part of this publication may be copied, photocopied, reproduced by means manual, mechanical or electronic, stored in an information retrieval or other electronic system, broadcast by radio or television or reissued in any form or format without the prior, written permission of the Publisher (ELM Publications), as administrators of the copyright on behalf of the author.

If you wish to copy any part of this book, you must apply in writing to ELM Publications and pay a licence fee to do so.

Printed by St Edmundsbury Press, Bury St Edmunds, Suffolk, England. Bound by Woolnough Bookbinding, Express Works, Church Street, Irthlingborough, Northants, England.

ISBN 1 85450 085 6

British Library Cataloguing-in-Publication Data. A catalogue record for this publication is available from The British Library.

TABLE OF CONTENTS

Acknowledgements   *vii*
About the authors   *ix*
Mission Statement   *xi*

Chapter   **Page**

1   How to approach essay writing and debating 1

2   Getting in the right frame of mind 8

3   Collecting your thoughts 56

4   What do *I* think? 76

5   What does it mean? 92

6   For or against? 111

7   Yes, but 139

8   How to draw up a draft plan 157

9   Choosing the right words and expressions 191

10   How to begin? 221

11   To conclude 237

12   On the other hand 244

Appendix 1: Suggested answers 283
Appendix 2: Sources and notes 286
Mini dictionary 293
Bibliography 312
List of publishers 318
Index 321

Acknowledgements

The authors wish to thank all the newspapers listed in Appendix 2 for their cooperation.

Special thanks to Esther Chandré, Tina Dickson and Dr Stephen Instone for their most valuable help.

The cover illustration is by M. Le Cunff-Renouard.

About the authors

Madeleine LE CUNFF-RENOUARD is Senior Lecturer in the French Department of Birkbeck College (University of London).

Dolorès DITNER is Director of the Language Centre of University College (University of London).

Bronwen MARTIN is a part-time lecturer in French at Middlesex University and also teaches in the Extra-mural Department of Birkbeck College.

Mission Statement

'To let no day pass without exchanging views and critically examining assumptions is the key to success'.

Socrates

Chapter 1

How to approach essay writing and debating

* WHOM IS THE BOOK AIMED AT?

This book is a guide for advanced students of English. It is designed for those in their final years of secondary education, College and University undergraduates, as well as for civil servants, people in business, and the like, who have to:

- understand a discussion/debate

- make a point in English

- write an essay or analytical report requiring logical and coherent use of data

* HOW DOES IT CATER FOR SUCH A HETEROGENEOUS PUBLIC?

We adopt a 'graded objectives' approach presented through a wide range of topics:

- material has been carefully selected to meet the needs of students from various backgrounds.

- the strategies and learning devices encompass role-playing exercises and the rigorous intellectual exploration of some issues.

- the proficiency in English expected from the reader varies, according to the type of activities presented and the goals that each reader wants or has to achieve.

In order to give you open access to the book, we have designed it to be used either from beginning to end, or selectively, according to need, so that you can work through chapters of particular interest to you.

* WHAT ARE ITS MAIN CHARACTERISTICS?

- It presents a variety of viewpoints on some of the most important social and political issues today.

- It challenges the notion that oral and written work should be approached separately.

- It offers active tasks to the reader, speaker or writer.

- It, therefore, encourages you to assess your own perception or analysis of various issues.

- It stresses the importance of the process of thinking and analysing in a foreign language. High priority is given to communicative skills and many activities in the book are suitable for two learners.

- Its approach acknowledges that the learning process varies in tempo, mode, and method from one individual to another. These differences have been catered for in its design.

* WHAT ARE ITS OBJECTIVES?

The exercises and the questioning of ideas and values that we propose, would be meaningless if not done in a context of intellectual freedom. We therefore encourage:

- creative thinking

- critical awareness

- the right to question and analyse different opinions, sets of beliefs, values and attitudes.

Our main objective is to improve your proficiency in English. The book is also a guide on how to organise your thoughts and ideas. It acknowledges the fact that a debate or an essay is a game with rules; it is a ritual and, as such, a set of conventions.

The book emphasises the fact that competence, the ability to play this sort of 'game', is improved with practice; it is only if you train yourself to see oppositions that you will be able to work on them:

i.e.:
positive	negative
more	less
good	bad
true	false
unity	multiplicity
uniformity	diversity
material	spiritual
funny	sad
light	heavy
white	black
rich	poor
dependence	independence
individual	mass
quantity	quality
ease	effort

The more you allow yourself to play with words, the more you understand the way a text is articulated, the more you will realise how meaning is produced.

Our approach attempts to awaken your interest in recognising logical relations in an essay title as in any other text. These relationships, be they of implication, opposition, contradiction or exclusion, are very rarely obvious. First of all, we encourage you to analyse relationships, 'links' between ideas, statements and attitudes.

The structure of your essay, that is to say your argumentative strategy, should therefore be based on this analysis.

We must also stress that both debating and essay writing are based on the assumption that there is (somewhere, somehow) a listener and/or reader, real or implied, who will be prevented from understanding the argument if s/he is not pointed in the right direction by certain 'signposts', and shown the links and relationships established between them.

3

* STUDENTS' REACTIONS TO WRITING AN ESSAY

The following questions are, in our experience, the most commonly expressed by students, and in this order:

1. **"How do I choose a subject?"**

   Which question do I really think I can answer well?
   Which question do I know the most about?
   How do I know that I understand the subject correctly?
   Is it better to choose a subject that I am familiar with, and perhaps use examples that I have used before, or to choose something fresh and stimulating?

2. **"How do I find ideas?"**

   How should I organise them?
   How can I draw arguments to a conclusion (without reaching a certain point and getting stuck)?
   What am I going to do if I run out of steam?
   How can I find suitable examples to illustrate the thesis formulated?
   How do I eliminate irrelevant ideas/arguments?
   How can I avoid clichés?

3. **"How do I write correctly?"**
   "How do I express my ideas correctly?"

   Do I know enough vocabulary associated with the question to be able to answer it?
   Can I express what I have to say in a clear, harmonious way in English?
   How can I avoid repeating the same construction?

The present book is in fact structured to answer these questions:

- First it helps you to select an appropriate topic from a list.
  You are invited to read a large number of English texts and to do various brain-storming exercises. These are best done in pairs;

4

the process is more fun. It is challenging and that's what an essay is about.

- It then suggests different ways of exploring questions and topics, that is to say, helping you to find ideas and analysing them (yours and other people's).

- Finally, and only at this last stage, do we give useful expressions and constructions for writing an essay.

You are also concerned with the assessment of your work and although it is obviously impossible to take into account all policies, strategies, guidelines, expectations and standards in use in all institutions, it is, in our view, reasonable to say that there is a consensus about what a good essay or brief should be.

In assessing an essay, examiners look for:

- A coherent discussion of the points at issue in the subject.

- A correct way of presenting thoughts and ideas in English.

- Good communication skills, including the ability to make a point convincingly, to present your case in a logical manner, and to explore several aspects of a question, supporting each one with relevant examples.

- Accuracy in English.

A general essay is not judged on the quantity of facts, or the amount of information presented, but rather on the choice and the use made by the writer of the data available. It should also be stressed that nobody (however competent), has ever produced a detailed analysis on a particular issue in one, two or three hours!

The time scale of the exercise is in fact crucial as it determines the length and shape of the output, and demands an unavoidable selection of the data. This means, in practical terms, that you should:

- Train to mobilise stored knowledge quickly.

- Be capable of playing with words and ideas, exploring various ways of seeing a particular issue and of tackling the question by defining a word, making a statement, defending it, attacking it, finding examples for and against ...

- Arrive at a coherent and plausible presentation of your ideas and material.

- Write fairly complex sentences in order to be able to express what you want to say in your argument, which should lead to a conclusion to the debate, however provisional, modest or limited.

How then can you produce a meaningful text or argument in English? At first the task might seem ambitious, daunting, but it's rather like a game of tennis, or chess, in which each move is calculated, your opponent's reactions anticipated, your feet or your pieces placed strategically ... and hopefully winning! Thus the challenge makes you think about what you yourself and other people think!

Furthermore, we emphasise that writing an essay involves making a choice, as in everyday life:
e.g.- voting, selecting a hobby, a TV programme or a book
- assessing a film or a political broadcast
- defending a point of view
- making a case
- challenging a view held by others
- explaining one's choices etc.

In other words, writing an essay is a matter of entering into a debate where nothing can be taken for granted, where even what is called 'common sense' should be questioned.

To argue that only docile students have to be taught how to write essays is in our view a fallacy, and our aim in publishing this book is to encourage all students to develop their communicative and analytical skills, or to acquire them.

So as to set off on the right footing, and enjoy yourself in the process, imagine that you're talking to a friend, in a sustained and fairly analytical conversation. Try to:

1. Explain what you mean.
2. Understand what your friend is saying.
3. Convince your friend of your point of view.
4. See your friend's point of view.
5. Go beyond: that's right/wrong true/untrue
   i.e.: **explain** by using examples
6. Recapitulate your thoughts from time to time and attempt to come to a conclusion.

To enable you to move on from the analytical conversational stage and to put pen to paper, we have provided you with:

- a selection of texts and topics which raise important issues today.
- a variety of exercises which allow you to:
  recognise the key issues
  conduct a debate
  improve your powers of expression.

Chapter 2

Getting into the right frame of mind

This chapter aims at putting you in the right frame of mind to tackle an essay, and to show you that it's not such a daunting task after all.

If you go through all the exercises you will have the opportunity to:

- read a selection of texts and articles on different topics (about the Third World, business, urban violence, literature etc.).

- test and increase your range of vocabulary in certain areas.

- express your ideas on particular issues (eg. racial discrimination, the role of the media, women in society, etc.).

- discuss your views with others on various topics.

- write short statements and passages on these subjects.

It should also encourage you to go on playing with ideas and words and make you feel more at ease in English.

Throughout the book you'll be invited to perform 'active tasks' - Thus the emphasis will be on:

- interactive activities and games, involving communicating with someone else.

- fluency activities, including discussion, role-play and scope for ceativity.

- exchanges on meaning and values rather than on surface structures.

It may be a good idea to ask yourself:

Who is the sender (of the message)?

Who is the target (the intended receiver)?

What is the message (what is being said or sold!)?

The stimuli used are drawn from 'authentic' pieces/moments of social communication.

And, last but not least, a wide definition of 'Culture' underlines our book (this includes trade and industry as well as politics, aesthetics, etc.).

Repetition

You'll find a certain amount of repetition in the book (the same 'ideas' expressed in different ways; issues discussed from various angles again and again).

This has been done on purpose as it will help you to acquire more flexibility in English and to concentrate on key issues.

* WELL-BEING MEANS NEVER FEELING DEPENDENT ON YOUR CHILDREN

Read the following advertisement carefully:

WELL-BEING MEANS NEVER FEELING DEPENDENT ON YOUR CHILDREN

There's no other insurance available quite like Commercial Union's Well-being Insurance.

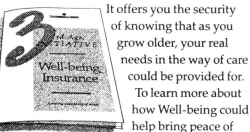

It offers you the security of knowing that as you grow older, your real needs in the way of care could be provided for. To learn more about how Well-being could help bring peace of mind, contact your usual financial adviser, return the coupon below or call the Well-being 'hotline' on **0800 100 155.**

Well-being Insurance
Assuring your peace of mind.

Please complete in block capitals and send to **CU 3rd Age Initiative, FREEPOST (BS4335), Bristol, BS1 3YX** or phone **0800 100 155** to arrange for us to contact you with further details of Well-being Insurance.

'I'd like to know more about assuring my peace of mind; please send me details of how Well-being Insurance can help me'.

Please print in BLOCK CAPITALS

Name Mr/Mrs/Miss/Ms _____

Address _____

_____ Postcode _____

Telephone: (Daytime) _____

      (Evening) _____ BSS1B

Date of birth _____

C_U
COMMERCIAL UNION

Commercial Union Life Assurance Company Limited. Registered in England No. 79678. Registered Office: St. Helen's, 1 Undershaft, London EC3P 3DQ. A member of Lautro and of the Insurance Ombudsman Bureau. 3rd Age Initiative and Well-being Insurance are Service Marks of Commercial Union Assurance Company plc.

What are, in your view, the various messages implied in the title of this advertisement? Select your answers from the following list:

1. Autonomy is the ultimate objective.
2. Everyone needs security.
3. Love is irrelevant.
4. Family values are old-fashioned.
5. Good insurance cover should be planned as early as possible in life.

Discuss your choice with someone else.

* **WHICH WORD(S) WOULD YOU ELIMINATE IN THE FOLLOWING STATEMENTS TO MAKE THEM PLAUSIBLE AND CORRECT (LINGUISTICALLY)?**

1. Nowadays, universities and hospitals **have to/dream of** become business enterprises.

2. As soon as they possess credit cards and a monthly mortgage, people become **amusing/conservative**.

3. Tax **fraud/pay** is widespread.

4. In recent years, the British hotel industry has considerably **reduced/improved**.

5. Skiing is still **a luxury sport/reserved for men**.

6. Politics has become a **poem/theatrical show**.

7. All forms of **pleasure/censorship** are unacceptable.

8. The rise of the extreme right is a very disturbing **phenomenon/game** in a democracy.

9. Graffiti are an **idea/art form**.

10. Luxury is a **bet/necessity**.

Discuss your choice with someone else.
(Suggested answers in Appendix 1)

* **SELECT A WORD FROM THE FOLLOWING LIST, WHICH YOU WOULD USE TO COMPLETE THE FOLLOWING STATEMENTS:**

proposals   subject   freedom   issues   carried out
research   limit   quality

1. The concluding paragraph suggests further areas of .... [1]

2. When discussing the question of .... [2] of expression, the Committee will refer to the .... [3] that were recently made to the governors.

3. On the .... [4] of research, the document stresses that its financing will raise important .... [5].

4. There is a .... [6] beyond which .... [7] is sacrificed.

5. The report refers to the study that was recently .... [8] on the efficiency of management.

(Suggested answers in Appendix 1)

* **WHICH TEN OF THE FOLLOWING WORDS AND EXPRESSIONS WOULD YOU FIND MOST USEFUL IN WRITING AN ESSAY ON THE FOLLOWING TOPICS?**

1. **Most modern societies are multiracial but relations between the different ethnic groups are often difficult.**

power	ceremonies
social inequality	habits
harassment	problems
victimisation	educational system
rejection	poverty
ghetto	overpopulation
exclusion	the rulers
traditions	the governed

way of life	the privileged few
integration	tensions
adoption	conflicts
domination	exploitation
inheritance	colonisation
justice	intolerance
equality	revolution
poverty	will
dignity	culture
tolerance	brotherhood
co-existence	respect for others
right to be different	authoritarianism
understanding	lack of understanding
cross-breeding	skin colour
cultural identity	autonomy
hatred	fear

2. Computers cannot solve every problem.

decision-making powers	utopian
imagination	tool
creativity	machine
unemployment	auxiliary
excesses	appendage
efficiency	obstacle
competence	toy
performance	saving
profitability	hobby
contemporary society	relaxation
precision technology	squandering
labour force	risk
dehumanisation	danger
automation	gadget
bureaucracy	measure
modernisation	decision
change	factor

rationalisation	criteria
market	disaster
communication	surplus
distribution	lack
production	consequence
marketing	cause
sign	result
resistance	sector
adaptation	field
reorganisation	characteristic
maladjustment	illusion

3. Everyone is aggressive but few people recognise this.

relief	strong
repression	weak
quality	pleasant
defect	unpleasant
character trait	positive
hatred	conflict
unrecognised	drama
praised	regulation
useful	control
useless	drive
encouraged	use
repressed	manipulation
primitive	archaism
worrying	authority
harmful	constraint
liberated	authority
concern	law
dangerous	human nature
calm	aggression
irascible	impulse

Compare and discuss your selection with someone else.

I		II	
1.	Marriage is an	a)	indefinable
2.	Beauty is	b)	to be deplored
3.	Poverty is	c)	outmoded institution
4.	The modern theatre is too	d)	dull
5.	Life in the country is often	e)	free
6.	The influence of communism is declining throughout the	f)	intellectual
7.	Text books should be	g)	world
8.	Our top priority must be to interest children in	h)	passive
9.	Computers encourage people to be	i)	reading
10.	Research funds should be	j)	butter?
11.	Why is Europe producing tonnes of	k)	politicians
12.	We are frequently being misinformed by	l)	increased

Compare your choice with someone else.
(Suggested answers in Appendix 1)

* WE'RE HERE TO MAKE LIFE EASIER

Read the following advertisement:

15

Get hold of it
if you want to make a go of it.

Starting a business is never easy. Before you set out, you have to plan every aspect.

That's why you'll find our new guide invaluable.

It covers everything from thinking and talking about it, to legalities and many of the problems you might face once you're up and running.

Last year, NatWest Small Business Advisers helped over 150,000 people set up in business. Which is more than any other High Street bank.

If you'd like to join them this year, make sure you get a free copy of "The Business Start-Up Guide".

Simply call us on 0800 777 888, return the coupon, or better still, call in and see your nearest NatWest Small Business Adviser.

🐿 National Westminster Bank
We're here to make life easier

National Westminster Bank Plc, Registered Office. 41 Lothbury, London EC2P 2BP. Member of IMRO.

Imagine you are about to start a small business. What 10 questions would you ask your bank?

Discuss your questions with someone else and select the five that you consider the most appropriate.

* SHE CAN'T EAT, SHE CAN'T SLEEP, SHE'S STOPPED WANTING TO CARE

Read this advertisement carefully:

Charter Nightingale Hospital, 11–19 Lisson Grove, NW1 6SH. Telephone: 071–258 3828. Charter Clinic Chelsea, 1–5 Radnor Walk, SW3 4PB. Telephone: 071–351 1272.

When someone loses interest in practically everything... their work, their friends, their family... and they feel like they are standing on the side-lines of life; depression could be the reason.

Depression can hit anybody... even the people who appear to have everything going for them; good looks, wealth, a great career. At least, that's how it appears to the people on the outside.

People suffering from depression seem to live in another world. Often family and friends, even the person who is suffering, think they'll snap out of it eventually. Unfortunately, that's almost never the case and unless you've actually suffered from depression yourself, you may never understand how overpowering it can be.

Over the years, the Charter Clinic Chelsea and Charter Nightingale Hospital have helped many people suffering from depression in a caring, discreet, and above all confidential, setting.

If you recognise yourself or someone you care about, Charter Hospitals offer a 24-hour Help Line and a free initial appointment service to help you talk through a problem and decide what your next step should be. Calling Charter Hospitals could give you or someone you care for a new lease of life.

The treatment offered is covered by most of the major medical insurance companies. If you don't get help at Charter Hospitals, please, get help somewhere.

What are, in your view, the main causes of depression? Rearrange the following list in order of importance:

war
unemployment
educational background
repressed feelings
personal relationships
violence
illness
urban life
political climate
psychological make-up
lack of energy
parenthood
stress
laziness
sexual inadequacy
ugliness

Compare and discuss your list with someone else.

Which of the following groups is, in your view, more likely to suffer from depression?

women - ethnic minorities - old people - children - the unemployed - celebrities - politicians - doctors.

Discuss your choice with someone else.

* **DEBTS OF HONOUR**

Read the speech below:

Other voices

AN IMPORTANT biological species is at risk of disappearing due to the fast and progressive removal of its natural habitat: Man.

We are becoming aware of this only now when it is almost too late to prevent it. The main responsibility for the destruction of the environment lies with the consumer societies. They are offsprings of the old colonial metropolises and of imperialist policies that also engendered the poverty and backwardness which are today the scourge of the overwhelming majority of mankind.

Although they comprise only 20 per cent of the population they consume two thirds of the metals and three fourths of the energy produced the world over.

They have poisoned oceans and rivers and contaminated the air; they have weakened and opened holes in the ozone layer and saturated the atmosphere with gases that impair climatic conditions with catastrophic effects that we are beginning to suffer.

Forests disappear, deserts grow, thousands of millions of tons of fertile soil end up in the oceans every year. Numerous species face extinction. Overpopulation and poverty lead to desperate efforts for survival even at the expense of Nature.

It is not possible to blame this on the Third World nations, which were only colonies yesterday and which today are still despoiled and plundered by an unjust world economic order.

The solution cannot be to check the development of those that need it most. Everything that today contributes to underdevelopment and poverty constitutes a flagrant violation of the ecology. As a consequence, tens of millions of men, women and children die every year in the Third World, far more than in the two world wars.

The unequal terms of reference, protectionism and the foreign debt are also an assault on the ecology and facilitate the destruction of the environment.

A better distribution of the wealth and technologies available in the world would be necessary to spare humanity such destruction. Less luxury and *wasteage in a few countries would amount to less poverty and hunger in a large part of Earth. Transfer to the Third World of lifestyles and consumer habits which ruin the environment has to be avoided.

Let human life be more rational. Let a just economic order be implemented. Let science work toward a sustainable development without contamination. The ecological debt should be paid and not the foreign debt. Hunger should be done away with, not Man.

When the assumed threats of communism no longer exist and there are no pretexts for cold wars, arms races and military expenditures, what is it that prevents the immediate use of these resources to foster development in the Third World and to avert the threat of the planet's ecological destruction?

Let this be the end of selfishness and hegemonism; the end of callousness, irresponsibility and deceit. Tomorrow it will be too late to do what should have been done a long time ago.

Fidel Castro was the best received - and least long-winded - leader at Rio, This is his speech.

* wastage

19

- Why does Fidel Castro consider the world economic order unjust?

- What does he think should be done to save our planet from destruction?

- Do you agree with the views presented here? If not, why?

* **PROFESSOR: CARE IN COMMUNITY CAN BE SUCCESS**

Read the following article:

Professor: Care in community can be success

CARE in the community for long-term psychiatric patients does work when well-planned and properly funded, but more needs to be done for the homeless mentally ill, according to a leading Hampstead psychiatrist.

Professor Julian Leff is director of a research team which has spent several years monitoring long-stay patients leaving Friern Barnet and Claybury psychiatric hospitals, due to be closed next spring.

The Friern-based Team for the Assessment of Psychiatric Services (Taps) has lost contact with only seven out of 500 patients it has followed.

His team's latest results, announced at a conference at University College Hospital yesterday, show that people taken out of crumbling Victorian institutions like Friern do not have to end up on the street.

None of the patients had got worse clinically or in terms of behaviour, most appreciated the freedom and less restrictive conditions and a great majority wanted to stay where they were.

One of the best things discovered by the Taps team was the number of people willing to act as good neighbours in befriending those returned to the community.

"If these provision programmes are well-planned and resourced, which this one is, then very few patients get lost. No patients got lost from staff group homes at all. So if we are prepared to give proper housing and professional care, they will not end up on the street," Professor Leff told the Ham & High.

In the first three Taps studies involving 300 patients who had been in psychiatric hospitals for 15 years on average, the researchers lost touch with five patients placed in temporary hostel accommodation or with relatives, and one who left a private nursing home.

In years four and five, involving a second group of about 200 long-stay patients, Taps lost touch with only one, who was an illegal immigrant and who is thought to have returned to his country of origin, said Professor

20

Leff.

However, the results of research involving psychiatric patients who spend short amounts of time in hospital, due to be presented at the same conference, were not expected to paint such a rosy picture of community care.

"A number of studies recently indicate very few homeless mentally ill people have had long periods of in-patient care. The great majority are in and out of hospital admission wards very rapidly.

"That in itself is a criticism of the system, there is inadequate aftercare for these people, but that is not a direct result of reducing the size of mental hospitals," he said.

Rehabilitation homes needed to be set up as a buffer between hospital wards and the community, to allow mentally ill people who may have been on the streets for a long period a stable environment in which to recover after times of crisis.

A study involving interviews with long-term homeless people to find out why they ended up on the streets was about to get underway, but would require tactful interviewing and a lot of detective work to find out why people lost touch with their families, said the professor.

The loss of old-style reception centres, shelters and relatively low-rent rooms, and the impact of the recession on casual employment could all be pinpointed as causes for the rise in street homelessness, he said.

Professor Leff is one of a few in the health service working with families of those who are mentally ill: "If we can keep the family going and supporting the patient we will probably prevent a lot falling into homelessness in the long run."

Should mental patients be kept in psychiatric hospitals or allowed back into the community? Give at least four reasons for their retention in hospital and four against:

FOR	AGAINST

Compare your list with someone else.

Write a short report containing at least four proposals for solving the problem of street homelessness.

Discuss your suggestions with someone else.

Read the following article:

Soaps show blacks as underclass

BY ALISON UTLEY

POPULAR TELEVISION soap operas and dramas are pronounced guilty of negative ethnic stereotyping, often portraying black characters as criminals, drug abusers or slave-like characters, in a new study.

Programmes such as *Neighbours* (only one black character), *Casualty* (two minor black characters, a nurse and a receptionist in the first series) and *The Paradise Club*, all came under scrutiny. Of all the popular soap operas, dramas, comedies and crime series monitored in the research a total of 902 characters included 3.3 per cent blacks and 1 per cent Asians. But no leading characters were assigned to ethnic minority actors, none portrayed a strong character or leader and few black or Asian parts featured regularly in their respective series.

"Many of the roles played by ethnic minority actors are stereotyped as the black villain, the Asian shopkeeper, or the black athlete, which simply perpetuate the orthodox racist imagery which already exists about ethnic difference," says Karen Ross of Warwick University.

"If only 5 per cent of television characters are black and Asian and those that are featured are villainous, adulterous, corrupt, poor and weak, then it is likely that the white viewing public will expect all members of such communities to be the same and act in similar ways."

To test this theory, Dr Ross questioned 650 young white viewers in the West Midlands who used television as a major information and entertainment source. The sample was chosen to constitute the so called television generation "brought up on a staple diet of televisual material".

Nearly three quarters of respondents believed the number of appearances of black and Asian people on television was about right. Commenting on characterisations, the majority preferred to see ethnic minorities portrayed as "ordinary people".

But black people were more than twice as likely to be perceived as habitually playing criminals.

Dr Ross said: "The way in which television treats ethnic issues is a result of deliberate policy and programme decisions regarding what is included and excluded, who is allowed to speak and who is not, quite apart from the type of language and imagery employed in television fictions."

All lack of black or Asian characters would not be so significant - the proportions equate roughly to the numbers in the population generally - if such roles displayed the full diversity of human experience in every day life. "It is the enactment of normal ordinary everyday life that is missing from popular television fictions*were actors are allowed to act outside their skin rather than in constant reference to it."

The BBC's *EastEnders* is criticised in the research by Dr Ross. During the period of viewing (1989) five ethnic minority characters were featured. Characters comprised the unpopular Asian family which owned the local grocery shop, forced to leave the series after adultery shamed them - they only featured in the cast list once in the *Radio Times* during the four week review period; the Turk Ali Osman who lost everything through gambling; Vince who sold stolen property and a Chinese schoolteacher in a one-off appearance.

Television is Black and White by Karen Ross, Centre for Research in Ethnic Relations, University of Warwick.

* where

What do you think about the following statements? Find examples proving or disproving these declarations:

- Television programmes represent male standards and values.

- Television strengthens social prejudice.

- The media image of the working class is idealised and false.

- Television strengthens the status quo and reinforces the values of a materialist, consumer society.

Compare your answers with someone else.

- What other forms does racism take in our society apart from its presence in the media? Give at least five examples.

* SPARKS FLY OVER JEANS AD'S 'RISK' TO MACHO MEN

Complete the following article:

The phenomenally ..... Levis 501 advertisement campaign, which took buttoned-fly jeans from costume museum back to high ....., has been attacked as sexist, ... and sizeist - but yesterday it was denounced as dangerous, writes Maev Kennedy.

James Tye, director general of the British Safety Council, said the latest ad was "totally mindless and highly dangerous" and is writing to the Independent Broadcasting Authority demanding that it be ..... .

The story line is a role-reversed Cinderella, as a young woman with a pair of jeans goes in search of the man with ..... enough hips.

She finds her ..... fit in a workshop, a young mechanic already conveniently half out of his ....

Instead of a fairy tale Mr Tye saw a ..... trap "in which the Prince Charming character is seen to have total disregard for Health and Safety laws" with the "semi-naked ..... mechanic standing in a shower of sparks". It would incite dangerous copy-cat exploits ..... apprentices.

Stef Tiratelli of Bartle Bogle Hegarty, the agency that ..... the campaign, said: "When we launched Launderette (their first Levis ad) we didn't expect people would start taking all their clothes off in ....., and we would not expect people to start ... this one."

You may need to use these words:

copying, death, banned, among, successful, macho, devised, mindless, narrow, public, fashion, perfect, incite, boiler-suit, ageist.

Compare your answers with the original in Appendix 1.

- How do you think advertisements influence people?

- Give an example of an advertisement that you consider particularly effective.

* WOMEN'S WORK REMAINS UNDERVALUED REPORT CLAIMS

Read the article below:

Celia Weston
Labour Correspondent

SEX discrimination is so deeply embedded in the labour market that women will not achieve equal pay unless positive steps are taken to improve wages in female-dominated occupations, according to an Equal Opportunities Commission report published today.

The research, the first of its kind, details why women's work is undervalued and the likely costs and benefits of achieving equal pay.

It says that major gains for women workers are unlikely to be made through individual equal value cases taken under the tribunal system laid down by the present Equal Pay and Sex Discrimination Acts.

The 1984 equal value amendment to the law was intended to help combat the effects of job segregation. It allows a woman to claim the same pay as a man doing a different job if the work is found to be of equal value.

Its impact has been limited, the report says. Women still earn less than 77 per cent of men's hourly earnings and an even lower proportion of men's pay if weekly earnings are taken into account.

The commission has in recent years urged the Government to streamline and update equality legislation, including provision for successful individual cases of equal pay for equal value being applicable to all workers in similar jobs.

The report, The Economics of Equal Value, challenges as a myth the view that the British economy cannot afford to pay women a fair wage. It says although equal value pay has implications for labour costs, the assumption that the economy cannot afford it emphasises direct costs while playing down the competitive advantages of productivity and human development.

"If women's wages were increased by 10 per cent, the estimated overall impact on the wage bill in manufacturing would be less than 2 per cent," the report says.

"Even in services, with its high share of female labour, it is estimated the wage bill would rise by less than 4 per cent."

Evidence from other countries showed that, rather than market forces alone, custom and practice, social values and systems of industrial organisation play a role in determining pay levels.

The report concludes that discrimination based on historical views of women's position in society is outmoded.

The Economics of Equal Value, EOC, Swan House, 52-53 Poland Street, London W1V 3DF.

24

- Do you agree or do you disagree with the statement that the 'British economy cannot afford to pay women a fair wage'?

Give your reasons.

- What are the attitudes or beliefs that lie behind sexual discrimination?

- Do you think employers should be legally bound to provide child care and paternity leave? What additional measures should be taken to achieve equality of opportunity at work?

- How can women's work be revalued at a time of high unemployment?

- Do you agree that our first priority should be the creation of a minimum wage?

- Are women undervaluing themselves at work?

- Is discrimination against women more obvious than any other form of discrimination?

- Women are paid less and live longer. Is there a link between these two facts?

Compare you views with someone else.

Read this article carefully:

Life should not be so sweet...

ATTENTION all health conscious shoppers! Watch out for different types of carbohydrates.

Nutrition labels that lump sugar and starch together can be confusing - even though both foods are rightly classified as carbohydrates, healthy eating means eating more starch and less sugars.

Lynn Stockley, manager of the Health Education Authority's nutrition team, says: "People think starch is particularly fattening and to be avoided. In fact, it contains about half the calories of fat and we should eat more of it.

"Both brown and white bread, pasta and potatoes are packed full of starch. But if you eat the brown version you're going to get fibre so there's an added benefit.

"Wholegrain varieties of starchy foods contain more vitamins and minerals and are more filling. If you fill yourself up with starchy foods, then you'll be less tempted by sugary or fatty foods. Eating less fat also reduces your risk of heart disease."

Sugar is not always listed on labels as sugar, and though many people worry about additives like E numbers, they do not worry about sugars which may be labelled as glucose, fructose or honey - amongst other things.

"Many people think honey is better than sugar because it's natural," she adds. "But in actual fact it's full of sugars. Honey is just as bad as sugars in causing tooth decay."

Lynn recommends that you eat less sugar. It only contains calories - it has no minerals or vitamins. If you cut it out you don't lose any nutrients.

If you do take sugar, eat sugary goods, or give it to the children, try to give it as part of a meal rather than in-between meals. Don't worry about a little bit of sugar in baked beans or tomato ketchup. But keep an eye on sugary drinks consumed between meals.

- Do you think that the food industry should be more health conscious?

- Suggest eight measures that should be adopted to improve the nation's health.

Discuss your views with someone else.

Read this article carefully:

Data 'posing grave threat to privacy'

Richard Norton-Taylor and James Erlichman

INDIVIDUAL privacy in Britain is under grave threat, Eric Howe, the Data Protection Registrar, warned yesterday as he announced the Government had imposed further cuts on his already stretched budget.

Mr Howe, the ombudsman for personal privacy, revealed in his annual report that the Metropolitan Police had refused to destroy 3,500 DNA profiles taken from people questioned but subsequently ruled out of criminal inquiries.

This was an example of how the rapid growth in the use of personal information, coupled with an explosion of computer technology, was intruding on people's lives, Mr Howe said. "There is a grave danger that individual privacy will simply be whittled away."

Mr Howe said the Government had cut his budget by 6.2 per cent when he needed more resources, especially to meet the expected demands of a European Community directive on privacy. "The future is fraught," he said. "The lack of any detailed knowledge of people's rights is a matter of real concern."

The Metropolitan Police had agreed to stop using the DNA profiles for "investigative purposes", but it had refused to destroy them on the grounds that it wanted them for "research purposes". Under existing legislation, police are obliged to destroy fingerprints held in similar circumstances.

The Department of Health had failed even to deliver a promised voluntary code to protect the confidentiality of patients' records, arguing that common law did so adequately. Mr Howe said he remained unconvinced.

He decided, however, not to oppose collection of HIV/Aids status by police — one of the "warning signals" on individuals kept on police computers.

The planned EC directive, unlike Britain's Data Protection Act, specifically establishes the right of personal privacy. But Mr Howe warned that its tough terms are being undermined by lobbyists for the direct mail and marketing industry, as well as by Whitehall. The Government is also strongly opposed to the EC proposal that legislation should cover personal information held on manual files as well as those held on computer.

The EC directive will not cover police and immigration data exchanged in the Trevi Group.

27

New threats to personal privacy cited by Mr Howe include the growing practice of "data matching" whereby one government department transfers information to another to build up a profile of an individual. These dossiers were recently described by a High Court judge as "the badge of the totalitarian state".

Mr Howe pointed out that Australia and Canada had set up independent bodies to scrutinise the collection of personal information by central government.

He warned of threats to the confidentiality of telephone users by the proposal for Calling Line Identification, pressure for the wider use of information gleaned from driver and television licences, suggestions for a national database of the DNA profiles of the whole male population, and a proposal from the census offices for a national population register.

The report also refers to successes, including action against local authorities for collecting irrelevant information and obtaining information unfairly for poll tax forms.

Eighth Report of the Data Protection Registrar, HMSO, £10.95.

- Do you think that personal privacy is a fundamental human right that should be guaranteed by law?

- Why might it not be in the individual's interest to have personal data held on file or computer?

- What are the fundamental characteristics of a totalitarian State?

Discuss your views with someone else.

* NOISY FROGS

Read the article below:

> People in south and west London have complained to the London Wildlife Trust that incessant noise from French frogs is disturbing their sleep. The frogs, which have appeared in gardens in Chiswick and Putney, croak far louder and longer than native English frogs.

Sunday Times, 15 November, 1992

Which of the following issues are raised here?

1. the power of the media
2. noise pollution
3. ecological disaster
4. the Franco-British love-hate relationship
5. nationalism
6. animal rights

Compare your choice with someone else.

What are, in your view, the main causes for complaint in an urban environment? Select 2 answers from the list below:

1. heavy traffic
2. lack of public services
3. lack of privacy
4. poor housing
5. violence
6. high crime rate
7. noise pollution
8. absence of parks.

Discuss your views with someone else.

Read the following article:

Treaty with Aborigines 'threatens safety'

THE former chief justice of the High Court, Sir Harry Gibbs, has attacked the proposed treaty with Aboriginal people, saying that it threatens the existence of Australia as a nation.

In the opening address to a new society aimed at preserving the Australian Constitution, Sir Harry warned that the treaty could lead to the development of independent Aboriginal nations in the strategic central and northern parts of Australia.

Sir Harry, who retired as chief justice in 1987, is overseas, and arranged for the speech to be delivered on his behalf to the society's opening on Friday.

He said Australia may admit that Aboriginal people had been the victims of crimes and blunders, but legislative power existed to provide justice to Aborigines.

"It does not follow that a generation which was in no way responsible for the crimes or the blunders of the past should be so racked with guilt that we would imperil our sovereignty and place the very existence of our nation at risk," Sir Harry said.

The chief executive of Western Mining Corporation, Mr Hugh Morgan, used the conference to attack the High Court for making decisions since Federation that had changed the Constitution away from what its founders had intended.

He particularly attacked a decision handed down last month that effectively established sovereignty to the Meriam people over the Murray Islands in Torres Strait.

Mr Morgan said that when the implications of the decision became known it would lead to a national fight that had not been known since the fight over conscription in World War I.

"The court has placed itself at the epicentre of what will become the most divisive debate in Australia, a debate concerning the territorial integrity of Australia as proclaimed in the Constitution," he said.

The society has been named after Australia's first chief justice, Sir Samuel Griffith, who was also one of the key architects of the Constitution.

It has been established with the stated aims of opposing both the power of the Federal Government over the states and of Cabinet over Parliament.

Do you agree or disagree with Sir Harry Gibbs' viewpoint? Give your reasons.

Read the following article carefully:

● *No money to repair our architectural gems*

By CHRIS GOODALL

ISLINGTON'S architectural heritage is in danger of crumbling to dust because of a cash shortage.

The council's conservation officer Alec Forshaw this week warned councillors that the 21 council-owned properties on English Heritage's register of listed buildings at risk are in urgent need of repairs if they are to survive for future generations to admire.

Heritage officials met council representatives last October and called for action to save the historic properties.

"It was felt important that if the council were to persuade or take action to enforce private owners to repair their listed buildings, the council itself must be seen to be setting a good example," Mr Forshaw said.

But he admitted that council funds to save the buildings "are virtually nil."

The 21 "at risk" buildings include Finsbury Town Hall – the headquarters of the former Finsbury Council until 1965. The town hall is presently occupied by Clerkenwell Neighbourhood Office, the registrar of births, marriages and deaths, and the area repair team. But the first floor public hall, widely regarded as an architectural gem, is vacant as is the former council chamber.

Mr Forshaw said there had been recent roof leaks and evidence of poor repairs and blocked drains.

Another building on the list – the Lloyd Dairy in Amwell Street – was "in very poor condition and has been badly neglected by the council", warned Mr Forshaw.

Temporary scaffolding erected five years ago to protect the defective roof was "now itself contributing to the deteriorating condition".

It has cost the council £25,000 to rent the scaffolding for the past five years.

Labour Councillor Kevin Arthurs described the report as "extremely worrying" when it was discussed at a meeting of the housing sub-committee.

"We're under pressure from the Government to sell, but the Government makes it difficult for us to sell these properties."

To what extent do you think that the problem raised in this article is a political one?

Discuss your views with someone else.

* JUST AS YOUNG AS YOU YOGA

Read the article below:

PENSIONERS as old as 87 are as graceful as gazelles from their weekly yoga class where "hula-hoop" hip swivels feature in the routines.

For some of the elderly people at Holloway's Alsen Day Centre in Durham Road it's "a way of life". Pictured left, Olive Hyslop, 87, said: "I'm the best hula-hoop dancer in the class. I do quite a bit of trotting about and this keeps me really healthy."

And Betty Carter, also 87, re-marked: "It's wonderfully relax-ing – I sleep like a baby at night."

The group enthused that yoga helps keep arthritis at bay. And 78-year-old Betty Abrahams commented: "The breathing ex-ercises are marvellous for my asthma – I go months without an attack now." **Pictures: Tony Gay**

Health

Do you agree that the following issues are raised in this article? Do you consider that some of these concerns are more important than others? If so, why?

1. community care
2. the care of senior citizens
3. women and health
4. self-help groups
5. the integration of ethnic minorities into the community
6. health consciousness

Discuss your views with someone else.

Read this article carefully:

Police chief says justice is 'a game'

A CHIEF Constable said yesterday that the judicial system was in danger of collapse and needed an urgent overhaul to restore public confidence.

Charles Pollard, of the Thames Valley force, said the legal system was in a critical condition and beyond its sell-by date. The adversarial system of justice had led to a clash of cultures between the police and lawyers, he told the International Police Exhibition and Conference at the Barbican in London. "Many practitioners would say that the criminal trial in this country is rather like a game, akin to any other sporting contest.

"It is also a theatre in which the players rely as much on their acting skills as cold analysis of the facts. It is not designed to get at the truth. Rather it is a contest between two sides aimed at reaching a decision in which the truth sometimes seems incidental." This amazed most laymen, who always assumed that getting at the truth was what trials were for.

Key aims for a new system of justice were acquittal of the innocent and conviction of the guilty, seeking the truth, supporting the rights of the public, accountability and holding the principles of quality and value for money in high regard.

"What is needed is a new brand of justice to take this country into the next century which seeks truth and not confrontation: which treats people with dignity, not indifference, and above all one which contributes towards solving society's problems instead of providing an arena for adversarial virtuosity."

* Decisons in trials were based on only some of the facts in contrast to inquisitorial style systems where all relevant facts were considered as evidence.

In Britain, many "facts" were treated as inadmissible for reasons associated with the historical development of the law centuries ago. The system was ritualistic and highly formal, epitomised by the dress and language of the participants, often seeming at odds with the real issues and problems people face in their daily life. It was expensive, backward-looking and not user-friendly.

"Taken together these characteristics create values which are the very opposite to those required for a rational, objective, dispassionate trial process. The rules and rituals seem to the laymen to be contrary to common sense. "That some of the professional participants — not just police but also judges, lawyers and scientists — sometimes get their values misplaced is surely inevitable. That mistakes are occasionally made is unsurprising."

* Decisions

- What are the weaknesses of the English judicial system?

- Has it any strengths?

- How does the English legal system differ from that of your own country?

- Do you agree that "laws grind the poor and rich men rule the law"? [O. Goldsmith].

- What measures should be taken to reduce the number of miscarriages of justice?

- Do you think that police pay should be linked to performance? Give reasons for your answer.

- How can governments influence the course of justice?

- Do you think that the law treats women and other disadvantaged groups fairly? Support your answer with example.

Discuss your views with someone else.

Read this article carefully:

Aids study group vows to fight fear

NOT everyone will be infected by HIV, but it affects us all nonetheless, HIV/Aids counsellor Mary Hughes told a workshop at Golders Green Unitarian Chapel on Saturday. The workshop was held in the hope of challenging negative attitudes towards people with the virus.

"We are all suffering from life and we are all going to die of it," was the philosophical stance taken by bereavement counsellor Sara Groves. "My attitude is changing all the time. I came to have my attitude changed."

The day, at which participants were encouraged to examine their own assumptions and feelings about HIV/Aids, was organised by the Positive Unity project.

The project is a partnership between the Unitarian movement and the charity Positively Women, the only organisation in the UK providing emotional assistance by women with HIV/Aids for women with the virus.

Ms Hughes, who organised the event, dismissed talk of "high-risk" groups. "The 'high-risk' group is the human race. There are only high-risk activities.

"Because of the misinformation and misunderstanding which has been promoted and surrounds HIV and Aids, and because the virus seems to threaten us through our most intimate activities and relationships, we can become infected by a condition just as deadly to ourselves and others as any virus. This condition, this infection, is called fear — and at its most acute stage it can cause hatred, intolerance and death."

The Unitarians are trying to break down the ignorance, fear and prejudice surrounding HIV/Aids.

Mary Burns, the co-chairwoman of the chapel in Hoop Lane, Golders Green, said she did not enjoy talking about Aids because it was such a sad thing. "I would rather think about more positive things."

But she felt it important to inform herself about it for the sake of her grandchildren. "I am sure it is going to be a problem for them when they are growing up. I feel it is through the younger generations in my family that I am affected. I would like to be able to answer questions. They would expect me to be able to give them honest information."

Peter Buxton, a trained nurse currently studying at the British College of Naturopathy and Osteopathy in Netherhall Gardens, Hampstead, said: "It would be good if people could sit down and talk about Aids in the same way as we talk about chronic bronchitis, a bad back or any other diseases. When you say 'Aids' it is still something special and that is not quite right. You want specialist care but you don't want special attitudes towards it."

-   Make a list of ten negative attitudes towards people with Aids.
-   List ten measures that should be adopted to combat this prejudice.
-   Discuss your views with someone else.

Read this amusing article:

A MERMAID like the one Daryl Hannah made famous strayed from Loch Ness

IT'S MER-ACULOUS!
Half-woman, half-fish washes up on beach

SCOTSMEN ARE flipping their kilts over a beautiful mermaid who surfaced and flopped up on the sands of a remote beach on the wild coast of the North Sea!

And experts say the creature strayed from Loch Ness, legendary home of Nessie, another magical creature.

A witness to the eye-popping discovery described the mermaid as a "slender girl-fish with long blond tresses and a white tail fin."

And she may even have been ALIVE when she was found by two early morning joggers.

Officials are trying to muzzle local residents, but Jean Tauffer, 31, told **The EXAMINER**: "I spoke to one of the men who found the body.

"He's been ordered to keep very quiet about the whole business.

"He said he and a friend were jogging along the beach around sunup when they stumbled

'She was blond and beautiful!'

across something partially hidden by sand.

"When he started.to brush away the sand from her lower body, he nearly collapsed with shock.

He found the woman had a pure white tail fin. But apart from that — and the slightly greenish color to her skin — she looked quite human ... and very beautiful!"

At Drumnadrochit, Scotland, underwater experts searching the murky depths of Loch Ness for its legendary monster think the mermaid may well have been driven out to sea by all the frenzied activity.

Said one diver: "The mermaid could easily have swum out of the loch, passed through a series of interconnected, underground caves and ended up in the North Sea."

Why do you think journalists do not always tell the truth? What other factors influence them?

Discuss your views with someone else.

Read the following article:

Riotous rage of the have-nots

Jock Young on how the politics of despair spread from blacks to disaffected whites

TWO YOUTHS stole a police BMW motorbike in Hartcliffe, Bristol, on Thursday night; in the subsequent police chase they crashed, and were killed. Trouble ensued: crowds of young people, white and black, set fire to the local library and community centre, and looted shops. The following night, there were more riots. It is a familiar pattern, repeating what has occurred in depressed estates from Teesside to Salford.

After the riots of 1981 and 1985, the immediate response, from all parts of the political spectrum, revolved around race. For the right, an unassimilated black minority was simply displaying its inability to act in an orderly British fashion. For the left, the problem was racism: a minority barred from jobs because of prejudice and treated unfairly by police, had been driven beyond their tether. Both interpretations conveniently forgot that many of the rioters, in Brixton and elsewhere, were white.

We can now see the secondary nature of the race factor. In the 1980s it would have been possible to pinpoint the sites of rioting by marking on the map where there were concentrations of blacks or Asians. Brixton, Tottenham, Handsworth and Toxteth all fit this pattern. Now the dots on the map are more widespread: in cities or districts with no black concentrations: Meadow Well on Tyneside, Coventry, Oxford and Ordsall in Salford. As the recession has spread, the white population of depressed areas has joined the ranks of the violently disaffected.

Riots are the politics of despair: the collective bargaining of the dispossessed. Whether in Brixton or Los Angeles, whenever a part of the community is economically marginalised and feels politically impotent, riots occur.

But history never repeats itself, and the causes of riots today are specific to the modern recessions. First, there is a notion of consumer citizenship. With political and social rights, the affluent societies of the West have fostered new expectations. Advertising and the rules of an economy based on mass consumption teach us that if we are truly to belong to our society we must possess its glittering prizes. Hunger no longer propels the riot: in its place is the video-recorder, the BMW and the mountain bike. Kids may be robbed, not for their pocket money, but for their trainer shoes or designer clothes.

Second, although black youths were certainly to the forefront of the riots in Britain of the early 1980s, this was simply because they were the first to face the cutting edge of the recession. It is class, not race, which unites rioters today. The distinction was clear in Los Angeles, where the targets were not only whites and Asian business people, but also better-off blacks.

Much play has been made of the word "underclass", which, in the work of the neo-conservative Charles Murray, has the resonance of a group which has lost all motivation and, shored up by welfare, is unwilling to help itself. But there is another definition of underclass, which does not contrive to blame the poor for their own misfortunes: those young people who face a lifetime on the dole, whose welfare benefits are being cut, who regard the local police as persecutors, who are impotent to make any change in their lives and who, perhaps most pressingly, are chronically and endlessly bored.

The police recognise that their task is made more difficult by the recession. As the Avon and Somerset constabulary put it in the Operational Police Review: "Is it a coincidence that, at the depths of the 1980-81 recession, when unemployment began to rise sharply from its 1970 base, the first urban riots of the modern era occurred in St Paul's, Bristol, and Brixton? Is it again a coincidence that, as unemployment approached its peak, a series of disorders occurred in 1985 in Brixton, Tottenham and Hansworth?"

However correct their diagnosis, much is lacking in police practice. Survey after survey on poor housing estates reveals widespread experience of gratuitous police violence, assault and the improvisation of evidence. It is not just in the headline cases that such lapses occur; there is a vast undertow of malpractice. And the antagonism between police and youths becomes a game. A status-symbol motorbike is stolen; the police chase which ensues is an entertainment feature on the estate; two young men die. The riot which occurs in protest is irrational in its targets. The library, the community centre and the local shops: the infrastructure of the community — *their* community — is attacked.

Riots and disturbances will not go away, and the people affected are not just an underclass on some far-distant estate. Beneath the overt riot is the vast slow riot of crime which affects us all. Last year more than five million offences were known to the police; in 1980 it was 2.5 million; in 1950 half a million. Crime is no longer a chance misfortune but an ever-present threat, yet ministers still blithely blame lack of parental discipline and the decline of religion: anything to avoid the economic explanation.

It is riots and crime which confront the "haves" with the despair and hopelessness of the "have nots". No society can permanently exclude so many people from the rewards and prospects which the majority takes for granted, without bearing these consequences.

Professor Jock Young, of the Centre for Criminology, Middlesex University, is co-author of 'What's to be Done about Law and Order?'

- What does the author consider the principal causes of riots today?

- How is the word 'underclass' defined?

- How does the government account for the increase in crime?

- What measures do you think should be taken to solve the problem of urban unrest?

Discuss your answers with someone else.

Read the following article:

Mystery of the 'missing' royal car

BUCKINGHAM PALACE is tight-lipped about a beautiful coupe it bought from Czechoslovakia in 1938, *writes Eric Dymock.* It was discovered during research into a new book on Skoda by the authors Ivan Margolius and Charles Meisl, but their requests for information from the royal mews met with no response. The car was ordered from Carrosserie Sodomka in Czechoslovakia, but its recipient and subsequent history remain a mystery.

"It is possible that it was bought for the Duke of Windsor," Meisl said. "Or it may have been a gift for another royal family. Either way the palace isn't saying."

Sodomka constructed bodies for other makes besides Skoda, and the stylish royal convertible was built on an American La Salle chassis. The shape followed contemporary French coachbuilders' style with faired-in headlights, flowing wings and chrome "streamline" decoration.

The Windsors' preference for large American cars, instead of the rather staid Daimlers in which the royal family had ridden since the turn of the century, may explain the palace's reticence. As Edward VIII, the duke took delivery of two Buicks, built in a Canadian factory, within a month of George V's death. The break with Daimler was explained by the king's wish to encourage empire trade.

Skoda Laurin & Klement, by Ivan Margolius and Charles Meisl, Osprey Publishing, £25. Phone 0933 410511.

Who do you think is the target reader of this article? Select one or more answers from the list below:

1. a man
2. a French coachbuilder
3. a fan of Royalty
4. a thief
5. a car lover
6. a film producer
7. somebody interested in history
8. an MI5 agent
9. a car dealer
10. a scriptwriter for a TV series

Justify your choice and discuss it with someone else.

* THE GALLIC SYMBOL OF FAILURE

Read the article below:

France is currently reeling with - on top of everything else - the newly imparted knowledge that they have less sex than the British: twice a week for them, 2.5 times for us.

Myself, I never bought the myth that the French had the best sex, any more than I swallowed the line which said they also had the best wine, women and song - despite the decades of propaganda from Piaf to Provence.

Unlike, say, the Italians - who must number among the more beautiful women under the age of 40 than any other country in the world - French women don't really look any better than ours, once you take away the trimmings.

Flirt

They simply accessorise as if their lives depended on it, and flirt as if their livelihoods did too.

French culture is bankrupt, their Champagne is becoming undrinkable, their best chefs are all over here and they have to import their sex stars from Pinner.

Their country is lovely in parts - but so what? If Romania appears to be 'Italians trapped in Hell', then France is surely quite like Italy awash with Romanians.

The Mail on Sunday, July 12, 1992

- How do you think the statistics given in the above article were obtained?

- Do you think opinon polls are reliable? If not, why?

Discuss your views with someone else.

* BOARDS' LINGUISTIC SILENCE SPEAKS VOLUMES

Read the following article:

Boards' linguistic silence speaks volumes

By Paul Taylor

MOST directors of the biggest UK companies fit the stereotype of the insular Brit unable or unwilling to communicate in a foreign language.

They lack both the language skills and the overseas work experience necessary to face the challenge of international competition and global markets, according to a survey published today.

The latest board of directors study by Korn/Ferry International, the executive search firm, says that fewer than one in five boardroom directors of leading British companies speaks a foreign language and two thirds have no experience of working abroad.

Of the 581 directors of 179 UK listed companies who responded to the survey, 84 per cent spoke no foreign language. Fourteen per cent spoke one foreign language and 2 per cent spoke three or more. The proportion of directors with language skills was no higher in companies that generated more than half their business overseas last year.

Questionnaires were sent to the 335 UK companies in the Times European 1000 list and the next 500 largest British companies.

Mr Michael Brandon, a Korn/ Ferry International director and author of the study, said: "Unless British boards take rapid steps to acquire the necessary international skills and experience, UK Ltd is in danger of becoming a foreign subsidiary."

Perhaps the occupants of British boardrooms could learn a lesson or two from the UK's top exporting companies. A straw poll conducted by the FT yesterday among Britain's 10 most successful exporters showed that they generally bucked the survey's findings.

Rolls-Royce, Shell UK and BP said virtually all their directors had been based overseas at some stage, and most had at least a conversational grasp of another language. Of Shell UK's 12 directors three are Dutch nationals "who speak English better than the English". However top marks go to Mr David Simon, BP's new chief executive, who read modern languages including French at university, speaks three other languages fluently, and studied for his MBA at Fontainebleau.

IBM UK said the majority of its directors would have conversational French at the very least since most had worked at the company's European headquarters in Paris, and Ford UK said all but two of its 10-man board had worked overseas. Ford boasts a German-speaking chairman in Mr Ian McAllister together with a native German speaker in Mr Albert Caspers, and a Spanish-speaking personnel director.

ICI said it did not know the level of language skills among its eight non-executive directors but of the eight executive directors, four had more than one language.

At Pearson, the FT's parent company, three of the 13 board members are foreign nationals, another is a foreign resident and only one director speaks no foreign language.

However, another board member makes up for this by boasting four languages, including Hausa from north Nigeria.

The study also examines the composition of the British boardroom, the balance between executive and non-executive directors, and the composition of audit and remuneration committees.

Other main findings are:

● Only 11 of the 581 directors were women and no company had more than one woman on the board. Eight of the 11 women were non-executives.

● Three quarters of UK companies had separate chairmen and chief executives – as recommended by the Cadbury report on corporate governance. In a quarter of those companies, the chairman was a full-time executive playing a leading role. There was still, however, an overall majority (55 per cent) with chairmen who were either part-time or non-executive, or full-time but not playing the leading role in the organisation.

● As the concentration of power and the level of involvement of the chairman reduces, it becomes more likely that the majority of the board will be non-executive. Among companies with non-executive chairmen, 55 per cent had a non-executive majority, but among companies with a strong chairman role, the proportion was less than 20 per cent.

● Just under 60 per cent of the top executives of the largest companies with turnover of £1bn or more have university degrees, while roughly one in five is a qualified accountant.

The 1992 Board of Directors Study UK. Korn/Ferry International. Tel: 071-930 4334. £90.

Imagine you are a dissatisfied company director. Write a short report explaining the necessity for fundamental changes in the training of future executives and in the composition of the boardroom.

Read the article below:

Prisoners of corporate culture

BY ROGER TRAPP

EXECUTIVES grappling with such concepts as change management are unlikely to find the thought consoling, but an industrial anthropologist assisting the parliamentary and scientific committee on Japanese industrial policy says that the notion that corporate cultures can be changed is based on a misunderstanding of human behaviour — and therefore is likely to fail.

"The idea that it is possible to change a company's culture, that it is merely a matter of individual willpower, is itself a cultural phenomenon — one peculiar to our Western society," says Alexandra Ouroussoff. "It is a consequence of our tendency to overestimate the power of human reason to change human behaviour."

We look to Japan for ideas about how to improve business practice, yet more often than not we select the evidence to suit our own cultural prejudices. Concentrating on such issues as staff canteen seating plans evades the more fundamental question: is the company being efficiently run? "I do not believe that eating arrangements have had a long-term inhibiting effect on our national economy. Economic performance and cultural values are much more subtly linked."

Ms Ouroussoff has worked in industry for three years, studying her subject in the same way a conventional anthropologist would tackle an exotic society. As well as gaining a combined Ph D in social anthropology and industrial relations, she has spent a year as a post-doctoral fellow at the London Business School, as part of a detailed study leading to a forthcoming book.

Although the book's title, *Illusions of Rationality, the Cultural Perpetuation of Industrial Inefficiency,* has a distinctly pessimistic tone, she insists it is not meant in that spirit.

"But our ability to achieve effective changes depends on our ability to unmask malignant patterns which interfere with rational choice and make change impossible."

Drawing on her experience of a British-based multinational, she says that the tendency to overestimate the extent to which behaviour is determined by conscious choice and individual willpower can lead "managers of change" to perpetuate the very problems they are trying to solve.

By concentrating on the individual, social constraints on people are being ignored, with the result that the overall picture is distorted.

Managers do not just determine corporate culture, they are determined by it. A clearer insight into the values which sustain culture is necessary if change management is to be effective. Paradoxically, "the more we are aware of the things that constrain us, the freer we are to change them," she says.

- Why is it so difficult to change a company's culture?

- How do you think economic performance and cultural values are linked?

- How can business practice be improved?

Discuss your views with someone else.

43

* CAN'T PAY, MUST PAY

Read this article carefully:

Daniel Nassim examines the devastating impact of 10 years of the debt crisis in Africa and Latin America

Ten years ago, in August 1982, Mexico sparked the third world debt crisis when it announced that it could no longer repay its debt to the West. The debt crisis is little discussed today. Yet its impact on the third world has been far worse than that of the Western planes, tanks and missiles which destroyed Iraq.

Over the past decade, Western governments, banks and international institutions have imposed harsh terms on third world countries to ensure that they repay their debts. The peoples of Latin America and Africa have experienced a permanent regime of austerity, as a leading Western credit rating agency coyly describes:

'The key effect of the debt crisis has been a profound breakdown of routine economic norms in debtor countries. When a country must operate in circumstances equivalent to permanent bankruptcy reorganization, the economic behaviour of its citizens is bound to shift. To satisfy creditors, wealth must be relinquished, perhaps for reasons perceived as illegitimate, and without the promise of reward for such sacrifice.'

In other words, the third world has to tighten its belt still further to pay money to Western bankers and governments. In effect, the poorest people on Earth are subsidising the life-styles and economies of the richest. The result has been a massive shift of resources from the third world to the West. According to the UN: 'In 1983-9, rich creditors received a staggering $242 billion in net transfers on long-term lending from indebted developing countries.' (*Human Development Report 1992*)

Such figures are so large as to seem meaningless. Who can visualise the $1.4 trillion dollars that is owed by third world countries to the West? Yet this burden has a very real human effect on the lives of billions in the third world. The UN estimates that 2.3 billion people lack access to sanitation, 1.3 billion people lack access to safe water, and 1.2 billion barely survive in absolute poverty. It is truly the arithmetic of death.

Sub-Saharan Africa is the worst affected. The Gross Domestic Product (GDP) of 450m people is the same as that of Belgium (10m). Food shortages are widespread, clean water is scarce and infant mortality is high. Each year 150 000 African women die and a similar number suffer permanent disabilities as a result of problems in pregnancy and childbirth. An estimated 200m Africans have chronic malaria.

In some ways the situation of Latin America is even more shocking. During the seventies, the industrialising countries of Brazil, Mexico and Argentina were held up as models of capitalist development. But in the eighties GDP per person in the region fell by 11 per cent. During this period Chile—ruled by one of the most brutal dictatorships in the world—was regarded as the model debtor. The only country to record consistent positive growth was Colombia—thanks to the drug barons who run most of its economy.

Despite the common perception in the West, such poverty does not spring from 'natural' causes. It is not caused by African culture, a poor climate or corruption. It is primarily a product of the way in which the West has bled the third world, particularly through the forced repayment of crippling debts.

The debt crisis has played a large part in the spread of disease in Africa and Latin America. One of the most common ways of raising funds to pay debt is by cutting public spending. This in turn leads to reductions in vaccination programmes and more polluted water supplies, which allow diseases to spread and breed much more easily. That is why there have recently been the first epidemics of typhoid in Latin America this century.

Indeed all of the 'solutions' to the debt crisis ultimately involve an attack on the living standards of the mass of people in the third world. Public spending cuts have meant mass redundancies and an end to subsidies on staple foods. Real wages have been eroded, falling behind hyper-inflation. Imported goods, paid for with scarce foreign exchange, are only for the rich.

If the impact of the debt crisis is so terrible, why is this issue which once preoccupied the world's top bankers so little discussed in the West today?

The fact is that Western banks and governments were only ever concerned about the third world debt crisis inasmuch as it was a problem for *them;* they were never much interested in the dire problems facing the impoverished masses of Africa or Latin America. Seen in this light, it becomes clearer why the third world debt crisis has dropped off of the West's economic agenda. First, the Western financiers have managed to limit the damage it does to their accounts; and second, they have become preoccupied with other debt problems much nearer to home.

The various Western 'plans' for third world debt have been designed to bail out the banks rather than third world countries. The basic strategy has been to shift as much of the problem as possible on to the peoples of the third world, by imposing harsh austerity programmes through the International Monetary Fund and World Bank. The demise of the Soviet Union has given the West a freer hand to pursue this strategy in the third world than it would have had a decade ago. A couple of years ago, the *Financial Times* felt able confidently to note that the banking industry was 'past the worst of the third world debt crisis, which was itself the gravest danger facing it since the last war' (9 May 1990).

In the current slump, the attention of Western banks has also been diverted by a huge bad debt burden closer to home. Collapses such as those of the Maxwell empire, the Bank of Credit and Commerce International, the Heron Corporation and Mountleigh have all left the banks saddled with bad debt. Olympia & York, the Canadian company that owns Canary Wharf, alone owes as much money as Peru and almost twice as much as Bangladesh.

While Western capitalists try to extract the maximum repayments from the poorest countries on Earth to help finance their domestic crises, every day the third world is witnessing the economic equivalent of the Western massacre of Iraqis on the road to Basra. ●

LIVING MARXISM September 1992

Complete these sentences which are based upon the article above. You may need the following words:
concerned, barons, spread, bled, run, insomuch as, primarily, played, consistent.

1. Poverty is .... [1] a product of the way in which the West has .... [2] the Third World.
2. The debt crisis has ..... [3] a large part in the ..... [4] of disease.
3. The only country to record .... [5] economic growth was Colombia thanks to the drug .... [6] who .... [7] most of the economy.
4. Western banks and governments were only ever .... [8] about the Third World debt crisis ....[9] it was a problem for them.

(Suggested answers in Appendix 1)

Now answer the following questions with reference to the article:

- What effect has the debt crisis had on the people of Third World countries?

- Why is the Third World debt crisis no longer a burning issue for Western banks and governments?

- Do you agree or disagree with the arguments presented in this article?

Discuss your views with someone else.

Read the article below:

Votes of disabled 'denied'

AS MANY as 6,000 people with *disabiliies could have missed out on voting in the election in Hampstead and Highgate, according to The Spastics Society.

A report reveals the constituency's polling stations to be among the country's 20 least accessible for people with disabilities, contravening the Representation of the People Act 1983.

Problems include uneven pathways leading to the polling stations, a shortage of ramps and narrow doors.

The report claims that 11pc of schools used for voting in Hampstead and Highgate were accessible to people in wheelchairs. but said that half the public halls could not be reached at all, and as many as 60pc of the community centres visited had at least two problems.

Brian Lamb. the society's head of campaigns, added: "The report provides overwhelming evidence that people with disabilities are disenfranchised, ignored and marginalised during the General Election."

* disabilities

How can facilities for the disabled be improved? Make a list of 10 suggestions.

Discuss your list with someone else.

* PUB REGULARS ... FRIENDS INDEED!

Compare the following two articles:

Pub regulars brighten up kids' lives

SICK children at Westminster Hospital have received a £1,000 gift from kind-hearted customers at The Eclipse pub in Barnsbury Road, Islington.

Two brave regulars had their heads shaved to raise money and the rest of the cash came in from sponsored darts matches, raffles, quiz nights, lucky dips and auctions.

The Eclipse's publicans, Brian and Jean Roberts, presented the mammoth cheque to Jennifer Jones, who represented the children's hospital.

Friends indeed!

FUND-RAISING group the Friends of Whittington Hospital donated an incredible £87,000 to the hospital during the year.

The group's chairman Sam Swallow announced at a recent meeting that highlights were the donation of two ultra sound scanners — one for the maternity department and one for general use — costing a total of £27,000, and two Pegasus beds for very sick patients.

How would you raise funds for a hospital? Give at least 6 suggestions.

Compare your views with someone else.

Read this article carefully:

Pond plan intended to enhance environment

RECENTLY there has been some concern about the City Corporation's proposals to refurbish the facilities at the mixed bathing pond on Hampstead Heath. The main fear appears to be that the corporation will ruin the intrinsic character and charm of the pond by making "improvements". I want to allay the fears of pond users and reassure them that we have taken on board their concerns in drawing up the plans.

The existing pond facilities are over 50 years old, there is no mains water supply or drainage, the building is dilapidated and unsightly, the floor is uneven, there are no proper toilets, no showers and no hot water to the hand basins. We appreciate that the ponds are a natural facility and that the last thing required is some ghastly hi-tech complex, but we do feel that a few modest improvements will add to the safety and comfort of the swimmers and be more aesthetically pleasing to the local environment.

The main aspects of the work are:

● The compound will be replaced with a similar construction of the same height to the existing one, except that it will consist of dark green profiled steel sheeting instead of corrugated iron. The reason for this is that the area will be significantly smaller than the existing compound and the surplus land will be returned to the Heath.

● The uneven, cracked concrete floor in the compound will be replaced with a new one.

● Mains water supply and drainage will be provided.

● The chemical toilets which currently have to be emptied by the attendant will be replaced with proper flushing facilities.

● Cold water showers are being installed where none exist at present.

● Hot water will be provided to the hand basins.

The message we received from users is that they like the spartan facilities, and this is reflected in the plans. All the proposed changes received the support of the Heath's Consultative Committee. We have recently carried out exactly the same type of work on the men's pond, and the improvements have been extremely well received by the users.

As with all Heath matters, it is the corporation's objective that the mixed pond is preserved as a centre of enjoyment and relaxation for all its users. We firmly believe these modest improvements will enhance, not spoil, that enjoyment.

The letter from A. Alvarez in last week's Ham & High expressed three particular concerns — about consultation, the roof of the building and the tree. I would like to assure Mr Alvarez and others that: consultation did take place when the plans were publicly on display at Camden Town Hall and our own offices at Aztec House; the partial roofing at the existing facilities will be retained but renewed, and there is no question of chopping down the stunning copper beech tree.

GORDON WIXLEY,
Chairman,
Hampstead Heath
Management Committee,
Members' Room, Guildhall, EC2.

- Can you identify a similar problem in your local neighbourhood?

- Suggest ten measures that should be adopted to solve the problem.

Compare your answers with someone else.

Read this article carefully:

Superior persons

The modernist avant-garde and the rank and file

TERRY EAGLETON

John Carey

THE INTELLECTUALS AND
THE MASSES
Pride and prejudice among the literary
intelligentsia, 1880–1939
246pp. Faber. £14.99.
0 571 16273 8

The tidal wave of literary modernism which broke over Europe in the early decades of this century did little more than lap the edges of traditional English culture. There *was* of course a flourishing modernism in these islands; but it was largely the product of the literary exiles and expatriates – of those displaced, peregrine souls who from James and Conrad to Eliot and Pound were charitable enough to write most of our great modern literature for us. As cosmopolitan outsiders, these men could bring fresh, estranging perspectives to bear on the native culture, and thus had their finger on the modernist pulse; but because what attracted some of them to England was its civilized, traditionalist milieu, in contrast to their own "inorganic'" or politically turbulent homelands, the modernist art they created was often enough of a conservative or elitist kind. To this extent, English modernism wrote large the paradox that stamped much of its European counterpart: radical aesthetics, reactionary politics.

Why did England prove so resistant to modernist experiment? For one thing, it was the oldest industrial nation in the world, with a well-entrenched heritage of realism in art, empiricism in philosophy and doughty common sense in its routine social values. This was hardly the most fertile breeding-ground for the scandalous avant-gardism of a Breton or Mayakovsky. For much the same reasons, it was less easily bowled over by the shock of the new – for it has been claimed that modernism thrives best in industrially backward

societies anxiously or euphorically caught up in rapid technological change. In Europe, much artistic experiment was fuelled by political revolution, as art, like politics, strove to imagine beyond the limits of the given; but the more settled political conditions of Britain lent themselves less obviously to such utopianism. It is surely no accident that the most adventurous outbreak of literary modernism in Britain, in the early years of the century, occurred in backward Ireland – in a politically unstable corner of the British Isles that was living through the traumatic impact of modernity on deep-rooted tradition. Finally, modernism is nothing if not cosmopolitan, crossing national frontiers as cavalierly as it moves between different art forms; and Britain's inward-looking imperial identity was hardly enthused by the pretentious antics of a bunch of arty foreigners. While modernism was sweeping Europe, the phenomenon of English Literature was being considered at Cambridge; and few avant-garde works were granted leave to apply. The two greatest home-grown English modernist writers were for different reasons at odds with this Little Englandism: a provincial miner's son who abandoned England as soon as he could, and an emancipated woman who cast a cold satiric eye on the Establishment.

By the 1930s, then, with Auden and Orwell, realism was back in the literary saddle; and since then, English critics as diverse as Frank Kermode and Donald Davie have found occasion to defend plain speech and social democratic values from the lures of a spiritually rootless experimentalism. They have now been joined by John Carey, whose new book, *The Intellectuals and the Masses*, focuses on modernism's odious elitism. Professor Carey sees rightly that modernism and "mass" culture were born more or less at a stroke – that the former is, among other things, a desperate last-ditch reaction to the supposed debasement of language and literature by mass art, literacy and education. His book is a spine-chilling record of the modern writer's raging contempt for ordinary men and women, all the way from the eugenicist zeal of a Wells or a Yeats, and the misanthropic ravings of a D. H. Lawrence, to the sour snobbisms of Virginia Woolf and the Hitlerite leanings of Wyndham Lewis. It is a sobering, if hardly original indictment, exposing as it does the complicity between the finest of literary artefacts and the most brutally regressive of social values.

As an account of modernism as a whole, however, Carey's thesis is drastically one-sided. His mistake is to reduce that extraordinarily diverse, contradictory movement to its Olympian disdain for the masses, and to view this, moreover, as a calculated conspiracy: "The early twentieth century saw a determined effort, on the part of the European intelligentsia, to exclude the masses from culture. In England this movement has become known as modernism." What, then, of the radical modernism of the Futurists, Dadaists and Surrealists, or the populist strain of some North American variants? Are Tatlin, Meyerhold, Brecht and Carlos Williams to be categorized along with Lewis and Pound? Carey's narrowly Anglocentric perspective edges such inconvenient questions aside; it also obscures the fact that, while much modernism belonged on the political right, it was nevertheless a *radicalism* of the right. Its distaste for suburbia and liberal democracy was often enough coupled with views which the Orwellian Carey might himself well share: a hostility to inert traditionalism and rampant commercialism, a protest against oppressive forms of authority and uniformity, an iconoclastic way with the sacred cows of state and religion. Modernism, to be sure, is in part a scream of outrage against mass society, and as such a deeply self-interested aesthetic; but does this then imply, as Carey seems to hold, that there was simply nothing in its sense of how common men and women were being manipulated by a profit-hungry press, or how their lives were being blighted by a soulless commercialism? Is the true champion of the people one who attends to such exploitation, or one who dismisses it as the fantasy of alienated intellectuals? Is the choice really one between Nietzsche and Lord Northcliffe?

The Intellectuals and the Masses is a good deal stronger on documentation than on argument. It is concerned to show how the modern concept of the masses was gradually constructed; but it passes over in silence the innovative work of Raymond Williams on this topic, and thus fails to ask itself how Williams could be at once a relentless critic of such dehumanizing jargon and a vigorous advocate of modernism. Carey's writing is usually at its best when assembling, in pokerfaced, drily sardonic style, the smug, pretentious or blood-curdling opinions of others, leaving his own critical stance suggestively implicit. There is more than enough to curdle the blood in this compendium of loathing and arrogance; but the acerbic Careyish wit has given way here to a curiously flat presentation, which is really too irritated to be enticing. When it comes to the masses, some modernists indeed showed all the signs of monomania; the risk of this generously motivated book is of merely reproducing that tunnel vision with a different moral inflection, rather than analysing its complex historical roots.

Terry Eagleton is Thomas Warton Professor-elect at the University of Oxford.

Answer the following questions:

- Why, according to Terry Eagleton, was England so resistant to modernism?
- What does John Carey think of modernism?
- How do his views differ from those of Terry Eagleton?
- In what way can modernism be considered a radical movement?

What do you think about the following statements? Find examples proving or disproving these declarations:

- Modernism is a combination of radical aesthetics and reactionary politics.
- Artistic experiment is often fuelled by political instability.
- English literature is predominantly inward-looking and imperial.
- The modern writer is scornful of ordinary men and women.

Discuss your views with someone else.

Read the article below:

Forlorn sameness of naturalism

Forum

Steven Berkoff

●●●●●●●●●●●●●●●●●●●●●●●●●●●●

I T WAS a fascinating experience to be led by the Guardian's stalwart critic, Michael Billington, through his mini-Open University lecture on naturalism (Review Guardian, June 25) as he once again untangles the knotty skein of literature and puts John Guare firmly in his place.

What was fascinating was Guare's remark about divesting the theatre of the "cancer of naturalism". Well said! But having seen the play in question, Six Degrees Of Separation, at the Royal Court, it may be that by Yankee standards his topical play is daring, but his work is still rooted in naturalism and worse. It reflects and appeases the audience — which is naturalism's most sinister vice — with its ghastly mirror image of the yuppy audience that supports it. Mr Guare has a long way to go before he can consider himself anti-naturalistic and his role model might be Eugene O'Neill, whose Emperor Jones and Hairy Ape both laid bare the grovelling turpitude of mirror-image theatre. Both plays are testaments to the power of drama when divested of the need slavishly to copy the day-to-day details of bourgeois life so beloved of our critics.

Curiously your critic name-drops the giants of literature as if to demonstrate the rich soil of naturalism — but confusing the novel and the drama. The two are utterly different. Literature is by nature imaginative and free-flowing and Guare was talking about the static nature of the play.

Naturalism means reproduction of the external world and this world is the only valid one for those who don't want to be taken anywhere else. It is a world that lives from the head up and can be seen trundling out of its forlorn sameness in all major theatres. It likes amateurism which is naturalism's strongest forte. It treats its audience as idiots with its belief in stage blood and dry ice to suggest battle. Though there is a tendency to minimise the need for sets in a nod towards that unknown void, it still claims huge grants for its decor since it doesn't really believe in the power of the performer. Naturalism is not very fond of the art of movement and shape, choreography and ensemble since the naturalistic director knows next to nothing about the workings of the body. He has spent so much time trying to be a literateur and an expert on iambs and line endings.

In the A to Z of the arts, naturalism is still at "A" and yet there are many ways to perceive experiences without giving them titles. And Mr Guare doesn't consign 120 years of achievement to the ashcan, which is rather a tendentious statement and one which of course the fierce defender of naturalism would make. Heavy and missing the point.

Theatre art can be a complex and powerful experience, whether it's called naturalism or constructivism. But an audience likes to be stimulated and repeating the same old formula over and over again may be a reason why theatre will eventually die out.

Film is the art of naturalism or even the endless maw of TV seems religiously devoted to it, though I remember a braver time when I could see Buchner and Orwell as regular occurrences.

Naturalism is what you do when you don't know anything else. When you have little skill for anything else you automatically revert to the copying of everything around you. It is the art of the cave-drawing. That there is such a reverence for naturalism today suggests to me a fear of the unknown and a contempt for the difficult. Since your critic throws some names around in his gang, allow me the same privilege. Eisenstein, Max Rheinhart, Kazan, Samuel Beckett, Tennessee Williams, Ionesco, Eugene O'Neill, James Joyce and Kafka. Kafka is a realist of sorts but, like all great writers, uses the outer layers of naturalism as a structure to create his inner world. It is this outer world that the naturalist clings to.

Whilst the theatre's naturalistic movement, Your critic claims, began in the 19th century, it may have been a worthy reaction to stilted drama and it may now have become as stilted as that which it replaced. Hitler was very prone to naturalism too. Finally, great thoughts make themselves felt in whatever signature the artist chooses.

-   What criticism does Steven Berkoff make of naturalism?

-   What do you think should be the ideal relationship between theatre and audience?

Read the following article:

The creative critic

Claire Messud

Playing in the Dark: Whiteness and the Literary Imagination, by Toni Morrison (Harvard University Press, £11.95)

THE creative writing of a critic tends often to result in something other and uncomfortably hybrid. So too with the criticism of the creative writer; and it is not without trepidation that one turns to the analytical musings of Toni Morrison.

But Playing In The Dark is enhanced rather than confused by its writerly preoccupations. A slim book of three essays, it addresses the nexus of American thought since Emerson: the constitution of American identity, and, specifically, the "self-conscious but highly problematic construction of the American as a new white man." Morrison's thesis — concerning the "parasitical nature of white freedom", where freedom is intrinsic to American identity; and the fact that "Africanism is inextricable from the definition of Americanness" — is not of itself new. The enslavement and debasement of black peoples as a precondition for white Enlightenment notions of humanity and individualism has been widely documented, by Franz Fanon, Edward Said and others. And yet, Morrison's daring — as a writer, a black woman —in addressing the issue in contemporary America is a measure of her integrity and courage.

Many African American critics, such as Henry Louis Gates Jr or bell hooks, have turned their backs on the interaction of white and black in American literature (and in America at large), to address instead pressing and neglected issues of black culture, literature and semiotics. In so doing, they ride a wave of separatism which, while perhaps necessary, is historically inaccurate: America is profoundly and inescapably *about* the relationship of blacks and whites, and an attempt to grapple with that relationship is seminal to any exploration of American identity, regardless of race.

Morrison is not interested in this separatism. In these essays she examines "the impact of racism on those who perpetuate it". Through readings of Poe, Twain, Cather and Hemingway, she identifies the creation of an 'Africanist' character in white American writing, where Africanism is "a term for the denotative and connotative blackness that African peoples have come to signify, as well as the entire range of views, assumptions, readings and misreadings that accompany Eurocentric learning about these people." Not dissimilar to Said's Orientalism, this character has served as a blank slate, an Other on to which white Americans have projected everything that transgresses the limits of white identity — such that it provides "the means of thinking about body, mind, chaos, kindness and love".

Morrison's reflections, while not original, are vital not simply to conceptions of racial identity but also to those of American literary production. But the relationship of criticism to literature is similar to that of whiteness to blackness: criticism, an authoritarian discourse, constantly circumscribes and displaces literature, making a myth of it. The only redemption from the historical opposition of whiteness and American "Africanism" will not come from criticism and critical books like Morrison's, but in the creation of *literature* by, for and about African Americans. Which is why one is grateful, ultimately, that Morrison is a novelist rather than a critic.

Claire Messud is the deputy editor of Guardian Women.

- Do you agree or disagree with the statement that 'the relationship of criticism to literature is similar to that of whiteness to blackness: criticism, an authoritarian discourse, constantly circumscribes and displaces literature, making a myth of it.'?

Give your reasons. Discuss your views with someone else.

We hope that by now, you'll be more aware of what is important in the initial stage of essay writing, and which particular skills need to be developed.

You would therefore be well advised to test your vocabulary resources in areas which you and your fellow students can identify as being broadly representative of today's issues.

We also hope you will have discovered that one of the best ways of identifying issues and finding arguments for or against a particular question, is to discuss both your priorities and your points of view with someone else who may not share them, and to whom you will then have to justify your own position. Of course this applies to any intellectual exercise and is not limited to foreign language learning. But the challenge here is twofold:

1. *to react to issues* which happen to be raised in English society today.

2. to react to these issues *in English*.

The following chapters will build on the skills you have practised in this chapter and will hopefully help you to write a full essay in English.

Furthermore, we would recommend that while you're working with this book you read the English press regularly (see Chapter 12) and listen frequently to English-speaking radio and TV programmes, especially those which contain debate and discussion.

Chapter 3

Collecting your thoughts

On first reading, essay titles often look difficult and abstract, impossibly removed from our way of expressing thoughts and ideas in daily life.

Under examination conditions, when you are confronted with a particular issue,

e.g.-   capital punishment

-   freedom of the press

-   the national interest

-   fashion etc.

the artificiality of it all just seems to be too much!

But when you come to think of it, in informal conversations at home or with a group of friends, we all tend to say things which could go like this:

* Cars should be banned from town centres.

* People don't think these days, look, they all dress alike.

* Alcoholism is awful, isn't it? The sale of spirits should be strictly controlled.

* Newspapers are boring, they all say the same thing.

* One should leave one's family at the age of 18.

* We don't really know what is happening in the nuclear industry, do we?

* Why should Britain stay in the Common Market?

* This crime is so appalling that one is forced to bring up the issue of capital punishment.

* These days it's really impossible to have anything repaired around the house.

* All television series are American; if they aren't (American) they copy the American model.

* Have you read any good books recently? I haven't ... Books bore me anyway.

The Context

In order to understand opinions, statements or questions, it's a good idea to imagine the context in which they could have been raised (who said what to whom and when?).

Do the following statements sound as if they are public or private; in other words, were they made:

1. publicly (by politicians, broadcasters, journalists, public figures etc.)?

2. privately (at home, amongst friends etc.)?

3. both publicly and privately?

Please tick the appropriate box:

Table 1

	Public	Private	Both
1. Unemployment is a tragedy.			
2. Football is not what it used to be: it's too violent			
3. Market forces rule our lives			
4. The sciences are much more important than the arts.			
5. Everybody is racist.			
6. All newspapers are biased.			
7. Most people do not care about their neighbours, they only think of money!			
8. Yes, it is important to learn foreign languages.			

It may not be very easy to distinguish between public and private statements, since expressing an opinion (whether it be 'true' 'authentic', 'sincere' or 'genuine' or not), is part of 'usual' exchanges between human beings. What differs is the manner in which they are expressed (the choice of vocabulary, the tone, the register ...., ... whether the statement is personalised or not, whether it occurs in the course of a heated argument or as one of the many 'clichés' we produce ...)

In order to be more aware of the way you say things (i.e. how you use language differently in certain situations, such as writing a personal letter, or an essay, or a publicity leaflet etc.; talking to a friend, your parents, a teacher, somebody you have just met in a club ...),

1. tick the appropriate box in the chart.

2. ask a friend to do the same exercise.

3. compare and discuss the results.

Table 2

Statements	You			Your friend		
	Formal	Informal	Both	Formal	Informal	Both
1. Everybody should learn and know how to use a computer these days.						
2. It is much more pleasant to live in a small town than in a big city.						
3. Smoking should be banned from all public places.						
4. Society is more divided than ever.						
5. There isn't enough money spent on public services.						
6. People don't want to work these days.						
7. Shops should be open on Sundays.						
8. Nobody reads books nowadays.						
9. I hate watching the news.						
10. Love is what matters in life.						

Although most essay titles look formal and remote, when you think about the ideas expressed and the questions raised, it's not usually so difficult to attribute the utterance (which has become an essay) to *a real speaker* and to imagine the context in which it was produced.

How would you say the following in your mother tongue?

Table 3

English	Your mother tongue
1. Politics is a game.	
2. Love is a myth.	
3. The media is American.	
4. Is happiness possible?	
5. Art is reserved for an elite.	
6. How would you describe democracy?	
7. Good novels are extremely rare.	
8. People are no longer interested in poetry.	
9. The history of Europe is still to be written.	
10. Everybody's dream is to become rich.	
11. Terrorism is a problem of modern times.	
12. Trade unions have lost their credibility.	
13. Education should be the same for all.	
14. What is popular culture?	
15. What are the negative aspects of tourism?	

Discuss your perception of cultural differences with someone else.

Now that you've started to play with words and ideas in English, let's go a step further. So as to encourage you to

1. express and develop your reactions
2. understand how two English students reacted to a particular question/essay title
3. express yourself in English

We are going to use a statement which was originally heard on the radio:

* CONTEMPORARY MUSIC TURNS PEOPLE INTO MORONS

1. What are your first reactions to this statement? Write them down in note form.

2. Now read John and Margaret's reactions to the same question. They are both 18 years old English students

* What exactly is meant by *contemporary music*?

a. Rock music
   Soul music
   Reggae music
b. All the new groups and experimental orchestras who are looking for fresh sounds by tapping bottles, brandishing sheets of metal etc.
c. Contemporary songs (words and music).
d. Present-day jazz groups or orchestras that play classical music.

In other words, what type of music are we talking about?

* The term *morons* refers to individuals who are completely mindless and incapable of any rational act. It is an extremely pejorative expression.
  There is no doubt that having your ears blasted for hours on end cannot be considered a very healthy or constructive activity, let alone a relaxing one.
  But, on the other hand, the fact that you can understand a few words in another language or even whole songs, means that listening is not entirely unproductive. Violent rhythms can also be a means of exorcising the barbaric impulses that are in all of us .....
  This said, the question must now be raised: who exactly are these people who are being turned into morons? Is it all classes and ages who are being affected? Each generation has different musical tastes ... We need only think of the arguments about music that go on in almost every household.

* To say that contemporary music, rather than music in general, turns people into morons implies that, in the past, music had a different function. What was this function?

- to make people more 'thoughtful', more 'civilized'? I bet! Music is supposed to have a calming effect on people. But on

61

the battlefield, musicians have never been successful in stopping the fighting. The enemy has never laid down arms in order to listen to music!

- to make life more pleasant, more romantic? How true! How nice it is to dine tête-à-tête to the sounds of soft music wafting gently through the air!

- to entertain people? There is no doubt that in the past, as in the present, the principal function of music has been to entertain.

Once the parallel between contemporary music and music of the past has been established, we must consider what is meant by the concept 'entertainment'. There have always been some forms of entertainment that are noble and edifying and others that are more primitive, violent or idiotic.

If we look at the words of contemporary songs, they do, indeed, appear very simplistic. It may, however, be interesting to note that English songs that are successful abroad are not usually the same ones that make the charts at home.

* I shall conclude by saying that music is no more likely to turn us into morons than televised gameshows or soaps.

3. Now write down ten statements on this topic: (either your own statements or ideas expressed by Margaret and John that you agree with).

    i.e. - What ideas are the same?

         - Do you have different opinions: If so, *why*?

         - Deliberately take opposite sides to the argument (as in a Court of Law), one of you defending contemporary music and the other attacking it.

         - Play the devil's advocate, whereby one of you systematically refutes what the other says.

Do you agree or disagree with the following statements? Why?

Table 4

	Agree	Disagree	Give two reasons justifying your answer
1. Television is a threat to literature.			
2. Poetry cannot be translated.			
3. In the modern world, you have to be aggressive and competitive.			
4. There is nothing worse than stupidity.			
5. Knowing how to sell something is an art.			
6. Everyone ought to learn at least one other language in primary school.			
7. We cannot understand what is happening at present if we have no concept of history.			
8. To successfully conduct a business transaction, you should speak the language of your client.			
9. Tobacco is less dangerous than cars or nuclear waste.			
10. Order is necessary but too much of it is a bad sign.			

Compare and discuss your answers with someone else.

Let's now move to some other topics on which you will express and develop your reactions.

* SHOULD INHERITED WEALTH BE ABOLISHED?

- Give an order of priority to the following questions as indicated in column II.

- Then draw up your own questionnaire (by selecting at least five questions) and submit it to people around you.

63

Table 5

	Give an order of priority to these questions by renumbering them
1. Should inherited wealth be abolished?	
2. Do inequalities in wealth go hand in hand with inequalities in education?	
3. Do you think that with the present system of inherited wealth there can ever be genuine equality of opportunity?	
4. Do people with inherited wealth have less entrepreneurial spirit?	
5. To limit equality should we put an end to the practice of handing down vast fortunes from generation to generation?	
6. Do you think that a government would ever be willing to abolish inherited wealth?	
7. Do you agree that it is the State itself that, through taxation, benefits from this system of inherited wealth?	
8. Would you like to leave something to your children? Yes/No? Why?	
9. In your opinion is inherited wealth: - a right? - a principle? - the luck of the draw? - a scandal?	
10. Are people liable to become lazy if there is no possibility of handing down their possessions to their children?	

1. Compare the reactions/opinions of the group you have interviewed.

2. Is there a consensus in the group?

3. Were conflicting ideas expressed?

4. Write a brief report or a short article, based on the group's answers and reactions.

* FASHION IS A FORM OF TYRANNY

Which two of the following statements on fashion are the closest to
your own opinions on the matter?

1. Clothes are first and foremost the expression of our
   personality.

2. Fashion is a language. We have first of all to learn the basic
   rules. Then we can each create our own style.

3. Our clothes reveal our true personality.

4. Whoever says 'no' to fashion, says 'no' to other forms of
   tyranny.

5. Fashion blunts our critical faculties.

6. Why should we follow the fashion?

7. Can people follow the fashion without being rich?

8. Who determines what is fashionable?

9. Fashion tends to stifle our personality.

10. Fashion contributes to social inequality.

11. To what extent are we aware of fashions?

12. When we think of fashion, we think mainly of clothes.

13. Is it possible to respect someone who is badly dressed and
    badly groomed?

14. Why do so many people wear clothes that do not suit them?

15. Media stars create fashions which we blindly imitate.

16. The lives of many young people are governed by fashion.

17. We can guess people's age by their clothes, hairstyle and accessories.

18. Fashion is always excessive and extravagant.

19. The fashion industry keeps the economy booming.

20. Only extroverts follow the fashion.

21. Fashion is a game which makes life more interesting and more fun.

22. Why is plastic surgery so popular?

23. Fashion excludes fat people.

24. Old people do not need to be fashionable.

25. Many feminists refuse to wear smart clothes and jewellery because they associate these with the exploitation of women. But what do they want to prove - and to whom - by opting for ugliness or slovenliness?

26. Everytime you change your hairstyle, you produce all kinds of remarks and comments. Why?

27. Many people who are interested in art, especially the visual arts, are scornful of the fashions and dress anyway they want.

28. Whatever people say, men are more interested in fashion than women.

29. Why are so many fashion designers nowadays men?

30. Fashion is frivolous and takes our mind off serious matters.

31. Tastes change and fashion not only expresses these changes in

the field of consumption but also in the field of culture and of ideas.

32. There are also fashions in food (to eat healthy, natural food, for example); fashion is, therefore, a historical and social phenomenon.

33. Fashion seeks both to reveal and to hide the body (e.g. the mini-skirt).

34. There are fashions for the rich and fashions for the poor.

Compare your choice with somebody else.

If your choice is different, can you find two other opinions that you both find acceptable?

* SPORT IS NECESSARY; IT CHANNELS OUR NEED FOR VIOLENCE

(1) Is sport necessary?
(2) Can any physical activity become or be called a sport?
(3) Is there a relationship between sport and violence?
(4) Do you think that the media devotes too much time to sport and shows too much violence on the screen?
(5) Are all sports violent?

Do any of the following sentences answer or illustrate one of the five questions above?

* Is there a link between mental stability and the practice of sports? In other words, 'mens sana in corpore sano'?

* Sport can regulate violence in the sense that it enables people to give expression to impulses that would normally be repressed.

* Has competition replaced the original aim of sports, that of developing a healthy body?

* Why have our football grounds become the scene of violence?

* Playing games is a very human activity. It gives people the opportunity to fight and to compete with each other.

* Some sports like boxing appear to celebrate the cult of violence. Should they be banned?

* Sport has become a spectacle; people no longer practise sports, they sit down in front of the television and watch others play.

* Does the media attach too much importance to sport?

* **WOMEN ARE FULL INDIVIDUALS**

   (1) What is an individual?
   (2) Do women and men have the same rights?
   (3) Do women earn as much as their male colleagues?
   (4) Are there more men than women in top professions?
   (5) Should women stay at home to look after their children?
   (6) Do boys and girls choose to study the same subjects at school?
   (7)
   (8)
   (9)
  (10)

Add four more questions to the above list, concerning women in society, their role and their rights, by selecting (or adapting) some of the following statements:

* What is meant by 'full individuals'?

* Have women sufficient knowledge to assume their rights as citizens?

* As long as nature demands that they have children, can women really be full individuals?

* In the past, with a few exceptions, women have never distinguished themselves in the artistic, intellectual, political or economic spheres. Is this state of affairs going to change?

*   Although they have the same qualifications as men, women are frequently refused employment.

*   Employers still continue to employ men in preference to women.

*   Men still do not share the housework or take responsibility for the children.

*   Should women allow themselves to be treated as objects?

*   Women always have to fight for financial independence.

*   Women become aware of their individuality too late in life to reap the full benefit.

*   Women will always remain enslaved to men because of their maternal instincts.

*   How can women avoid the traditional female role of daughter, mother and wife?

*   Women do not discover their 'individuality' in the world of work. It is simply another form of slavery.

*   It is only by working together with men in a common cause that women will discover their own individuality and dignity.

*   Are the same jobs open to women as to men?

*   Why does a woman change her name when she gets married?

*   Are women taxed the same as men?

*   Is contraception solely the responsibility of women?

*   Women enjoy being kept by men.

*   Will a woman agree to her husband staying at home to do the housework and look after the children?

* Sexual difference does exist but all citizens should be equal before the law.

* As long as there is a danger of being raped, women will remain potential victims.

* Should women learn the art of self-defence?

* Single women represent a danger - for other women.

* Why is the relationship between mother and daughter so difficult?

* **OUR AGE IS DEPRESSING**

(1) Is there any reason to feel depressed about the world we live in?
(2) If the answer is 'no', how can you explain that some people feel this way?
(3) If the answer is 'yes' explain why ...
(4) What do we mean by 'our age'?
   What is typical of it, socially, politically etc.?
(5) Is society today more depressing than it used to be? If yes, when did this change occur? Why?

Here are some thoughts on the matter ... Read them carefully.

* Why should we describe an age of rapid technological development and social reform as depressing?

* Nowadays culture is available to a much wider public.

* Culture should bring us happiness.

* The plagues of past centuries were just as serious as those that threaten us today.

* It is up to us to put an end to this nuclear madness and make our world a happier place to live in.

* If our age is depressing, we should be making every effort to improve our personal well-being.

* The working day has been shortened and people have more leisure time. So why should our age be depressing?

* We should stop saying that our age is depressing. Things will not get better by complaining about them.

* Look at the people in the street: they hardly ever smile, they are always in a hurry and worried. Why?

* Although on average, people earn more than in the past, they are not any happier. Why not?

* Why do so many people dress in black? Are they in mourning?

* In the past, many people worked hard and earned little but they always helped their neighbours. Today, this is no longer true.

* Life today is too noisy, too hectic, too competitive. People are always tired.

* Depression can be caused by all kinds of abuse: drink, tobacco, food, loud music etc.

* When we read Miles Kington, we are reminded of how important laughter is for our health.

* Everyone is afraid of their neighbour. That is why our age is so depressing.

* Nowadays, popular festivals tend to degenerate into fights and the police are called in. Can't people enjoy themselves peacefully?

* Most people find life difficult because they do not have enough money. It's not the age that is depressing but the conditions under which we live.

* In the city, people do not know each other and are barely polite. In the country, they are more friendly - they greet each other at least!

* The planet is threatened with extinction. How can we not be depressed?

* Young people have no hope. Their future is clouded by unemployment and Aids as well as the threat of war.

* Drugs continue to wreak havoc upon people's lives.

* Newspapers bring us only unpleasant news and this makes us all the more depressed.

* Fighting is going on everywhere in the world! Peace is impossible.

* Young people are worried and so they resort to violence.

* The eighties marked the end of an era of social stability.

* Is it acceptable that so many people are still dying of hunger in our age?

* Our age has seen an increase in the powers of the police.

* We all live in Hell and the only way out is death.

* People nowadays spend all their time buying, consuming or fighting. Our age is truly depressing.

* **TOURISM IS ONE OF THE EVILS OF OUR TIME.**

* Has modern transport changed the nature of tourism?

* Tourists only go to picturesque sites such as Land's End and Canterbury.

* Have package tours killed real tourism?

* The tourist industry is an important sector of the modern economy. It employs a large labour force.

* Why are we always attacking tourists? They are always very generous with their money. The only flourishing business nowadays is tourism.

* Is there an unhealthy side to tourism? Is it a modern form of colonialism?

* Why does the media make such a fuss whenever the tourist industry is affected by a political crisis or the fall of the dollar?

* Hotels, restaurants and souvenir shops all live off tourism. Do we want to increase the number of unemployed?

* Tourism is a means of getting to know different races and different customs.

* Undoubtedly, some tourists are drug traffickers and more severe measures should be taken against them.

* Most tourists behave in a courteous manner. So what are we complaining about?

* You find some hooligans among the tourists but this is inevitable.

* With the exception of football hooligans, English tourists are welcome everywhere in the world.

* Can we get to know the people of another country after only a short stay in their land?

* Tourism is an important source of pollution.

* Do we go abroad for educational purposes or to enjoy ourselves?

* The tourist industry is concerned more with profit than with the protection of the environment.

* Taken as a whole, tourists often give the impression of being idiots.

* Package tours leave no room for initiative.

* Are there places which have been spoilt by tourism?

* Tourism is a seasonal activity. Out of season many towns are dead, the beaches are deserted and the people unemployed.

* Why are there so many tourists nowadays?

* There are very few tourists who change their habits and mode of thinking when they travel.

* Some monuments are completely hidden by the crowds in the tourist season.

* Some people bemoan the fact that tourism is no longer reserved for the wealthy.

* People still enjoy independent travel.

* Campsites spoil the countryside.

* Everyone does the same thing at the same time.

* Everyone goes to the same places! Our civilisation has lost all sense of originality.

As revision for this chapter, match a solution (in the right hand column) to the list of problems listed on the left, by writing the corresponding number beside the answer which you consider to be most appropriate.

Compare your solution with someone else.

Table 6

Problems	Solutions
1) Old people feel isolated in the city	a] Crime prevention centres that are better adapted to modern life should be created
2] Girls are more interested in their appearance than in social and economic problems	b] Bill posting should be limited to particular streets or areas
3] Prisons are ancient and overcrowded	c] Crèches and nursery schools should be established
4] The urban landscape is spoilt by advertising	d] The Church has always said that nobody has the right to kill another human being. The State must now ensure that this message is understood by all
5] Some people clamour for the return of the death penalty	e] The legal system should be modernised and made more accessible to people
6] Culture is the privilege of the few	f] All the countries of the world should collaborate to put an end to terrorism
7] Mothers of young children often feel cut off from the rest of society	g] There should be more libraries and books should be cheaper
8] People read less and less	h] Everything should be done to reduce social inequality
9] Many citizens are reluctant to resort to justice	i] Day centres for children and the elderly should be created
10] Everyone lives under the threat of terrorism	j] The world of politics should be open to women
	k] Neighbourhood Self-Help committees should be established
	l] Girls should be encouraged to choose the same subjects at school as boys

This chapter has explored various ways of seeing and saying things, describing or assessing a situation and analysing a problem.

This is the first step of essay writing: an awareness of the many viewpoints that various people may have on a topic.

Chapter 4

What do *I* think?

Certain issues are more widely discussed by people than others. These become topical for a certain period, such as unemployment for instance, which has been at the forefront of the social scene for some time. Even if you are not a specialist in politics or sociology, you can't help but be aware of recurrent issues which are continually mentioned.

Opinion polls are an artificial way of canvassing opinion, but they at least provide a way of finding out how people view a problem and what they consider to be of primary importance. For example, a questionnaire may ask you whether you consider AIDS as being more (or less) important than poverty.

The various topics presented in this chapter have been drawn from surveys either published in the press or conducted by ourselves.

Our aim here is to invite you to express *your opinion* on the selected issues.

Give your rating of the issues listed, numbering them from 1 to 10 according to the degree of seriousness that you attach to them:

Table 7

List of recurrent issues	Your rating (give each issue a number 1 -10)	Justify your own selected order of importance
A) Social inequality (including racism and poverty)		
B) Unemployment		
C) Drugs		
D) Urban violence		
E) Nuclear power		
F) The inadequate funding of education and training		
G) International terrorism		
H) World hunger		
I) Pollution		
J) Aids		
K) War		

Compare you choice with someone else.

Here are some ideas expressed by our sample students at British Universities on the same issues:

A.   Social Inequality

Do you agree with them?	Yes/No
* It is nature that is responsible for social inequality: physical and intellectual inequality is inherited from our parents.	
* The most important problem is that of social inequality because it affects many different types of people.	
* Because property and possessions can legally be handed down from father to son, the rich remain rich and the poor remain poor.	
* It is a thirst for power that drives human beings to dominate those who are weaker than themselves.	
* Inequality is biological and genetic, society can do nothing about it.	
* Famine in some countries of Africa indicates to what lengths the selfishness of rich countries can go.	
* Instead of using the aid and subsidies they receive to improve the living standards of their own people, governments of the Third World prefer to grow rich and to live in luxury.	
* It is only wise people who, having reached a certain stage of detachment, no longer try to grow rich.	
* The motives which lead us to acquire knowledge and power are noble: they only become dangerous and destructive when they do not take into account the aspirations of others.	
* In Western countries, advertising makes the poor envious of the rich.	
* We live in a consumer society where we are urged to buy more and more products. Those with limited purchasing power are tempted to steal.	
* Poverty usually means a poor education.	
* Children from disadvantaged homes are forced to leave school as soon as possible so that they can support themselves or their family.	

Continued . . .

Do you agree with them?	Yes/No
* Social inequality is defined by the place (country/city) where we live, by the area and by the type of housing.	
* Often people from other countries and cultures have great difficulty integrating into society.	
* Immigrant workers are isolated in their country of adoption. They are accused of taking the jobs and the houses of the indigenous population and this xenophobia makes them victims of continual harassment.	
* In strip-cartoons, the baddies are often portrayed by coloured people, whilst in advertising, blacks are frequently presented as noble savages.	
* Racism stems from a need to assert one's superiority and a distrust of people whom one feels are different.	
* There are some people who are racist but who know how to hide or to control their feelings. There are others, however, whose prejudice must be overtly expressed and it is their behaviour that poses a threat to social stability.	
* Parents cannot be forced to love their children but there ought to be laws requiring them to feed them properly and to give them a good education. Some children, rich and poor alike, are disadvantaged from birth: their parents do not look after them.	
* It is impossible to force people to be tolerant: we must accept, therefore, that racism is only harmful when it becomes violent.	
* Inherited wealth and the colour of one's skin are not the only causes of inequality. It must be recognised that there are other things, such as intelligence and beauty, which are not distributed evenly.	
* In every community, there are some people, for example, writers, actors and footballers, who are more gifted than others and it is because of these 'talents' that they become rich. They do not all come from privileged homes, indeed, far from it.	
* In whatever manner social inequality manifests itself, one fact is certain: the most obvious source of inequality is money.	

Which measures would you now adopt to remedy social inequalities? Select your ten most appropriate suggestions from the list below, numbering them in order of importance:

Possible remedies to social inequality:

* Martin Luther King said that nobody renounces his privileges without putting up a fight. We could, none-theless, try to eliminate the greatest disparities between people.

* People should learn at school to be more liberal and more tolerant.

* We should try to improve the living conditions of those who are at the bottom of the social ladder by striving for a better distribution of wealth.

* Children should be taught from a very early age that all people are equal and that the value of a human being does not depend on colour or nationality.

* The anti-discrimination laws should be strengthened and constantly revised.

* The media should broaden its horizons and introduce us to completely different ways of living.

  Economic and diplomatic pressure should be brought to bear on racist governments like South Africa.

* The government should devote more money to improving the lot of the poor.

* It is at school that we learn to know and to respect others. Education should, therefore, be a top priority for governments.

* Given that human beings have the natural tendency to be selfish and greedy, they should be taught to have better moral feelings both at school and at home.

* Mothers from disadvantaged homes should be given financial support to enable them to stay at home to look after their children.

*   Young people from disadvantaged backgrounds should have the same opportunity to acquire a good education.

*   Social inequality could be abolished by increasing the wages of the poor. A guaranteed minimum wage should be introduced everywhere.

*   Everyone should develop self-respect and a respect for others.

Discuss your choice with someone else.

B.   Unemployment

Which two of the following points of view on *unemployment* are closest to your own evaluation of the issue?

*   Developments in technology are responsible for unemployment.

*   Mechanisation, the use of robots and computers, has clearly improved industrial productivity but it has also led to a reduction in the required manpower.

*   Because of an absence of retraining programmes, graduates are going to swell the ranks of the unemployed.

*   How can the number of unemployed be calculated? Many people moonlight but still receive unemployment benefit.

*   Unemployment is a complex problem which economists and politicians are unable to resolve.

*   Our industries cannot compete with cheap imports from the developing countries where the labour force receives a derisory wage. This creates unemployment that is exacerbated by a lack of investment.

*   More and more women wish to work and are, therefore, joining the unemployment register.

* While the demand for employment increases, the number of vacancies is diminishing in many sectors.

* Unemployment is an offence to the dignity of man.

* Unemployment may be inevitable in the modern world but that does not excuse laziness or dishonesty.

* Some people prefer to moonlight rather than to have a poorly paid job.

* A fundamental revaluation of work is necessary if a solution to the unemployment crisis is to be found.

* As we cannot curb technological development, nor demand that women stay at home to reduce the number of unemployed, we must increase industrial productivity, restrict the number of imported goods, control the rate of inflation and redouble our efforts in the education and training of young people.

* The government should encourage the unemployed to look for work by rewarding them when they find their first job.

* How can unemployment exist when the streets are dirty, the roads full of potholes, and the parks badly maintained? Unemployment is a political problem.

* Taxes should be increased so that the unemployed can be recruited by the State to help in the protection and renewal of the environment.

* The government should help small and medium-sized firms by reducing their tax burden.

* Different working patterns should be devised with more flexible hours and more frequent leaves of absence.

* If there is less work, it should be more evenly distributed.

81

* People should be taught to develop interests apart from work: but is this possible in a consumer society?

* In contemporary society, people are denied a fundamental right: the right to work.

* Unemployment threatens both white-collar and manual workers.

* When people are unemployed, they regress.

* A leisure policy would include the introduction of evening classes and of retraining courses. If we cannot eradicate unemployment, we can at least help people make the most of the situation.

C. Drugs

Which of these points of view would you put forward when discussing the problem of *drugs*:

(i) with your friends (of the same age group)?

(ii) in a fairly formal conversation, at a social gathering with people you don't know?

Insert (i) or (ii)

1) They have always existed: De Quincy and Coleridge took opium and Utrillo drank the turpentine he used for his painting. Before 1982, it was sensitive people, such as artists and scholars, who were attracted to cannabis as a palliative to humdrum everyday life.

2) Nothing ventured, nothing gained: one can understand the attraction of drugs.

3) Women often take drugs as a rebellion against the traditional female role. They are also tired of the platitudes and affectation that characterises feminist meetings.

82

4) At first sight, drugs seem harmless and appear to solve the problems of many unhappy maladjusted people. There are several types of drug addicts: some take drugs because they are depressed, others to be "with it" or to imitate others.

5) Students who are worried because of their exams can easily be tempted.

6) It is often at school that we discover drugs and develop a liking for them.

7) The drug addict is like the smoker: he lacks self-control. Unfortunately, his needs are more harmful.

8) Drug addicts are to be pitied.

9) Basically, drug addicts choose to die: in their desire to escape life's constraints, they slowly destroy themselves. Paradoxically, their fear of war, of family dissension or of unemployment, puts them in the camp of the living-dead: they find a thousand reasons for hastening their descent into Hell.

10) Drug addiction, like Aids, is a curse which affects all social classes. Dependency entails an ever increasing expenditure of money and addicts will stop at nothing to satisfy their needs.

11) Heroin produces a strong physical and psychological dependency.

12) The use of narcotics has become so widespread that the governments of the developed countries have finally decided to intervene.

13) The dangers of soft drugs have been underestimated as they can easily lead to the use of hard drugs. It is also in the interest of drug traffickers to persuade young people to buy more expensive narcotics.

14) It must not be overlooked that drug magnates create jobs, reduce the level of unemployment and bring in foreign currency.

15) Drugs have already been prohibited by law; it is up to the customs officers and the police to collaborate more closely in the arrest of traffickers.

16) Drug traffickers should be punished more severely and their property confiscated.

17) The State should give economic aid to the governments of drug-producing countries in the hope that they may be persuaded to confront the problem themselves.

18) A change in attitude towards drug addicts is required. They should not be regarded as criminals but treated as victims who need to be understood and helped by the community.

19) The creation of detoxification and rehabilitation centres for drug addicts should be a top priority for all governments.

20) Given the magnitude of the problem, it is the State that should control the circulation of drugs. To reduce demand they should be distributed under medical supervision. This would prevent addicts from themselves becoming traffickers and it might curb the general demand.

21) We cannot insist too strongly on the necessity for preventive measures. Schools should face their responsibility in this area as they are duty-bound to protect children. There is no doubt that the stories of young people who have themselves experienced the disastrous effects of drugs would be much more effective than any lecture or sermon from an adult.

22) In order to satisfy children's natural curiosity for new experiences, schools should provide stimulating courses. The educational system is not solely to blame for delinquency and drug addiction, but if children had more say in their curriculum, numerous problems would be avoided.

23) Everyone should be made to feel that they have a positive role to play in society. This requires a considerable effort on the part of parents, teachers and political leaders.

24) Every individual of a working age should have a job; unemployment and drug problems are linked.

25) In order to eliminate the problem, the cause of the evil must be found. A full-scale research programme, financed by the State, is, therefore, urgently needed. Its aim would be the detection of high-risk groups.

26) The drug problem cannot be examined in isolation. It must be placed within a wider context of crime, social inequality and juvenile delinquency.

Now select three of the above points of view which you consider to be the most:

	Insert reference number
* practical?	
* Utopian?	
* irrelevant in the society you live in	

What do you consider to be the most urgent problem of all?

If asked for advice by your Government, what suggestions would *you* make to solve the drug problem?

Get together with a friend and discuss your final assessment of all the points on the drug problem, and see *where*, *how* and *why* your ideas differ.

D.   Urban Violence

From the following list of statements relating to urban violence select what you consider to be:

	Insert ref. no.
* One cause for urban violence	
* Two suggestions which may contribute to solving the problem	

1) Although violence is more concentrated in the city than in the country, it exists everywhere. It is the result of social inequality and is also the expression of emotional and religious conflict.

2) As long as there are rich and poor, rulers and governed, there will always be violence.

3) Overpopulation and a shortage of living space leads to violence. An experiment conducted on rats shows that a colony of rats needs a certain amount of space to live. If they are locked up and no longer have enough room to wander around, their behaviour changes: the females are more likely to miscarry and to neglect their offspring who die. The young males form gangs that fight among themselves and attack females. At the time of copulation, the male who is normally gentle towards the female, becomes violent and aggressive. Human beings, when they are crammed into cities, behave in a similar manner.

4) In all industrial as well as developing countries, there is a mass exodus towards the city. Living conditions of displaced populations, of immigrant and unskilled workers are often deplorable and this frequently leads to violence.

5) Delinquency can equally well be caused by difficult home situations and by failure at school.

6) The anonymity of human relations in high-rise flats, a sense of alienation and of social injustice, together with the temptations of a consumer society, are the principle causes of urban violence.

7) Racism aggravated by unemployment, can lead to violence.

8) Racial minorities often live in ghettos and they are frequently in conflict with people of surrounding areas.

9) The media incite people to violence insofar as they present violence in cartoons, films, serials and news items.

10) Most adults must like violence otherwise how can the plethora of violent images in the cinema or on the television be explained?

11) There exist a great many remedies to urban violence. First of all, each individual should be given a job. Then, more houses should be built that are spacious and less noisy. Centres for educational and sporting activities should be established so that adolescents can be kept busy and let off steam.

12) To promote good relations between different social groups, town councils should devote a large share of their budget to the organisation of festivals.

13) There should be a policy to rehabilitate former convicts, drug addicts and delinquants. The living conditions of prisoners should also be improved so that they can prepare themselves for life outside prison.

14) The number of local police should be increased to protect individuals.

15) Jobs should be created in those areas that have been particularly affected by unemployment.

16) More jobs should be created in community welfare.

Write a short text (100 - 150 words) justifying your answer.

Compare your text with someone else.

E. Nuclear Power

Which of the following ideas on nuclear power are most likely to have been expressed by:

1) a pacifist?

2) a supporter of nuclear energy and weapons?

	Insert 1 or 2
* Whether we like it or not, we are living in an age of nuclear power.	
* Our resources of natural energy are almost exhausted.	
* We must distinguish between the peaceful and military use of nuclear power.	
* For the first time in our history, we have the means of destroying the whole human race.	
* Every country dreams of possessing the nuclear bomb.	
* Is nuclear power more horrific than Nazism?	
* Scientific progress, such as the use of nuclear power, can lead to human catastrophe.	
* A nuclear war could be planned and controlled and may not be any worse, perhaps, than other forms of combat. The real risk, on the other hand, is that of mechanical failure and of human error. Someone presses the wrong button and the whole of humanity is destroyed.	
* Since the discovery of the nuclear bomb, no country is safe; frontiers no longer have any meaning.	
* One point of view is that nuclear weapons are responsible for the peace of the last forty years.	
* Supposing that nuclear disarmament were possible, who is going to take the first step? What head of government would run the risk of being disowned by his/her people?	
* The zones of political instability such as the Middle East could alter the balance of power and indirectly bring about a nuclear war.	

*   The reduction of nuclear weapons is an impossible dream: it is too late to increase or to develop the arsenal of conventional weapons.

*   Heads of government should be surrounded by a committee of scientists and intellectuals whose role would be to prevent a nuclear disaster.

*   Non-nuclear research should be developed and other forms of energy should be exploited such as the sea, sun and wind.

*   The ideal solution would be a simultaneous, synchronised disarmament.

*   Can summit meetings between heads of government stop the arms race? Should we put more trust in a rapprochement between nations to put an end to this madness?

*   A large part of scientific research is nowadays linked to military and nuclear programmes.

*   Why do we always need to destroy each other?

Which ideas on nuclear power would *you* have expressed?

F.   Inadequate Funding of Education and Training

Carefully read the following opinions on education:

*   Technological advances mean an increasingly expensive training: the necessary equipment such as computers and videos is very costly.

*   Teachers should be constantly updating their skills.

*   In an attempt to woo the electorate, governments prefer to release funds for short-term projects rather than invest in the future of the country, viz. in training and education.

89

* People prefer a reduction in taxes to investing in educational programmes.

* In our society, teachers have neither status nor power.

* There exist three possible sources of funding for education: government taxation, local taxation and, increasingly, parental financial contribution.

* More and more parents are prepared to make enormous sacrifices to pay for the education of their children.

* In periods of crisis, it is education that suffers.

* In the long run, there is nothing more important than education: it lies at the heart of all healthy societies.

* The wealth of a country lies first and foremost in its people.

Now answer the following questionnaire and give reasons for your choices:

	Yes/No/Why, (qualify your answer)
* Education should be completely free and universal.	
* Education is a top priority; more money should be devoted to it than to defence.	
* Education should be state-run, compulsory and of a universal standard until the age of eighteen.	
* Continuing education should be a right in so-called advanced societies.	
* More value should be attached to the teaching profession.	
* Schools should eliminate and not strengthen social inequality.	
* Schooling, like life, is the luck of the draw.	

* As there is an enormous wastage of resources and of energy, the school system should be completely reorganised.

* Some children want to grow up quickly. For them school seems a waste of time.

* Because most people are not interested in educational and training programmes, governments are able to ignore them.

Discuss your reactions and opinions with someone else.

G.   International Terrorism
H.   World Hunger
I.   Pollution
J.   Aids
K.   War

Which one of the above international problems do you consider to be of most importance? Why?

Which are most frequently:

a) on television or radio?
b) in the press?
c) in conversation around you?

Why?

How would you try and solve any two of the four major international problems, if you were:

a) a head of State?
b) a scientist?
c) a lawyer?

Read an article from the press relating to these four problems.

Discuss the issues at stake with a friend and compare your opinions.

As you will no doubt have realised, our aim in this chapter was not to cover the whole spectrum of topical issues. Our intention was to invite you, as the title of this chapter indicates - 'what do *I* think?' - *to think along critical lines*.

Chapter 5

What does it mean?

Most essay titles, from the point of view of vocabulary and grammar, don't look too difficult.

Look at this list:

1. What is democracy?
2. How can we make democracy function more effectively?
3. What is a social class?
4. Do social classes exist?
5. Why do women play so little a role in political life?
6. Who has power?
7. Do women have equal opportunities?
8. Society is more authoritarian than twenty years ago.
9. If you were the head of government, what would be the first thing you would do?
10. Voting is a waste of time.

In most cases you may understand a given problem but find it difficult to go *beyond* answers such as these:

Yes/No
don't know (I'm not interested)
true/untrue
agree/disagree

However, to discuss the issues raised by a question is not always easy; most people say that they find it difficult to:

- relate what they know (from their daily experience and reading etc.) to questions raised by an essay title.

- speculate (do some creative thinking) on a word or a concept that they aren't sure about (e.g.: 'democracy', 'social class').

- express their ideas and thoughts (because they think them naive or clichéd).

- find relevant examples to illustrate their argument.

These problems are best overcome if essay writing is approached as a game based on the following strategies:

1. Sit in a circle as a group, and exchange ideas on a given subject: this will give you confidence through self-expression.

2. Either as a group or with one other person, play with words and ideas, discuss their various meanings.

3. In groups of two, spend half the time trying to explain something to the other person, and then reverse the roles, using a different topic.

4. In groups of two, take a decided stand on a particular issue and try to convince the other person that you are right.

5. Pretend to be in a courtroom, one speaking for and the other against: the onlookers will be able to appraise both sides of the discussion.

6. Play devil's advocate and contradict systematically whatever is being said by people around you.

7. Try to express opinions you don't share.

8. Select press-cuttings on a given topic and try to assess why and how the viewpoints differ etc.

Understanding an essay title can be fun! 'What does that mean?' dares the players not only to juggle with words but also to understand their meaning.

* AN ESSAY TITLE IS IN FACT A QUESTION.
(or a series of questions...)

This may not be obvious at first glance, but since you're asked to explain, agree or disagree, approve or disapprove, let's assume that beneath every statement there are, in fact, several questions ...

e.g.: ... **'art is reserved for an elite'** ...

- Is art reserved for an elite?
- What is an elite?
- How do we define art?
- What does 'reserved' mean? Who reserves what for whom?
- Does the question refer to the practice or to the consumption of art, or to both?
- Is the majority of the population insensitive to art?
- What is the make-up of the majority of people who are interested in art?

... **'politics is a man's business'**...

- Is politics a man's business?
- Do politics concern men?
- Do women have the right to vote?
- Are women interested in politics?
- Are all men interested in politics?
- Is politics compatible with the role of mother?

... **'generous people are rare'**...

- Who says or who thinks that generous people are rare?
- What meaning can be attached to generosity?
- Can generosity be assessed?
- What must we do to be generous?
- Do the rich deserve credit when they are generous?
- Does society encourage individuals to live only for themselves?
- Is it in our nature to be generous?

94

... 'in the business world, foreign languages are indispensable'...

- Do people in business who speak English need to speak another language?
- If we want to win new markets, should we persuade and charm our potential customers in their own language?
- Why is the business world a special case?
- Has everyone a gift for languages?
- Are there many people in the business world who can count in the language of their overseas clients?
- Do multinationals make multilingualism inevitable?
- Can monolingualism be defended in our age?

... 'tourism is also an industry that pollutes'...

- To what extent is tourism an industry?
- Which industries are the greatest source of pollution?
- Can tourists be taught to be cleaner?
- What type of pollution does tourism produce?
- Is the environment threatened by tourism?
- Should access to particular sites (natural, historical) be forbidden?
- Does tourism cause less pollution than many other industries?

... 'the gap between rich and poor continues to grow'...

- Does this mean that the rich become even richer and the poor poorer?
- Does the statement refer to countries or to individuals?
- How can wealth or poverty be assessed?
- How can this gap be measured? Is it between countries or between the citizens of a same country?
- Are there examples of countries or of people who were poor but who have become rich?
- Is wealth increasingly concentrated in the hands of a few? If so, how can this phenomenon be explained?
- Who could organise a better distribution of wealth either on a world-wide basis or in a particular country?

* WHEN AN ESSAY TITLE IS A QUESTION, IT RAISES FURTHER QUESTIONS.

The following essay titles are questions but they all call for further questions ...

e.g. Is justice the same for everyone?

- Are all citizens equal in the eyes of the law?

- Is justice the same in all countries?

- Is equality a myth? Etc.

Select five essay titles and find three further questions for each one of them:

1. Are multinational companies a threat to the State?

2. Have rich countries the right to dissociate themselves from the fate of poor countries?

3. Is social inequality a characteristic of all societies?

4. Why is it so difficult to reduce unemployment?

5. "Image" seems to be a keyword in our age: what exactly is meant by the image of a person, of a society or of a government?

6. Politics seems to be governed more and more by television; is this good or bad?

7. Is real power nowadays concentrated in the hands of the banks?

8. Why has international terrorism developed during the past twenty years?

9. What is meant by democracy?

10. Does justice necessarily serve class interest?

11. Does the law treat everyone the same?

12. In our society, all citizens are supposed to be equal in the eyes of the law. Is this really true?

13. Why do so few women attain key positions in the industrial and political sectors?

14. With the precarious employment situation of today, should everyone be given a sound general education?

15. Do you think that one of the paradoxes of advanced societies is that the number of people who do not know how to read or to count is increasing?

16. How can the head of a firm reconcile the need for profit with the well-being of the employees?

17. Can a society founded on individualism survive?

18. What is the role of unions in contemporary society?

19. In the second half of the twentieth century, should everyone be able to speak at least two languages?

20. Should the principal aim of an educational system be to provide equal access for all?

21. Is it true to say that the political distinction between left and right has become meaningless?

22. To be effective, should nuclear disarmament be accompanied by a reduction in the number of conventional weapons?

23. Will the future of the world be settled in space?

24. Is it true that contemporary society rejects all forms of

extremism? Does it want to be governed by people of dialogue, negotiation and consensus?

Discuss your questions with someone else.

* AN ESSAY TITLE IS A 'MESSAGE' TO WHICH YOU ARE ASKED TO REACT.

An essay is an exercise in *intellectual awareness*. Don't be put off by the elitist overtones of this. We can all see our own beliefs, behaviour, thoughts, wishes and aspirations in such terms as: good/bad, shared/personal, free/hemmed-in, avoidable/unavoidable, stupid/clever (the list is endless ...). We can also see other people's attitudes, judgments, opinions and acts in the same way.

For instance, were you to be

-   a leftwing or a rightwing politician in power

-   a UK or a USA citizen

-   a boss or a manual worker

-   a teenager or a grandfather

-   an atheist or the Pope

-   an old man or a young woman

you would give a different answer to a particular question, depending on who you were. And since essay titles are usually quotes from what people have said or written to someone else, there is no reason to feel at a loss in dealing with what is basically a *'message'*.

Carefully read the following list of essay titles and try to see them as **'messages'**, from a **sender** to a **receiver**.

Write down your reactions or questions
1. to the message itself
2. as the sender
3. as the receiver

Table 8

Essay Titles 'messages'	Your reactions and questions		
	to message	as sender	as receiver
All literature worth its name produces a profound sense of unease.			
Humanism has disappeared from contemporary literature.			
Literature improves our self-awareness.			
Poetry is no longer fashionable.			
Good theatre no longer exists.			
The cinema has taken over from the theatre.			
A book should not be more expensive than a cinema seat.			
Libraries are like museums: they smell musty.			
Museums should be free.			
Culture will always be reserved for a minority.			
Popular culture should be valued more highly.			
You have to be rich to be cultured.			
Appreciating culture requires an effort.			
Television encourages us to be lazy.			
The art market is one of the scandals of our age.			

Continued . . .

Essay Titles 'messages'	Your reactions and questions		
	to message	as sender	as receiver
The artist frequently has financial problems.			
The world is hungry and has no time for culture.			
As soon as someone opens their mouth, you know to which social class they belong.			
People often try to change the accent they were born with.			
Social differences appear in the way people express themselves.			
Should children be given pocket money?			
Should children be encouraged to practise sport?			
What is the point of buying the same newspaper everyday?			
Everyone should look after themselves and not worry about others.			
Children should learn to be independent at a very early age.			
People should be taught tolerance and patience from early childhood.			
Young people are no longer interested in social issues.			
Everyone wants to make a profit.			
The stability of the family is threatened.			

Continued . . .

Essay Titles 'messages'	Your reactions and questions		
	to message	as sender	as receiver
The State should take care of the have-nots of the consumer society.			
Jealousy is a sin.			
Political debates should be public.			
Power corrupts.			
Madness is a social problem.			
Everyone needs to be loved.			
Courage is an ambiguous feeling.			
Heroic acts are often reckless acts.			
Literature and art are not concerned with the socio-political.			
What kind of pleasure does reading a good novel give us?			
All speech is violence.			
The family is not an out-dated institution.			
Do we learn as much from life as from books?			
Tell me who your friends are and I'll tell you who you are.			
Sexual freedom cannot last.			
Why should advertising be condemned?			
The unemployed are idle lay-abouts.			

Continued . . .

Essay Titles 'messages'	Your reactions and questions		
	to message	as sender	as receiver
Everyone tells stories, and therefore lies.			
How can we strike the right balance between authority and freedom?			
We all talk too much.			
How can we assert our right to be lazy?			
Can you stop someone from committing suicide?			

It's important to know what types of topics are likely to come up in exams. Essay titles are traditionally classified into different categories:

e.g. 1 Aesthetics
      2 Moral & philosophical
      3 Socio-cultural and political.

Such a classification is somewhat off-putting as it seems to imply that an expert's knowledge is required to discuss certain subjects. There is no doubt that some students are, from that point of view, better equipped than others. But it should also be stressed that the general essay examination is not a content paper, contrary to the belief of many students. It is possible to write a good essay by presenting coherently and convincingly your own point of view. Let's take an example:

You may be tempted to disregard titles you feel you know little about, such as subjects you label as 'philosophical' and/or 'moral'. On the other hand, you may feel quite confident in choosing subjects which seem more accessible, such as topics on the media and current affairs. In fact, it is very likely that, when discussing a question about the media, you will raise 'philosophical' and 'moral' issues. Using your own experience and knowledge to deal with a problem does not necessarily mean that the basic 'moral' and 'philosophical' issues at stake in the title have been left aside! The main purpose of the exercise is to produce a coherent argument or discussion, raising the points at issue as you see them in the essay title. Therefore it's vital to try and understand what is meant (and could be meant) by the topic.

Here are a few examples:

…'**indifference stands indicted as one of the great faults of modern society'**…

Rather than balking at the task ahead, and blindly assigning this topic to a category (e.g.: politics), it is better to begin to dissect the title gradually, by asking the following questions:

1. Who is talking?
    a humanist?
    a moralist?
    a Christian?
    a politician?

2. What are other kinds of 'faults'?
    Cruelty?
    Violence?
    Insanity?

3. Who practises this indifference?
    The individual?
    The community?
    Or both?

4. Who condemns it?
    How?
    Why?
    The media?
    Heads of State?
    Teachers?
    Social Workers?

5. Why should indifference be as serious as that?

6. Are we capable of influencing the causes of indifference?
   What are the causes?
   Are there remedies to indifference?

7. *What is exactly at stake here?*

...'do you think that the literary work - novel, poetry, drama or song - helps us to escape reality or, on the contrary, to understand it more fully?'

1. Who is talking?
   a writer?
   a reader?
   a singer?
   a songwriter?
   an interviewer?
   a clergyman?

2. What is reality?

3. When could this have been written?

4. How can literature help in understanding life?

5. *What exactly is at stake here?*

... 'we dream our lives rather than live them'...

1. Who is talking?
   a philosopher?
   a writer?
   a journalist?
   a priest?
   an old man?

2. How can one dream one's life?

3. What are the similarities and differences between dreaming and living?

4. If one dreams, one is not responsible for one's acts... Wouldn't the consequences of this be the end of society?

5. Some people dream a lot, but can everybody be called a dreamer?

6. Do fantasies and dreams play such an important role?

7. *What is at stake here?*

Try now to raise the same types of questions on five of the following topics:

1. Illiteracy is on the increase.

2. People are the slaves of convention and have great difficulty in changing their habits.

3. It takes two to laugh.

4. Our minds and our conscience are being manipulated by the media.

5. Happiness is only a word.

6. Literature still has the capacity to surprise.

7. The literary text is also a social document.

8. Cruelty towards animals is a sign of our inhumanity.

9. Vivisection is one of the disgraces of our day.

10. Can wars be prevented?

11. Given the rise in violence, everyone should learn how to defend themselves.

12. All mothers dream of having a son.

13. To succeed in life, women should either be more cunning or more gifted than men.

14. Money rules the world.

Would you raise different questions on the following topics? Have the questions listed below dealt effectively with the subject? Which ones would you select? Are some irrelevant?

...'thinking is not enough, we must act'...

* Can we determine our fate?

* Is an idea of any value if it remains hidden?

* Are ability and desire synonymous?

* Can knowledge of the world be acquired through thought alone?

* Is it wise to act without thinking?

* Is commitment a personal duty?

* Why should thought precede action?

* Can we think and act at the same time?

* Action is dangerous, unspoken thoughts are harmless. Television interviewers are content to ask questions: is it wise to adopt the same policy?

* Should we risk our freedom, indeed our lives, by expressing our opinions in a dictatorship?

* Should politicians be entrusted with all the important decisions?

* Does freedom of speech encourage action?

*   Do the media provoke thoughtless action?

*   Are politicians more interested in talking than acting?

*   Action is undoubtedly important but what should be done?

*   What would happen if everyone acted?

*   Is fear the real problem?

*   Is someone who thinks but does not act a coward?

*   Do we find it difficult to refuse help to someone in distress?

*   Should we keep quiet if we find a book or film revolting or dangerous?

*   Why in this age of unemployment is it so difficult to get everyday items repaired? Why do new ones always have to be purchased?

*   Why are so many people reluctant to come to the help of victims of violent attacks?

*   Why do people do the opposite of what they say?

*   Who can tell someone else what to do?

*   We need people who think and people who act. Why should the same person think and act?

*   If we stopped thinking, would we return to a barbarian age?

*   Is it true that when we stop thinking, we become senile?

...'art is the expression of man's nobility'

*   Is art useful?

* What is the ultimate aim of art?

* Can the perfection of a work of art be defined?

* What are the criteria for recognising a work of art?

* Should art portray the sociopolitical values of its time?

* Can masterpieces be compared?

* Are art and life compatible?

* Is Beauty the promise of happiness?

* Are we all capable of understanding or of recognising a work of art?

* Can everyone afford to buy a work of art?

* How can art be made available to all?

* Does art put man in the position of God?

* Does the fact that they are inspired mean that artists are superior to everyone else?

* Is genius a gift from Heaven?

* Why are artists so often flawed individuals?

* Is it through art that we learn about our history?

* Is art really universal or does it have frontiers?

* Which is the more wonderful: to produce a child or to create a work of art?

* Does the nobility of man lie in his creative powers?

* Is the artist a magician?

* Can the great literary works of our time be understood by everybody?

* Can a poem be understood without any technical knowledge of poetry?

* Is drama accessible to all?

* Can everyone appreciate the theatre of the absurd?

* Is cinema an art-form?

* In the past, was art "for" all?

* Is modern art more difficult to understand than classical art?

* What does "understand a work of art" mean?

* Where can we find out how to appreciate modern art?

* Should art be accessible to all?

* Is modern art intentionally obscure?

In this chapter we have stressed the importance of reading an essay title very carefully in order to unlock its meaning (which may not be apparent at first glance). You may have experienced the feeling that you missed out something in what somebody told you; you're not sure that you correctly understood the 'message':

- What did s/he mean?

- Did s/he mean that?

- How could s/he mean this?

- But then if s/he meant this or that ...

\- Why did s/he say this/that afterwards? etc.

This shows that even in a dialogue when people are talking to each other, misunderstandings occur. When you start writing an essay, this initial phase of reading the title again and again is of vital importance.

In the following chapters, and in particular in Chapter 10, more guidelines are given on how to make the most of this reading.

Chapter 6

For or against?

In this chapter, you are invited to explore the pros and cons of various issues, both by assessing your own thoughts and opinions on a given subject, and by contradicting someone else's views.

Don't be discouraged by what may appear to be repetitive; we have included statements which are equivalent in meaning:

e.g.: naive people are gullible,

naive people believe everything they are told,

because if you don't know a word, you are given the opportunity of conveying the same meaning by using a different turn of phrase. Ideally this should enable you to increase your range of vocabulary (and hopefully help you to acquire your own style in English).

But beware (!), this could also lead you to select a series of statements or questions which are so close in meaning that you could end up with no arguments at all ...

On the whole you'll find the learning process in this chapter more of a game than anything else.

There are many ways of disagreeing ... Try to acquire some of them by doing the following exercise: match up the statements in column I with their endings in column II.

I	II
1. On the contrary, the British	a) claim that prices have fallen
2. Not at all! Literary criticism	b) politicians are sincere
3. It is quite wrong to	c) have a greater sense of humour than the Australians!
4. It is naive to think that	d) is extremely boring
5. How can one support	e) the premise of his argument
6. I cannot accept	f) a statement that is blatantly untrue
7. I would like to challenge	
8. We must reject	g) the views expressed by the speaker
9. There is no point in trying to prove	h) all forms of extremism
10. This statement is somewhat	i) controversial
	j) to a fanatic that he is wrong

Answers in Appendix 1

* **THE TWENTIETH CENTURY IS POWERLESS IN THE FACE OF THIS TRIPLE THREAT: THE WORLD IS HUNGRY, THE RICH ARE GROWING RICHER AND THE NATURAL BALANCE OF THE PLANET IS BEING UPSET.**

Contest this. You believe, on the contrary, that people CAN and MUST DO something! Find 5 points in the list below to defend your opinion.

* Europe has tonnes of butter and piles of wheat and other produce: all we have to do is to transport this food to those who need it.

* The gap between rich and poor countries is grotesque and immoral.

* The rich should pay more taxes.

* There should be a universal ban on the sale of arms.

* We should combat defeatist attitudes.

* People are willing to sell their souls in the pursuit of money.

* If there were less money spent on defence, there would be less poverty in the world.

* What makes us think that we are living in a time of peace?

* Everyone should go to the same schools and the same hospitals. In that way the privileged would see how the majority of the population live.

* There are too many people in the world: a means of controlling population growth should be found.

* The arrogance of some people knows no limits! They do not hesitate to impose their laws on the whole of humanity.

* People should be taught how to resist all forms of oppression, domination and exploitation.

* We all want to feather our own nests.

* In our age, we can think the unthinkable: the end of the world.

Discuss you choice with someone else.

* 'BT LOOKS TO EURO TV SATELLITE LINKS'

Read the following article carefully:

BT looks to Euro TV satellite links

Nicholas Bannister
Technology Editor

BRITISH Telecom has targeted the provision of satellite news-gathering facilities for broadcasters as one of the first areas to exploit following the start of the liberalisation of Europe's telecommunications industry.

Yesterday it announced the start of a full-time SNG service in Germany in conjunction with a Ludwigshaven-based company, AKK, and is currently in talks with other companies in France and Holland.

Until now broadcasters wishing to use major satellite links into or from Germany have had little option but to use the services provided by the state-owned Deutsche Bundespost Telekom (DBT). When deregulation of Germany's telecom industry started, BT obtained a satellite operating licence that now enables it to challenge DBT's position.

Steve Maine, director of BT's visual and broadcast service operations, said there was a rapidly growing demand from television companies and other industries for satellite news gathering links — which he claimed were quicker and cheaper than land lines in many circumstances.

Until now BT has only been able to provide SNG services on a one-off basis for specific events planned in advance like football matches. Now it will be able to offer a permanent 24-hour-a-day service in Germany.

Mr Maine said: "Entry into the 835 million mark German broadcast services market provides BT with a lucrative toe-hold in Europe. There are relatively few players offering the sort of service BT and AKK can provide.

"The new service will allow BT to expand internationally. The long-term aim is to build European business and exploit BT licences in Germany, France and Holland."

One of the key advantages for international broadcasters will be access to BT's dedicated satellite capacity on the Intelsat, Eutelsat and Panamsat satellites. BT claims it will be offering broadcasters cheaper access than that provided by DBT.

BT's £1 million investment in hardware for the German operation includes equipment at AKK in Ludwigshaven that provides the necessary audio and visual links with the satellites.

Mr Maine said that broadcast services was a rapidly growing business. "In the next five years I foresee broadcast services doubling in size, and that 70 per cent of that growth will come from overseas," he said.

Clients of BT's visual and broadcast services include CNN, NBC, ABC, BBC World Service TV, BSkyB, and ITV regional companies.

Do you agree or disagree with the following statements?

	Agree/Disagree
* The monopoly of national broadcast services should be abolished.	
* We need more satellite news gathering links.	
* Joint broadcast ventures with European countries should be encouraged.	
* Everything should be done to combat the influence of the North American media.	
* In the future, television will take over the role of art and literature.	
* There is no room for the small independent television company in the Europe of the future.	

Compare your answer to someone else's.
Discuss the points you disagree on.

* THE MEDIA HAVE BLUNTED OUR CRITICAL FACULTIES

1) If you agree that the media have made us less critical, find five points which would illustrate this argument from those listed below.

2) If you disagree, pick out five points disproving this.

* The media deaden our mind.

* The press, radio and television bombard us with news and events, so that we no longer feel concerned.

* The images pass so rapidly before our eyes that we no longer have the time to think.

*   It's very easy just to switch on the television.

*   It is only intellectuals who can resist the influence of television.

*   There is nothing more pathetic than to see someone slumped in front of their television set.

*   In the office and in the playground, television is the principal subject of conversation.

*   Television programmes are seldom analysed. They are briefly mentioned in conversation and then usually in simple terms of praise or condemnation.

*   The media convey an abundance of superficial knowledge.

*   Through watching their televised speeches, we become aware of the true nature of many public figures.

*   A politician can lie on television and, the next day, it is forgotten.

*   Television reduces everything to the same level whether it be politics, gameshows or soaps.

*   Much of our everyday behaviour is influenced by advertising.

*   Television presents us with a make-believe world.

*   The media are an agent of social uniformity.

*   The media equip us with all the information we need to fight oppression.

**   'SCHOOLS GO INTERNATIONAL'**

Read the following article:

Schools go international

Institutions are reflecting business trends, writes **Roger Trapp**

LIKE the management consultants that many of their graduates become, business schools are highly susceptible to trends. One of the latest ideas to capture the imagination of the management education business is going international. It is a rare institution that does not now stress how cosmopolitan it is in outlook, content or make-up.

In the past, only the Fontainebleu-based L'Institut Européen d'Administration des Affairs (Insead), with its stringent language requirements and conscious international attitude from its foundation 30 years ago, could be said truly to fit this description. In recent years many others have been striving to obtain the status. The Cranfield School of Management and the London and Manchester Business Schools are already world-renowned names.

Lesser-known institutions, some of them attached to the former polytechnics, have now set out down the international road.

The institutions are responding to the increased globalisation of business. This is partly related to the imminent arrival of the single European market, but also has a lot to do with the continued investment in Europe by US and Japanese companies and the development of the Far Eastern economies.

"We talk to managers all the time and they tell us that their job is becoming much more international," says Cranfield's director, Professor Leo Murray. So, to a large extent, the impetus for this broadening of outlook is coming from the companies that the schools serve, but it is also derived from the schools' sense of where business is going.

Some might see the trend as a response to the business's overcrowding at a time of recession in many of its markets. The Association of MBAs reports that in the past five years the number of business schools offering MBAs has doubled to 82, while the number of graduates produced every year has increased by about the same proportion, to 5,000. "Internationalisation is the flavour of the month," says the organisation's director, Roger McCormick, pointing out that he is concerned about the effects of this massive growth on quality.

But the lesser-known should not be seen as a safety net for those applicants who fail to gain a place with more prestigious institutions. "Applicants shouldn't discount those that don't have a high national or international profile," he says. Schools with strong knowledge of their hinterland, say, can be attractive.

'We make sure that the whole spirit is international'

Few seem prepared to confine themselves to local roles. What they offer may vary from language training to high percentages of non-British students, but they are mostly concerned to stress their internationality. Students can be exposed to foreign ideas and methods without paying the high fees and living expenses that come with attendance at such centres as Harvard or Stanford in the US or even Insead.

The high level of English speaking among European managers means that it is little problem for them to study in Britain. But the same cannot generally be said of their British counterparts. In

117

recognition of this, the recently renamed Brighton University has started a Euro MBA. A 16-month programme instead of the normal 12, it takes students with appropriate work experience and O-level or equivalent in one of the four main European languages. Participants are then, while following a conventional business studies syllabus, made fluent in their chosen language and sent to the appropriate country to be taught for a final term.

The management school at Lancaster University also offers intensive language tuition overseas combined with instruction in business studies with local students. It has built on existing links with schools in continental Europe, Asia and North America to offer a qualification that combines a conventional undergraduate MBA with working in two European countries. "This is addressing a double demand — from companies and from students who see themselves as European managers," says Gerald Watts, director of the university's MBA programme.

Few courses can be as global in make-up as that at Stirling University. Headed by Professor Errol Alexander, an American with experience of running his own companies as well as of academe, the current MBA course numbers a Thai prince and a former Garda officer among its 30 to 40 per cent overseas contingent. But it is particularly popular in the Far East, where, says Prof Alexander, it is considered to be on the same level as Harvard.

Describing the course as a "smorgasbord MBA" that has a particular emphasis on negotiating skills, Prof Alexander sees the 12 months' duration as a particular advantage in attracting students who might otherwise head for the US.

Many schools are strengthening links with industry. For instance, at Insead, Dominique Héau, associate dean responsible for executive education, talks of the well-established relationship with the computer company Digital as "a learning alliance" and predicts similar developments with other companies.

At Cranfield, where the proportion of overseas students has grown to about 40 per cent, Prof Murray comments that "We've got to deliver what the market needs", while adding that he and his fellow academics must also give a lead.

"We make sure that the whole spirit is international," he says.

* Fontainebleau

Do you consider that:

	Yes/No
* The twinning of educational institutions should become official policy throughout Europe.	
* All schoolchildren should be allowed to receive their education in at least two countries of the European Community.	
* Educational qualifications should be mutually recognised among all member states.	
* Whatever their nationality, teachers should be allowed to work in the European country of their choice.	
* All children should learn at least one foreign language in primary school.	
* The nations of Europe have a common history: their differences are minimal.	
* A voucher system should be introduced throughout Europe enabling students to study at the university of their choice.	
* Links between university and industry should be strengthened.	
* All university degrees should possess a foreign language component.	
* British companies should adopt a more international outlook.	

Discuss your answers with someone else.

* 'BRITAIN LAGS FURTHER BEHIND COMPETITORS, STUDY SHOWS'

Read the article below:

Britain lags further behind competitors, study shows

Ruth Kelly

BRITAIN'S international competitiveness has dropped even further behind other leading industrialised nations and its education and training system is completely unsuited to the needs of an industrialised economy.

So says the latest World Competitiveness Report published today. Produced by the management development institute, IMD, and the World Economic Forum, it places the UK 13th of the 22 industrialised countries, compared with 10th last year. It has now been overtaken by Ireland, Belgium and Sweden.

According to the study, Britain's education and in-company training is worse than in any other developed country. Young people in Britain have the least appropriate attitude towards studying and choose to "have fun" instead, it adds.

Although the report finds that the tax burden is light and fiscal policies are conducive to innovation and initiative, it ranks the availability of skilled workers in Britain 21st and says that managerial rewards encourage short-term thinking in industry to a greater extent than any of the UK's rivals.

This is compounded by poor public funding of non-defence research and development which is ranked 20th and by the fact that more companies plan to cut back on R&D spending over the next two years than in any other country except Canada. But the report finds that Britain is more open to inward investment than any industrialised country except the US.

It also concludes that the domestic economy has become too dependent on services, with only Finland, Norway and Sweden more reliant on the service sector. Growth in services soared in the last decade and its rate of expansion was outflanked only by Turkey but this growth has been at the expense of the manufacturing base, which the report finds has been seriously eroded over the last five years.

France has climbed up from 15th last year, and now stands just behind Britain. "France is still behind the UK in internationalisation, government and finance, but it leads the UK in management, science, technology and qualified people — so building for long-term competitiveness," the report says.

Japan retained its place as world leader and the report ranks its performance ahead of Germany and Switzerland. But Japan has become more protectionist, the study says, and has dropped from first to sixth place for integration into the international economy.

Recession has taken its toll on the overall competitiveness of the United States and it has fallen from second place in 1991 to fifth this year. "Most alarming is the drop in the quality of its people, from second to seventh this year," the report adds.

The study also ranks the ability of the newly industrialised economies to compete internationally on a separate league table. This shows that Singapore, for the fourth year running, continues as the strong leader, followed by Taiwan and Hong Kong.

World competitiveness scoreboard

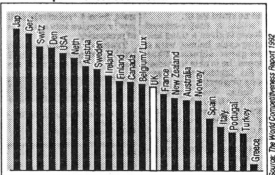

Source: The World Competitiveness Report 1992

120

Are the following statements correct?

	Yes/No
* Britain's international competitiveness has dropped behind that of Ireland, Belgium and Sweden.	
* Britain's education and in-company training are better than in any other developed country.	
* Finland, Norway and Sweden are less reliant than England on the service sector.	
* France leads the UK in management, science and technology.	
* The recession has not affected the overall competitiveness of the United States.	
* Taiwan is ranked first in the league of newly industrialised economies.	

Check your answer with someone else.

* **'PAPERLESS DREAMS BURIED BY OFFICE REAMS'**

Read the following article:

Paperless dreams buried by office reams

Frontiers of work

Andrew Beven

THE Kafkaesque nightmare of bureaucracy — dimly lit offices knee deep in swirling triplicated paper and filing clerks — has haunted the 20th century. In the 1970s the computer industry opened up the possibility of a brave new world of bright, paperless, open-plan offices in which information was transferred silently, efficiently and instantly. But is it making the dream come true?

There have been three generations in the computerised automation of the office environment. The first, from the late seventies to the mid-eighties, was based on standalone computers such as word processors (WPs) and small Commodore computers for producing spreadsheets, and was about automating an individual and his task.

John Robinson, ICL's worldwide marketing manager for office applications, calculates this produced an 80 per cent efficiency increase on these particular tasks but affected only the lowest 20 per cent of wage costs.

The second generation encompassed small departments, which acquired a proprietary WP, electronic mail and database system. This did automate some managerial tasks, allowing them to share information and send memos instantly, but each manufacturer used its own language which made it more or less impossible for any of these integrated mini systems to talk to one another. If entire companies wished to communicate by computer they had to adopt centralised buying and one maker.

This "closed" approach had obvious advantages for the manufacturers, and until recently they refused to produce systems that did communicate, remaining hell-bent on global domination for their own models. A factor in forcing them to pay lip-service to an open systems approach is that many governments, among the biggest spenders on the information technology, will no longer allow tenders without such a commitment.

The third generation, then, involves open systems operating to international standards, and its object is enterprise-wide automation and communication. Customers can mix and match, choosing software from one and PCs or boxes from another.

That is the theory. But the reality, determined to a large extent by users who have already invested in existing "closed" equipment, is that these barriers are likely to be in place for some time to come.

The manufacturers conclude, with some justice, that the third generation has revolutionised the lives of office workers.

The flexibility and rapid information flow have reduced staff numbers but improved the quality of work and the skills needed to accomplish it.

There is of course a dark side to this boosted productivity, demonstrated by the eighties debate on screen-glare and attendant headaches, and the appearance and rise of RSI (repetitive strain injury).

The EC is issuing a directive recommending 15-minute breaks every hour and minimum seating standards, but there will be no laws to enforce these points in member countries. The threat of employee compensation costs may prove the best safeguard.

Mr Robinson is bullishly dismissive of such problems. "Any technology has drawbacks. Information technology cannot be compared with coalmining and pneumoconiosis. Surely nothing can be worse than the old typing pools."

He points to the manufacturers' work on more ergonomic PCs, but puts his main hope in the fourth generation of automation currently in development which will by the mid-nineties give us the multi-media office. This will have the ability to take not just text-based information but sound and video mixed within one file or "object" and accessible through, and altered by, the humble PC. The capacity to dictate to the machine by voice will, Mr Robinson argues, do much to alleviate RSI.

Generation four ties in with the work of academics such as Mark Lansdale at Loughborough University. Although at first sight his theories seem to have more in common with the traditional bureaucratic nightmare, he argues that the very messy desk is in its own way an efficient filing system because it gives the sort of context that aids memory.

This "volcano" model, with its clear central crater and a self-disposal system whereby the oldest and most useless items eventually reach the edge, fall to the floor and are removed by cleaners, is more flexible than the traditional manual filing system.

Dr Lansdale is attempting to incorporate the best aspects of the "volcano" into the world of information technology with the Memoirs database, which uses the way that people actually remember rather than the way that efficiency experts feel they should.

Memoirs can deal with both electronic documents and real ones, recorded by video camera. Their arrival and any subsequent handling are "events" which define the document and its passage through the electronic office. Just as with a perfect human memory, "events" are tagged, for example, by sound and paper colour as well as chronologically and by subject, so the user can construct the circumstances around something to hunt it down, as if on a messy desk. Fourth generation technology will make this practicable.

Undoubtedly the office environment has changed beyond all recognition since the mid-seventies but, has the paperless age drawn any closer?

An IBM spokesman suggested that it had never been an ambition, but Mr Robinson is more forthcoming. "There is, if anything, even more paper now, but the spirit of the paperless office is with us."

Frontiers is edited by Celia Weston

Imagine you have been asked to make some fundamental changes in the organisation of your office. What measures would you take to:

a) improve efficiency.
b) reduce stress.
c) provide a healthier environment for your colleagues.
   Compare your answers with someone else.

Read this short article:

WALL STREET

International news causes Dow to fall 4 points

NEW YORK — The stock market drifted through a mixed session restrained by weakness in overseas markets and uncertainty over events in the Middle East.

The Dow Jones average of 30 industrials dropped 4.33 points to 3,285.71, extending its loss for the week to 45.93.

In the Japanese market, the Nikkei index of 225 issues tumbled 3.4 percent, wiping out gains it had posted the day before. Major European markets also lost ground.

By yesterday afternoon, analysts said U.S. traders were reluctant to make big commitments as the White House considered what action to take in response to Iraq's defiance of U.N. weapons inspectors.

The economic news, meanwhile, offered a small respite from a recent run of adverse signals on the progress of economic recovery.

- Why do you think the economic situation is affected by political events?

- Give three examples from the recent past of a similar phenomenon.

Discuss your answer with someone else.

Read the article below:

What do you get if you cross a poem with an Apple Mac? **Glyn Moody** reveals all

The hyperpoem

COMPUTERS in poetry have a long if rather inglorious history of turning out sentences that rhyme. But John Cayley, whose installation at the Poetry Library on London's South Bank combines poetry with an Apple Macintosh SE, has no interest in that. "I haven't done a set of rule books for producing verse; they are tools for me to explore poetic language," he says.

Indra's Nets or Hololography, his collection of such explorations, is what he calls a "coverless book". It uses the Mac's Hypercard program to present pages of a book on screen. Clicking with the mouse on the page turns to the next page, clicking on the left or right edge of the book takes you to the contents or the index.

But this is no ordinary book: many of the poems it contains change each time you read them. The micro applies transformations to pre-existing base texts to arrive at new ways of thinking about them. The computer's role is crucial: "Some of the pieces can't be done any other way," Cayley says. "The simplest types of transformation are acrostical, so you replace each letter of a word by a word from the same

text that begins with that letter. But which word you take is partly random."

For example, one of the shorter base texts is an acrostic poem, where successive words begin with the next letter of the alphabet: "Another bloody clod. / Damn / Each Friday Gary had it" (from Overheard in the pub). Applying the transformation this becomes: "another / near absence time / had each realised" where the words used for each letter are taken from within the poem. In this way each text generates new versions of itself, with each part of it reflecting other parts. Hence the name Indra's Nets, which was "a network of jewels that not only reflected the images in every other jewel, but also the multiple images of others." The word "hololography" expresses this same idea of word (logos) holography.

As well as carrying out the transformations, the Mac displays the results a word at a time. With this system "you can force silent reading to be done at the speed the author wants." Similarly, for the more conventional poem Wine Flying — Cayley's first coverless book, and an appendix to Indra's Nets — "you can force people to read in different orders."

This is particularly appropriate for Wine Flying, a translation of a Chinese quatrain complete with the original text. Cayley, a professional translator of Chinese, notes that "Chinese poetry invites non-linear reading." This made the Mac's Hypercard system, with its ability to display words and graphics sequentially or to jump from one page to anywhere else, ideal.

Cayley aimed to produce tools to explore the nature of poetry. "One of the interesting things is how strongly the base text determines what is produced, and how persistent the meaning of the base text is, despite inflicting these horrendous and almost arbitrary transformations."

And are these "hyperpoems" art? "I don't really want to make any aesthetic judgments about the value of the work, that's up to other people."

Indra's Nets can be seen at the Poetry Library in the Royal Festival Hall, London, until September 30 or bought on disc as a Macintosh Hypercard stack from Wellsweep Press, 8 Duke Street, London SW1Y 6BN for £5.95. Tel: 071-839 6599.

- What positive contribution have computers made to society and to learning?

- What are their limitations?

- Can machine produced texts be called art?

- Can a computer be more creative than a poet?

  Compare your views with someone else.

126

* COURAGE IS AN AMBIGUOUS FEELING AND ONE OF THE MOST DIFFICULT TO ANALYSE

Divide the statements and questions below into two columns:

Column I = FOR   Column II = AGAINST

	I	II
* A man dives into the sea to save a drowning child. We can say without hesitation that his is a noble and courageous act.		
* We call courage the instinct that compels people to confront danger.		
* To win wars, we need courageous people.		
* If we suffer from vertigo, we cannot climb onto a roof or climb a mountain. Does this mean that we are weaklings?		
* The weak are rejected by society.		
* Descartes said that indecisiveness is the greatest evil.		
* Can courage be expressed in words?		
* Do people often mistake aggressiveness for courage?		
* Courage is not an absolute value but is defined by a particular age and society.		
* We all have the right to be afraid.		
* Courage is not a virtue we acquire. It lies at the very core of our nature. All thought and action require courage.		
* What is a courageous person trying to prove and to whom by committing his act of bravery?		
* We should demand the right to be lazy.		
* What makes courageous people want to risk their lives?		
* Courageous people want to prove to themselves that they are afraid of nothing.		
* Courage is altruistic.		
* To suffer without complaining is the most noble form of courage.		
* When we cease to strive, society collapses.		
* Knowing how to relax is a prerequisite of contemporary society. Do we need courage to make the best of our leisure time?		
* Every society needs heroes and nowadays football and tennis players are praised to the skies and proclaimed noble warriors! Do these modern heroes possess courage?		
* No-one is perfect and it is often ambition which is concealed beneath courage.		
* Can we live with someone whom we consider to be completely lacking in courage?		

Compare your selection with someone else.

* NAIVETY IS A FORM OF STRENGTH

Divide the statements and questions below into two columns:
Column I = FOR   Column II= AGAINST

	I	II
* Innocence is bliss.		
* For the innocent, life is uncomplicated.		
* Naive people live in a rose-tinted world.		
* Naive people take everything at face value.		
* Action stems from madness or naivety.		
* Naive people can be very charming.		
* Naivety is a form of stupidity.		
* Knowing how to preserve the innocence of childhood is an art.		
* Naive questions are often the most disarming.		
* Naive people always look wide-eyed at people and at things.		
* Naive people are exploited but as they are unaware of things, they do not suffer.		
* Naivety is often synonymous with inanity.		
* Naive people are gullible.		
* Naive people are excused everything.		
* People laugh at the naive.		
* Naive people are liked by those whose self-esteem needs to be boosted.		
* Naive people believe everything they are told.		
* For the naive, everything is for the best in the best of all possible worlds.		
* Naive people become involved without thinking in all kinds of ventures.		
* A little naivety is the prerequisite of happiness.		
* All religions require a certain amount of naivety from their followers.		

* THERE IS NO VIRTUE WITHOUT RELIGION

If a fellow student made this statement, which six questions from those listed would you elect to ask?

* First of all, what is virtue?

* In our age, who can be described as virtuous?

* Is it possible to still believe in virtue after the discoveries of psychoanalysis?

* Does everyone have the same definition of virtue?

* In whose interest is it that we are virtuous?

* Why should virtue be more important than goodness or generosity?

* Is it true that virtue is a cloak for hypocrisy?

* We are not born virtuous so how do we become it?

* The history of religions clearly proves that 'religious' people are violent; so why claim that religion is on the side of virtue?

* We are virtuous because we are afraid of authority. Is it true that all religions have an authoritarian figure whose role it is to condemn and to punish?

* Is saying that we cannot be virtuous without religion a condemnation of the human race?

* Why do we need religion?

* Is it true that fear of the Last Judgment makes us virtuous?

* Is it only religion that exhorts us to love our neighbour?

* Do you agree that there are enough examples of religious fanaticism to prove that religion and virtue do not necessarily go together?

* Are all religions of equal value?

Compare your choice with somebody else.

* **READING ENABLES US TO LIVE A FULLER LIFE**

Select five statements from those listed, which support the declaration made above.

* When we read, we withdraw from the world.

* Reading is a substitute for living.

* Reading is a form of escapism.

* Reading is merely entertainment.

* Reading encourages us to think deeply.

* Reading broadens our knowledge of other people.

* Reading is a form of self-discovery.

* To avoid becoming a moron like everyone else, there is only one solution: read!

* Reading demands a silence which is lacking in our world of noise.

* Reading is a means of acquiring the information that we need to cope with the modern world.

* When reading a good novel, we forget about the world around us.

* In our age, it is action and not reading that is important.

* Reading should not just be associated with the dreamers and the dissatisfied. It can enrich everyone's life.

* Why should reading have become so old-fashioned?

* Whom must we convince of the necessity of reading?

* Why do we find reading a chore?

* Reading is an erotic activity.

* Nothing can replace reading a poem aloud or in silence.

* Can we do without books? If so, at what price?

* Literary texts evoke in the reader an experience of beauty.

* Reading enables us to lead not fuller lives but better lives.

Compare your choice with someone else.

Which two of the questions below, on the same subject, seem to you the most relevant?

* Is reading essential if you want to live a fuller life?

* Does the author of the statement "Reading enables us to live a fuller life" mean that without reading, our lives are impoverished?

* Should the author of the statement have specified the type of books we should read to enrich our lives?

* Even if the illiteracy rate has considerably fallen in our so-called 'developed' countries, there still exists a large proportion of the world's population who do not know how to read. Should we conclude, then, that our lives are more fulfilled than theirs?

* Is reading the only cultural activity that can improve the human condition?

* Are there other cultural activities that can offer us the same treasures as reading?

* Is reading more than just a source of pleasure or satisfaction?

* How is it that so many people who know how to read practically never open a book?

Discuss your choice with someone else.

* WE MUST CHOOSE BETWEEN LIVING AND TELLING

In your view, which of the statements or questions below support the idea that there is no choice to be made between living and telling?

* Who says that we have to choose?

* You either tell stories or you act; you cannot do both.

* We all invent and tell stories.

* By recounting our experiences, we become aware of the passage of time.

* We can always have fantastic adventures - in our head!

* Is there a dividing line between life and the after-life?

* Does living mean doing things, is it action?

* Are novelists 'dead' because they tell stories?

* Is it possible to live without creating our own personal myths?

* We are in the throes of a great passion because we tell ourselves we are in the throes of a great passion.

* Even politicians make up stories (with goodies and baddies, obstacles and rewards).

* What worse fate could befall us than to lose our imaginative powers?

* Storytelling is lying.

* In the course of telling us what they have done at school, children re-live their experiences.

* A site worker does not tell stories, he plans and analyses: he acts.

Compare and discuss your choice with someone else.

* LITERATURE IS IN THE PROCESS OF DYING OUT

Which of the following statements support the above?

*   Human beings will always need the form of escapism that literature provides.

*   Writers are the outcome of a century's problems; literature, therefore, will always exist.

*   Literature is a form of exploration and there are no more places to be explored - the next stage will be the blank page.

*   People have stopped reading because of television.

*   We are moving towards an oral society.

*   Because we have so many gadgets doing our work for us, we have more time to read.

*   We need literature in order to overcome our isolation: it enables us to share our experiences with others.

*   Literature is an outdated mode of communication.

Discuss your choice with someone else.

Last but not least, draw up a questionnaire using the lead sentences listed, on one or several topics in the right hand column.

Select ten lead sentences	Choose ten issues
Are you for	nuclear power?
	free nursery education?
Are you against	
	a change in the laws on homosexuality?
Are you in favour of	sexual freedom?
	a United Europe?
Do you defend	
	television 24 hours a day?
Do you reject	the privatisation of prisons?
	the liberal/conservative/ labour party?
Are you opposed to	
	the economic policy of the government?
Do you agree with	the modernisation of the church?
	computer science in schools?
Do you refute	
	abortion?
Do you support	the isolation of Aids victims?
	sperm banks?
Do you disagree with	
	the use of condoms?
Do you approve of	**(INCLUDE WHATEVER MAY BE IMPORTANT TO YOU)**
Do you disapprove of	

What are your conclusions?
Compare them with someone else.

At this point you should be aware of opposite views on the same subject and should feel quite confident about writing fairly long and elaborate YES/NO answers to essay titles which are 'simple statements' like these:

- The media deaden our mind.

- Freedom of the press does not exist.

- The law is made for the rich.

- There is an increasing threat to world stability.

- The banks are too powerful.

- It is not just individuals who are mad.

- We need a United Europe.

- Contemporary society poses a threat to the couple.

- Marketing is a masculine occupation.

- Every society needs heroes.

- Naive people can be very charming.

- Virtue is a guise for hypocrisy.

- Reading enables us to live a fuller life.

- Storytelling is lying.

- Speaking and writing are always public acts.

- Schools should train pupils in the skills of communication.

- In the modern world, two cultures co-exist: a popular culture and a high-brow culture.

- It is wrong to say that young people are only interested in pleasure.

- There is no progress in the arts.

- It is only the human that gives rise to the comic.

- Politics is the continuation of war by other means.

- Freedom is the ability to say 'no'.

- Religion is a source of strength and discipline.

- For the State, security is the most important virtue.

- We cannot prove that anything is true.

- The concept of freedom is incompatible with that of the unconscious.

The fact that these essay titles can be defined as 'simple statements' does not mean to say that there is nothing to discuss; rather the argumentation is inscribed in and somehow shaped by the very formulation of the title.

Let's take one of the above titles as an example:

'There is an increasing threat to the world's stability'.

Once you have defined what you understand by 'stability' (Peace? Equality of resources among countries? Or both?), it shouldn't be too difficult for you to:

1) illustrate a YES answer. **YES**, the world is at risk because of:

- international terrorism

- the difficulties in establishing a real dialogue between nations

- an increasingly wider gap between the rich and the poor (countries and people)

- the nuclear threat, etc.

You could demonstrate that there is ample evidence that this is the case. You may even go as far as saying that the world is on the verge of collapse!

2) find several reasons and arguments to disprove this. **NO**, on the contrary, the world is stable today because:

- military conflicts are kept under control

- the capitalist ethos seems to make ground all over the world

- world leaders regularly discuss their problems

- people are better informed, etc.

In explaining these two sides and opposite views of a problem, you begin in fact **to draw a plan**, which admittedly is still binary and may seem oversimplistic, but it is:
a) a fair reaction to a peremptory and rather abrupt declaration.

b) the first step in gathering your thoughts, writing them down and organising them.

c) the only way to construct an argument.
   What does it mean? What is at stake here? What do I think about it? How could I present various viewpoints and my opinions in a clear, logical and convincing way?

The following chapters will build upon this first attempt at shaping an argument and give you some guidelines on how to discuss subjects which are expressed differently,

as straightforward questions

- What is meant by the term 'uncultured' people?

- Can silence have meaning?

- Is the Third World an idea or a reality?

in more complex statements

- Probably to each of us the sense of his own personality, the knowledge that he exists and feels, is the ultimate fact of life.

- The change of thought from one generation to another does not depend so must on new discoveries as on the gradual shifting, into the centre of vision, of ideas and feelings that had been but dimly realised before.

- Manpower is a key resource in society and there is thus a need for governments to consider *manpower* in the forefront of their industrial and commercial strategy and planning.

Chapter 7

Yes but . . .

In the previous chapter you were invited to formulate and illustrate contradictions and oppositions. Our objective in the following pages is to take you a step further by suggesting yet another approach to a question.

In brief, you are being asked to adopt a more conciliatory attitude, or as the case may be, put yourself in a more analytical, critical frame of mind (which does not entirely trust a binary model of the world and is not satisfied with the quality of thinking which limits itself to oppositions).

Some people appear to be rigid, some less so ... let's call the latter group 'flexible',

Which of the following utterances would you attribute to:
1) somebody with strong ideas (= Rigid = R)?
2) somebody with a more conciliatory attitude (= Flexible = F)

		R	F
1	People are generous because they feel guilty.		
2	What you are saying is absolutely ridiculous.		
3	I would be inclined not to agree with you.		
4	I think that I admire generous people.		
5	This idea is ludicrous.		
6	I don't agree with you but I can understand your attitude.		
7	It's completely wrong.		
8	This seems at first glance a rather peculiar idea.		
9	This is not completely true.		
10	How can you say such a stupid thing?		
11	I am not sure that I've completely understood what you are saying.		
12	What do we really mean by 'generosity'?		
13	We must have ideals.		

Continued . . .

14	Motorbike traffic should be controlled.		
15	We can only hope that our dreams of a New Europe will finally be realised.		
16	All forms of extremism should be condemned.		
17	Let's join ranks to create a New Europe!		
18	Why do we have so much difficulty in understanding our fellow human beings?		
19	Stupid people do exist and we should have the courage to admit it.		

Discuss your choice with someone else.

THREE PEOPLE ARE TALKING

A is always *for* something
B is always *against* the same thing
C is *neither for nor against* what is being discussed.

In the following statements find two sets of ABC (= two groups or three people discussing the same issue and holding different opinions).

		A	B	C
1	Sport is a necessary part of life.			
2	We should practise a little sport but not too much.			
3	Sport frequently degenerates into violence.			
4	It is international sporting events that produce the best pictures on television.			
5	It is unbelievable the way children are not punished nowadays as they used to be.			
6	People should not be given money before having earned it.			
7	Children should be punished but not too severely.			
8	Fear of punishment produces hypocrites.			
9	Children should receive pocket money from a very early age.			
10	All forms of punishment should be prohibited.			
11	Knowing how to look after your money is a sign of independence.			
12	Money is the root of all evil.			

Compare you choice with someone else.

In the list given below, identify five conciliatory reactions (i.e.: statements or questions which do not condemn or attack but which try to raise questions on a particular issue).

1) Young people are frivolous.
2) Sex has become a thriving industry.
3) If a firm is not making a profit, it should simply be liquidated.
4) There is no room in society for lazy people.
5) People are not naturally lazy, at least I don't think so.
6) People are racist because they are afraid, not because they are stupid or malicious.
7) Everyone has his or her moments of weakness; we must learn, therefore, to be tolerant and patient.
8) Why do we always have to make a choice? We should have the right to hesitate.
9) Before condemning someone, we should first try to understand their motives.
10) Truth is seldom obvious. It is only found after a slow and painstaking search.
11) We should be charitable towards others.
12) The extreme right is as dangerous as the extreme left.
13) We should always follow our passions.
14) It is foolish to be always comparing ourselves to others.
15) Why are we afraid to recognise our faults?

Compare your choice with someone else.

You are in a conciliatory mood and therefore say things which try to take into consideration explicit or implicit criticism ... Find in the list below five utterances which would be acceptable to you.

Match beginnings from Column I with endings from Column II:

Column I	Column II
1) We could also say that	a) the novel will continue to exist as long as people have the desire to read or tell stories.
2) Of course, we must recognise that	b) governments too have their part to play in this matter.
3) It is undoubtedly true that multinationals are gaining in power but	c) there is an increasing threat to world stability.
4) We should nonetheless ask ourselves if perhaps	d) this opinion can be justified.
5) We should also consider whether	e) women are paid less than men.
6) This is only partly	f) literature is being threatened by the mercenary policies of the big publishing companies.
7) This is rather a superficial statement. The matter is much more complex than	g) meets the eye.
8) There is a problem in accepting this opinion as it would make us took too	h) true.
9) Your argument is sound in some respects but	i) sectarian.
10) We should try to understand why	j) not in others.

Compare your choice with someone else.

Let's now practise with some exercises based on newspaper articles.

Read the article below:

Union calls for pupil's charter

David Ward, Northern
Education Correspondent

THE new chairman of Britain's most conservative teaching union yesterday urged John Patten, the Education Secretary, to take action on crumbling schools, growing class sizes and bullying.

He also demanded modifications to tests for seven-year-olds and advocated formal contracts between parents and schools.

Nicholas Griffin, chairman of the 40,000-member Professional Association of Teachers, challenged the assumptions behind the Parent's Charter and called instead for a children's charter at the association's Loughborough conference.

Pupils had a right to be taught by teachers who were not exhausted and demoralised.

On testing, Mr Griffin said "A way must be found of quantifying the complex concept of the value added by an institution to a child's development. Only then will comparisons made between the schools have any meaning."

He called for an extensive programme of repairs and reconstruction. Children and teachers had a right to expect it.

Action on class sizes was an "astonishing omission" from the Parent's Charter. Mr Griffin said no teacher should be expected to teach a class with more than 30 pupils. In proposing a home-school contract, Mr Griffin said: "Parents must now be held responsible for the indiscipline of their offspring.

"It is time that society realised it is the role of the teacher to teach, it is not the role of the teacher to be a surrogate parent or a social worker or, heaven help us, a policeman."

The critical mood was continued in the conference's opening debates when delegates voiced strong reservations about the national curriculum.

They agreed that teachers were obliged to spend far too much time on record keeping and that pupils aged five to seven should be obliged to study only three core subjects.

● *James Meikle adds:* Mr Patten today unveils school changes designed to last at least 25 years with the 17th piece of education legislation since 1979. Key proposals are expected to include limited powers for schools to choose pupils by aptitude in particular subjects, and attempts to revamp the expensive City Technology College programme through cheaper specialist schools.

Schools will be given greater encouragement to opt out of local authority control, possibly including joint opt-outs by secondary schools and their feeder primary schools.

Imagine you are a student in a secondary school. Draw up a charter of pupil's rights containing at least six points.

Compare your text with someone else.

* 'COURT REFUSES PLEA FOR THE RIGHT TO DIE'

Read the article below:

Doctors get approval to give woman blood transfusion

Court refuses plea for the right to die

Clare Dyer
Legal Correspondent

DOCTORS can continue giving blood to a critically ill 20-year-old accident victim despite her refusal to accept transfusions, the Court of Appeal ruled yesterday.

The case is the first in the British courts to raise the issue of an adult's right to refuse life-saving treatment.

Lord Donalson, Master of the Rolls, and Lord Justices Butler-Sloss and Staughton were told that the woman was in a "critical but stable" condition. They will give their reasons next week.

Lawyers expect the judgment to lay down important guidelines for doctors on how to approach patients who object to treatment.

The woman, named only as T, is heavily sedated and on a ventilator. Her condition deteriorated following a car accident and premature delivery of a still-born baby by caesarean section. The court was told she was brought up by her mother, a Jehovah's Witness, after her parents divorced. But she had rejected the sect.

She has been receiving blood and plasma since last week when her father, who does not belong to the sect, won a High Court order authorising doctors to give her transfusions despite her objections. Before the operation, in her mother's presence, she said she did not want a blood transfusion.

This week's appeal against the order made by Mr Justice Ward was brought on T's behalf by the Official Solicitor, David Venebles, who represents those unable to instruct their own lawyers.

His counsel, James Munby, QC, argued that adult patients of sound mind have a basic human right, protected by the common law, to refuse treatment, even if the result might be death. Lawyers for T's father and the two West Midlands health authorities responsible for her treatment contended that her refusal was invalid.

This was because she did not foresee that her life would be in danger, she was misinformed about possible substitutes for blood, and she was acting under her mother's influence.

Jehovah's Witnesses base their refusal to accept blood transfusions on a literal reading of biblical passages which forbid the intake of others' blood. A number of adult Witnesses have died in Britain after refusing transfusions and doctors have made children wards of court to get court sanction to administer blood.

The problem may be eased in the next few years by the development of artificial blood, according to a specialist in physiology, David Dennison, professor of clinical physiology at the Royal Brompton Hospital, London, said suitable substitutes for blood could be available within two years.

Do you think that adult patients have the right to refuse medical treatment, even if the result might be death? Give your reasons.

Discuss your views with someone else.

* 'DENY HOMOSEXUALS SOME PRIVILEGES, VATICAN TELLS US'

Read the following article:

Deny Homosexuals Some Privileges, Vatican Tells U.S.

By Laura Sessions Stepp
Washington Post Service

WASHINGTON — The Vatican has declared its support for discrimination against homosexuals in such areas as public housing, family health benefits and the hiring of teachers, coaches and military personnel.

In a statement sent last month to Roman Catholic bishops in the United States, the Vatican described homosexuality as "an objective disorder" and compared it to mental illness. It said the government should deny certain privileges to gay people to promote the traditional family and protect society.

"There are areas in which it is not unjust discrimination to take sexual orientation into account," it said, "for example, in the consignment of children to adoption or foster care, in employment of teachers or coaches, and in military recruitment."

In the statement, which was designed to counter gay-rights initiatives, the Vatican said Catholic authorities should not confine their views to Catholic issues or institutions. "The church has the responsibility to promote the public morality of the entire civil society on the basis of fundamental moral values," it said.

Catholic officials said the document was compiled from several earlier papers by the Vatican's Congregation for the Doctrine of the Faith. It was leaked to news organizations this week by New Ways Ministry, a national organization that works with homosexual Catholics. New Ways leaders said the Vatican's arguments were "based on several crucial misconceptions, unfounded assumptions and unproven claims."

John Gallagher, theological consultant to New Ways, called the pronouncement "unadulterated homophobia."

He added that the Vatican was dredging up "all the hard-core myths about gays and lesbians, playing to everyone's fears."

A Gallup poll in the spring showed that the percentage of U.S. Catholics who favor equal job opportunities for gay people has risen from 58 percent, in 1978, to 78 percent, in 1992.

Many U.S. bishops have been more conciliatory toward homosexuals than the Vatican's statement is. In a letter to their parishioners last year, the U.S. bishops said: "We call on all Christians and citizens of goodwill to confront their own fears about homosexuality and to curb the humor and discrimination that offend homosexual persons."

Homosexual activity is wrong, the bishops said, but "such an orientation in itself, because not freely chosen, is not sinful."

Do you agree or do you disagree with the viewpoint of the Vatican?

Give your reasons.

Read the following article:

Animal rights fellowship for priest who says their souls are immortal

Walter Schwarz, Religious Affairs Correspondent

AN Anglican priest who believes that animals have immortal souls is to hold Britain's first research fellowship on animal rights at Oxford.

The Rev Andrew Linzey, director of Essex University's theological centre, will study the theological and ethical rights of animals for five years at Mansfield college on a £200,000 grant from the International Fund for Animal Welfare.

Mr Linzey said standard Roman Catholic teaching recognises three kinds of soul: vegetable, animal, and rational, with only the last immortal.

"That is wrong because the Bible says animals have the breath of life which gives them a moral status and makes their souls immortal."

He said he aims to "rescue the status of animals from what has been the false teaching of the Church". From next October he will also research the ethics of hunting. He said it was only a matter of time before hunting was outlawed in Britain. "Already polls have shown that 80 per cent of people are against hunting with hounds."

Mr Linzey, author of Christianity and the Rights of Animals and other books, failed in 1990 to secure Synod approval for a motion to ban hunting from Church of England lands.

Recently he refused to conduct a Sunday service at his university's chapel in protest against the shooting of rabbits in the grounds.

Richard Moore, director of the welfare fund, said Mr Linzey's appointment would help put animal rights on the agenda of churches and the public.

"Cruelty to animals around the world is condoned and actively supported by churches, as in the religious fiestas in Spain where animals are killed."

Should animals be used in scientific experiments? List four arguments supporting the case and four against.

FOR	AGAINST

Compare your findings with someone else.

146

Read the article below:

Methodists embrace concept of a God without sexual bias

Martin Wainwright

METHODISTS overwhelmingly embraced the concept of a feminine God yesterday by adopting a report condemning past imagery of the deity as "almost stridently male".

They only narrowly defeated an attempt to make a new, balanced-gender liturgy effectively compulsory, after warning of a sinister tendency towards political correctness enforced by chapel "thought police".

Britain's largest nonconformist church will now "strongly encourage" feminine imagery on an equal basis with male language in prayers, hymns and other worship. The 600 delegates to the annual Methodist Conference at Newcastle upon Tyne overwhelmingly defeated two attempts to dilute the proposals or delay them for further consultation.

Dr John Harrod, from the Methodist college in Bristol, and chairman of the report committee, said Bible and prayer references to God as "father" should be understood as images of an ideal parent.

"I don't think the maleness is important. Indeed, the life of Jesus seems to challenge many traditional aspects of maleness," he said. "To en-courage feminine imagery when speaking of God does not marginalise men but makes things mutual."

The report, which quotes Isaiah's comparison of God's struggles over mankind with labour pains, was condemned by the Reverend Steven Wild, a Cornish minister.

"Methodism is in danger of imitating King Canute by telling God what to do," he said. "Jesus was sent by God and he called God 'Father'."

The Reverend Roger Ducker, chairman of Leeds Methodists, attacked the proposal to make the new language "essential", saying: "I very much fear that there is a sort of thought police imposing a political correctness. This is to my mind a sinister way of thinking".

The Reverend Norman Walwork from Cumbria warned: "If we adopt this proposal, many Methodists will start voting with their feet and move away from us."

Dr Pauline Webb, a broadcaster on religious affairs, appealed for a recognition of God's feminine side in the same way that prayers about the monarch changed gender according to the ruler's sex. She said: "Some of us older women are sometimes amazed when it is noticed we're in the congregation."

Adoption of the report is likely to have a rapid effect

on Methodist publications. Inclusive language, using alternatives to "men" and "he" is expected to be widely adopted in prayers and sermons. The conference heard that the word "humankind" was used more than 200 years ago in a hymn translation by John Dryden.

Methodist chapels also urged the reintroduction of income support for 16- and 17-year-olds, after an apparent collapse in the government's guarantee of Youth Training places.

Tom White, chief executive of the National Children's Homes, said that the withdrawal of income support left many teenagers who had missed out on YT without any means of support.

Do you agree or disagree with the following statements? Give your reasons.

1) The Church should encourage the use of feminine imagery in its forms of worship.

2) The present-day concern with political correctness is a sinister development.

3) The life of Jesus challenges many traditional aspects of maleness.

4) Women should never be ordained priests.

5) The Church is becoming too political.

6) Religious affairs make excellent television programmes.

List at least four words or expressions that are considered politically incorrect.

Compare your results with someone else.

Let's now move to essay titles.

* WE ARE FREE, BUT OUR FREEDOM IS CONSTRAINED

How would you defend this statement?
How would you define the phrase 'our freedom is constrained'?
Select five statements in the list below which would help you to write an essay on this subject.

1) Human beings are made up of needs.

2) It is our duty to respect others.

3) The individual is required to make sacrifices in the interest of society.

4) Social relationships are ritualised.

5) We must all respect the law.

6) Society has an obligation to protect private property.

7) Work is a necessary evil.

8) We produce objects to satisfy our needs.

9) Action is in our very bones.

10) We are repressed cowboys.

11) The most virtuous people are those who are the most useful to their fellow human beings.

12) Happiness is the reward for our efforts.

13) Happiness has its laws.

14) Politicians cannot ignore the question of human happiness.

15) In every society there are the rulers and the governed.

Compare your choice with someone else.

* WE ARE ALMOST ALWAYS BORED WITH THOSE WHOM WE BORE

In the list below find three conciliatory points of view to discuss this subject:

1) Isn't it true to say that we expect to be surprised by other people?

2) Few people can tolerate silence.

3) Most people want to be entertained and amused.

4) It is a well-known fact that most couples have nothing to say to each other. Does that mean that they are bored?

5) How can we recognise boredom?

6) Without desire, no communication is possible.

7) Politicians and teachers have to learn to live with the boredom they can see in their listeners' eyes.

8) All communication is narcissistic.

9) Most people like to hear themselves speaking.

10) Talking to a row of blank faces can be very frustrating.

11) Vanity is a much stronger feeling than generosity. We find it easier to forgive those who bore us that those whom we bore.

12) Patience is not a common virtue.

13) Why is it so difficult for human beings to find a common ground for agreement?

14) We expect other people to have a favourable image of us.

Discuss your choice with someone else.

* AS THE POWER OF SUPERSTITION WANES, GOVERNMENTS MUST STRENGTHEN THEIR GRIP ON AUTHORITY

Are there any statements in the list below, which neither support nor condemn the above declaration?

1) All political power is based on beliefs (divine right, equality etc.) that cannot, by their very nature, be proved.

2) Patriotic feeling is one of the best guarantees of the stability of the social order.

3) When the least privileged in a society start to identify themselves more with a social class than with the country as a whole, governments should become concerned.

4) Governments receive a mandate from the people which they must carry out if they want it to be renewed.

5) Governments are more often judged on their speeches than on their acts.

6) Power tends to corrupt; absolute power corrupts absolutely.

7) Can politics be defined as the peaceful resolution of conflict?

8) A democratic society is one in which the source of political authority and discipline has been universally recognised.

9) What we call national unity can only really exist in war-time.

10) Religion is the opium of the masses. (Marx)

Compare your list with someone else.

* 'LIFE IS NASTY, BRUTISH AND SHORT' (HOBBES)

1) It may be useful to give some thought to HOBBES' view on the subject!

> 'The condition of Man is a condition of War of everyone against everyone; in which case everyone is governed by his own reason; and there is nothing he can make use of , that may not be a help to him, in preserving his life against his enemies. It follows, that in such a condition, every man has a right to everything; even to one another's body'.
>
> Hobbes, [*Leviathan* (1651), Ch. 14]

Consider Hobbes' views further and compare them with those of any philosopher with whom you are familiar.

2) What are your own views on the subject?

Find five examples proving that 'war is a natural condition'.
Think of five situations which prove the opposite.

Discuss your views with someone else.

* I AM APPALLED BY THE MALICE OF OTHERS AND AMAZED THAT IT DOES NOT GO EVEN FURTHER.

- Read this statement carefully.

- What perception of humanity does it convey?

- Do you share the author's view?
  YES/NO? WHY/WHY NOT?

We recorded the reactions of a group discussing this title. Firstly, students were asked to comment briefly on the wording of this sentence. Here is what they said about the title.

* The sentence is well-balanced.

* The symmetry is striking.

* The word malice is a little old-fashioned.

* What exactly does the sentence mean?

* It's almost a paradox.

* 'Appalled' and 'amazed' are very strong terms which indicate the depth of the reaction.

* The ideas are very clearly put.

* The statement is a little ambiguous.

* It reminds me of Hume's discussion of the passions (*A Treatise of Human Nature*, Book 2, Part 2).

* The first part of the sentence is perfectly obvious but the second half is a little ridiculous and naive.

* It's much too general, I prefer the subject to be more precise.

* I find the style too self-conscious but the question is interesting.

* The problem with this type of subject is that it is too general and I find it difficult to think of any concrete examples of the word 'malice'.

* What I like is the 'I' in the sentence. It's somebody trying to say something and that immediately makes me want to argue; I want to prove to the speaker that s/he is wrong.

- Which reactions do you agree with?

- Did they miss anything? Can you think of anything else?

Here is what they said about the various issues raised by the topic:

1) On the one hand, the author is shocked that people should be so malicious, and on the other, s/he is surprised that the situation is not worse; the viewpoint is both optimistic and pessimistic.

2) This statement can only be discussed by referring to specific cases. We must begin by defining whom we mean by 'others' and what is meant by the term malice. We must next consider who is doing the judging. According to what criteria? By what right?

3) People can behave like animals and commit atrocious crimes. They are also, however, capable of self-control. It is this that surprises the author of the statement.

4) Even good fathers and model husbands can become great criminals.

5) Countries indulge in atrocities in war-time. This does not prevent them from sometimes coming to the help of the people they have just defeated.

6) Even if we admit that we are born evil, our instinct for survival remains very strong. This is true both for individuals and societies. Do people deliberately choose to risk their lives and freedom?

7) We live in society and every society is founded on principles. It is because of these principles that we are not more destructive.

8) But who exactly are these evil people? Doesn't society have a share of responsibility in all this? We could say that people become evil when they feel threatened, oppressed or unhappy.

9) Perhaps the author has succeeded in coming to terms with a traumatic past!

10) If we say that there is no love without hate, then it is logical to conclude that when we love someone, we are also harbouring evil thoughts.

11) There is so much injustice and suffering in the world that it is surprising that there are not more violent confrontations. If people were really evil, they would always be at war.

12) Evil is not the cause of all human conflict, that would be too simple. Moreover, without conflict, there is no life.

13) We are neither good nor evil but both: cruelty and tenderness coexist in each of us. Even parents can be sadistic towards their children.

14) There are, however, some pathological cases: people who are mentally disturbed, who want to destroy everything including themselves. But that's only a minority of people unless we consider we are all mad at times.

15) Without moral principles, we cannot control our instincts. We must now consider why the family, school and church have not been more successful in inculcating in individuals a moral sense.

16) Our relations with evil are complex. The term malice here suggests acts that are both reprehensible and blameworthy. People, though, find it difficult to agree on what is good and on what is reprehensible. Society has to constantly redefine its moral code.

17) Do the courts condemn 'bad people'? There are 'bad people' who are guilty, others who are innocent. Isn't that the central issue?

18) In TV serials and adventure films, there are always goodies and baddies. It is a somewhat simplistic vision of the world directed mainly at children: in reality, it is impossible to make this distinction.

19) We are horrified when we think of Nazism and the massacres of the Second World War.

20) It is perhaps a form of wisdom or maturity to accept that we can all be a little cowardly or cruel at times. This ought to make us more tolerant.

Does this list provide you with ideas which would enable you to explore some of the issues raised by the title (which may be implied rather than clearly stated)?

Discuss your ideas with someone else and try to assess where, how and why your understanding of the question differs.

How then would you organise your argument in an essay on this topic?

In the next chapters you will find some guidelines on how to plan an argument.

Chapter 8

How to draw up a draft plan

By now you should be familiar with ways of:

* agreeing, defending, supporting, approving
* disagreeing, attacking, criticising, disapproving
* seeing both sides of:
    an argument
    a question
    a remark
    a problem
    an issue.

The aim of this chapter is to help you to draw up a plan, that is to say to:

- organise your ideas in a logical, coherent order.
- eliminate thoughts and arguments which are either irrelevant or secondary given the viewpoint that you have adopted.
- explore further questions and issues discussed in previous chapters.

You may find it useful to return to chapters 5, 6 and 7 before approaching this one.

Let's first explore some topical subjects.

* THE CINEMA

Why and how do you (and people around you) choose a film? If there are not enough cinema-goers around you, you may be interested in the answers given to this question by a group of young people in a survey of April 1987.

What makes you choose to go and see a particular film?

	%
Subject of the film	22
Film stars acting in the film	17
Conversations with friends or colleagues	14
TV programmes about the cinema	10
Number of Oscars etc. awarded to film	8
Name of the producer	6
Film reviews in the press	5
Title of the film	5
Advertising in the press	4
Advertising on the radio	3
Posters in the street	2
Photos in the foyer	2
Cinema programmes in the newspapers	1
Don't know	1

Compare the answers given in the chart above with

- your opinion
- the result of your own survey

Use this information to start thinking about one of the following essay topics:

1) The cinema has nothing to do with literature.

2) The cinema is an art form.

3) Film-makers fulfil the same function as novelists.

4) Going to the cinema is a form of escapism.

5) The cinema is merely entertainment.

6) Avant-garde films have a minority appeal.

7) People no longer read, they prefer to go to the cinema or to watch television.

8) The cinema is an industry.

9) Epic films have replaced great popular novels.

10) People go to the cinema to see their favourite film stars.

11) The cinema is increasingly dependent on advertising.

12) Television poses a threat to the cinema.

Which topic did you choose? Why? Compare your choice with someone else and discuss the use you each made of the results of the survey (either yours or this one).

Now read the following article on the European cinema today. What do you consider to be the role of the cinema in contemporary society? Should film-makers "plunge into documentary forms"?

A lot of soap but not much froth

European cinema has life in it yet, reports
Derek Malcolm at the Venice Film Festival

VENICE, the oldest film festival in the world, hit upon a brave idea for its 49th edition. It is showing all the films that decorated its first programme back in 1932. And since that includes films by Mamoulian, James Whale, King Vidor, Lubitsch, Capra and Leni Riefenstahl, the new films have a great deal to live up to.

Will they manage to do it? It is very doubtful. Gillo Pontecorvo, the veteran director of The Battle Of Algiers, who reluctantly took over the festival as a stop-gap director for a year when the complicated political process by which Venice Festival directors are chosen broke down, has already got into trouble. Peter Bogdanovich, the intended president of his jury, cried off at the last moment and Dennis Hopper had to replace him.

Worse still, the Italian press, not easily satisfied at this political festival, has berated him for refusing to accept Clint Eastwood's **The Unforgiven** as a competition entry. Instead, Eastwood's most successful film with both public and critics for years was offered the doubtful privilege of a midnight screening, and was then sent, on the instructions of Eastwood to the Deauville Festival instead.

But that miscalculation apart, Pontecorvo's programme is interesting. It is crowned by the inclusion of the second edition of Edgar Reitz's Heimat, which continues, over 26 hours and 13 separate films, the story of German history as seen by ordinary people from 1960 — where Heimat 1 ended — into the turbulent sixties and early seventies. It is not in competition because there was no way the jury could see it all. But already it has made a considerable impression.

Called **Leaving Home: Chronicle Of A Generation**, Heimat 2 takes place in Munich, Reitz's home city, rather than in the small, imaginary town where the first film was chiefly set. And whereas Heimat 1 describes family life before, during and immediately after the second world war, Heimat 2 is about growing into manhood, life in the great city, friendship and love.

We have not seen all of it yet, but one of the differences between the two projects is that it does not much matter in what order you see the episodes of the second Heimat, since they are more self-contained than in Heimat 1. But it seems certain that this sequel to one of the European cinema's finest achievements over the last 25 years is going to be equally notable. A wonderful soap opera, which like its predecessor allows history to unfold in the most personal way, connecting ordinary people to great events with cumulative power and extraordinary complexity. Heimat 2 arrives at the London Festival in November and will almost certainly be shown on British television and in cinemas subsequently — a sign that European cinema is not yet dead, despite the prognosis of various cultural doctors.

The rest of the programme has already included two notable films from France: Claude Sautet's superbly acted love story, **Un Coeur En Hiver**, and Bertrand Tavernier's **L 627**, in which, mixing fiction with documentary, the director takes a hard look at France's special drugs squad and its methods. The Sautet film proves this director ought to be much better known in Britain than he is, and the Tavernier shows that his recent plunge into documentary forms has renewed and enriched his art as a film-maker.

Sautet's subject matter, as so often, looks obvious enough. Its hero is a violin restorer who falls in love with a beautiful virtuoso; but so does his partner. The triangular relations are played out almost in sonata form — Sautet is a musician as well as a film-maker — and Daniel Auteuil, André Dusollier and Emmanuelle Béart act with rare subtlety and precision. The first signs, however, are that the jury did not appreciate the Sautet ambience as much as the critics. If so, that may give the Tavernier film a better chance.

L 627 is gritty realism writ large: a sprawling but fascinating look at the drugs squad that takes a neutral stance but has shocked people in France, who regard the police as honest defenders of the law. The police agents we meet are mostly young, cynical and fond of practical jokes; they are also clearly racist and violent.

We have, of course, seen that kind of exposé before and what it lacks is a distinct style. But even so, it is a formidable portrait of a society on the edge of breakdown and of an underclass that has perhaps already given up hope. The pimps, prostitutes, dealers and drug-takers who inhabit the film do not seem very much worse than those that chase them. But they are more desperate. It is the kind of film that makes it virtually impossible for the audience to take sides, which is perhaps what Tavernier intended.

Another success, among a considerable number of failures, was James Foley's adaptation of David Mamet's play, **Glengarry Glen Ross**. It is not quite filmed theatre; but it is a brilliantly acted summation of one of Mamet's most powerful comments on the falsity of the American Dream. Jack Lemmon is superb as the old real-estate salesman pleading with his bosses to give him one last chance of a major deal, and so is Al Pacino as the younger salesman in whom they have more confidence.

If Lemmon does not get the Best Actor award, I shall be surprised. This edgy, emotional part fits him like a glove. Glengarry Glen Ross may be decried in some quarters as not quite proper cinema, but if acting and screenplay count for anything nowadays, who cares?

* THE FAMILY

Look at the chart below relating to one-parent families.

PROPORTIONS OF ALL FAMILIES WITH DEPENDENT CHILDREN HEADED BY LONE MOTHERS AND LONE FATHERS

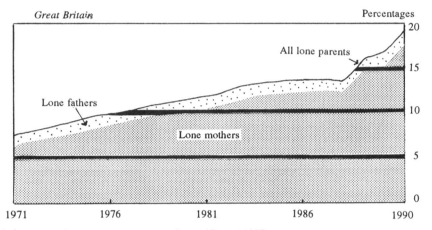

1 3-year moving averages used (apart from 1971 and 1987)

Source: Office of Population Censuses and Surveys

Your personal experience may contradict the picture given by these figures, in which case you will be well placed to write controversial answers on the following topics:

1) Is the number of lone fathers increasing?

2) Should the increasing number of lone mothers lead to fundamental changes in the social system?

3) Is the nuclear family still the norm in our age?

4) Is it true to say that the family is an out-dated institution?

5) How can we prevent single mothers and single fathers from feeling socially disadvantaged?

* EMPLOYMENT

Analyse the following charts:

EMPLOYEES AND SELF-EMPLOYED: BY SEX AND OCCUPATION, 1990

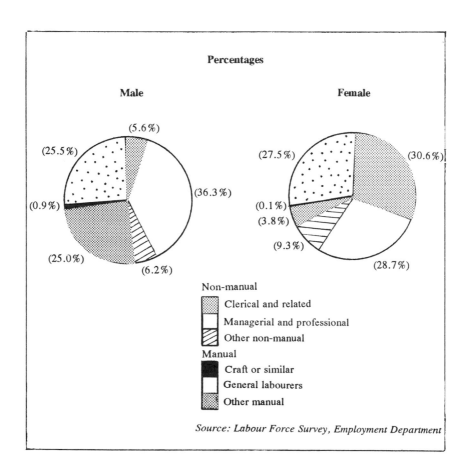

Percentages

Male   Female

(5.6%)
(25.5%)
(0.9%)
(36.3%)
(25.0%)
(6.2%)

(27.5%)   (30.6%)
(0.1%)
(3.8%)
(9.3%)
(28.7%)

Non-manual
   Clerical and related
   Managerial and professional
   Other non-manual
Manual
   Craft or similar
   General labourers
   Other manual

Source: Labour Force Survey, Employment Department

UNEMPLOYMENT AND VACANCIES

United Kingdom

Millions

1. Seasonally adjusted unemployment (claimants aged 18 and over).
2. About one-third of all vacancies are notified to job centres.
3. Vacancy data prior to 1980 are not consistent with current coverage.

Source:Employment Department

Can part-time or temporary work solve the problem of unemployment?

Answer this question by choosing six of the following statements which you consider to be particularly relevant, and do so in an order which, in your view, is a *logical* one.

	Your selection of statements 1 - 6
* Despite the advent of temping agencies, there is no decrease in unemployment.	
* Temporary workers are badly organised and badly paid.	
* People are prepared to do anything to earn a little money.	
* Are temporary work and trade unionism compatible?	
* Temporary work is a stopgap measure.	
* The power of the unions has greatly declined during the last few years.	
* Holidays and retirement are increasingly looked upon as a luxury rather than as a right.	
* The problem of employment and, therefore, of unemployment, is a political one.	
* Everyone has the right to work.	
* Temporary work is particularly suitable for women.	
* Low-grade jobs are badly paid.	
* People prefer to moonlight rather than go through temping agencies.	
* In times of high unemployment, job-centres provide few opportunities of obtaining work.	

Compare your selection with someone else.

* HOLIDAYS

Analyse the figures and diagrams given below and note what you find particularly striking.

PERCENTAGE ENTITLED TO ANNUAL PAID HOLIDAYS OF DURATION

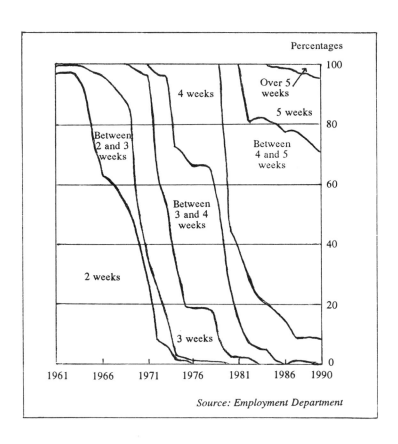

Source: Employment Department

HOLIDAYS TAKEN BY GREAT BRITAIN RESIDENTS: BY DESTINATION

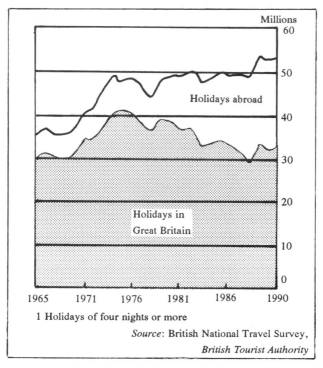

Millions

Holidays abroad

Holidays in
Great Britain

60
50
40
30
20
10
0

1965   1971   1976   1981   1986   1990

1 Holidays of four nights or more

Source: British National Travel Survey,
British Tourist Authority

Compare your notes with someone else.

Select *one* essay title from the following:

1)   Holidays are a waste of time.

2)   Beauty spots are polluted by tourists.

3)   Everyone takes their holiday in the same place and at the same time.

4)   Long holidays pose a threat to the economy.

5)   Holidaymakers are good for business.

6)   Wintersports are universally accessible.

7)   Not going on holiday fosters resentment in people.

8) Increasing the length of holiday-time is a progressive step.

9) Holidays are often very tiring.

10) Holidays with pay are one of the great advances made by the working classes.

Then pick up in the list below ideas which you will develop to write your essay.

* Holidays should be staggered.

* In summer, all you hear about are accidents and traffic congestion on the motorways.

* Family travel is dictated by the school holidays.

* There has been a rapid expansion in the sports and leisure industries.

* The growth of mass tourism has provided a boom to rural economies.

* Transistor radios should be banned on beaches.

* We all need peace and quiet.

* We have lost the taste for simple pleasures.

* Sun-worship goes to people's heads.

* Whether at home or on holiday, people always want to keep up with the Joneses.

* Snobs are attracted to the fashionable holiday resorts.

* It is fashionable to go on skiing holidays.

* People's attitudes change when they are on holiday.

* Two popular subjects of conversation in the office are television and holidays.

* Package holidays have destroyed all sense of initiative.

* There is nothing more depressing than to see endless rows of tents.

* Holidaymakers do not visit a country; they 'do' India, Egypt and Scotland in ten days!

* Tourism is an industry.

* Souvenir shops attract more holidaymakers than museums.

Compare you choice with someone else.

* **EUROPE**

Would you say that 'United we prosper'? Yes? No? Maybe?
Read the following article and pick up ideas and arguments you would like to develop:

United, we prosper

Debate on Europe is full of hypocrisy and ignorance. **John Palmer** hits back at the sceptics

THE advent of Britain's presidency of the European Community has been marked by smug predictions, from Bruges Group zealots and "moderate pro-Europeans" alike, that the high tide of European integration is — at last — starting to ebb. Good, we are assured, may yet come out of bad since the way is now clear for political power to be repatriated to where it properly belongs — Whitehall.

Of course, on the further reaches of the Euro-sceptical right wing, delight is unbounded. But, remarkably enough, the Thatcherite slogan that a "blow against the Maastricht treaty is a blow for peoples' power" has even found an echo among some who would not be seen dead sharing a platform with Baroness Thatcher on any other issue.

Much of the debate on European political union is suffused with hypocrisy, disinformation and ignorance. To cite but one instance of hypocrisy: a central charge against the Maastricht treaty is that it is undemocratic. This is in large measure true — but most of its undemocratic features were adopted at the spe-

cific demand of the British.

It was the UK government which resisted giving the European Parliament genuine equality of law making rights with the Council of Ministers. As a result, power in the proposed European Union, as in the present Community, will continue to be concentrated in the Council. This is the only legislature in the "democratic world" which passes laws behind closed doors and is in no meaningful way accountable to any democratic assembly.

The secrecy and unaccountability of the national governments who make up the Council is bad enough when they operate within the rules of the Treaty of Rome. But when the same governments meet outside the Rome Treaty framework in either of the two "inter-governmental" pillars established in the Maastricht treaty (again mainly at UK insistence) the absence of accountability is grotesque.

Decisions are to be taken outside the Rome Treaty in a range of critically important areas for civil and human rights — such as police and judicial co-operation as well as foreign and security policy. But, in the two inter-governmental pillars of Maastricht, the European Parliament does not even have the minimal rights of information and co-decision which apply under Rome Treaty procedures.

If British ministers are so concerned about the growing gulf between the decision makers and the people within the Community, why do they not make the legislative sessions of the Council open to the press and public? They could also give national Parliaments some meaningful role in European legislation by having MPs sit in the Senate of a European Parliament which was accorded real law-making parity with the Council.

Instead, the Government and its media acolytes have given the totally misleading impression that Westminster and the other national Parliaments can really control this burgeoning club of EC states. They do not do so now and they will have even less leverage if and when Maastricht comes into force.

The real threat of a centralised super state is to be found here, not in the alleged pretensions of Jacques Delors. It is the chronic weakness of the democratic, federal elements in the Maastricht treaty, not their excess, which poses the greatest danger to the popular legitimacy of the EC institutions.

THE paradox is that it was this in part which led the Danes to reject Maastricht. But if the treaty does collapse in the coming months it will be more difficult, not easier, to achieve democratic control in the Community than if it is — warts and all — accepted as a framework for future reform. Hence the delight of the far right.

To cover their tracks, the anti-Maastricht populists have mounted a campaign of lies, half truths and exaggerations to discredit the Commission — a civil service body which disposes of but a tiny fraction of the power wielded by the Council. John Major talks of an "intrusive Community" and his right wing Euro-sceptic back benchers of Delors' Bonapartist tendencies.

In the Tories' book, the single market cannot by definition be intrusive, whatever the disruption it occasions to the lives of individuals, industries and entire communities. It is only when the European Community seeks to place a minimal framework of elementary social rights or defences for the environment, that the outrage of the British populists is aroused.

The irony is that it has been national governments — not Brussels — which have been responsible for the Commission's excessive regulatory role over the internal market. The reason is that they do not trust each other. The absurdities of harmonised crisp flavourings or the volume of asbestos permitted in a billiard cue arise from insistence, by national government and industry representatives, that detailed legislation guarantees a level playing field in the single European market.

Would the UK be happy to see Paris take over the Commission's role in mergers and competition policy? Conversely, will the Danes or the Germans be happy to allow the British to determine the extent to which the European environment should be protected?

We hear much about the ineffectiveness of the European Community's policies towards Yugoslavia. But it was the UK which vetoed the European Union having its own defence role or being allowed to decide foreign and security policy by majority vote. As a result, the EC diplomatic caravan moves at the pace of its slowest camel.

The ignorance, however, is rooted in a longer term British inability to come to terms with the historical, economic and political dynamic behind European unity. The chimera of a serious alternative to European integration has assumed different shapes and forms during the past 40 years — from the empire, through the Commonwealth, the US special relationship and EFTA to the vague evocation of a depoliticised common market stretching from the Atlantic to Vladivostok.

The questioning of European Union and the Maastricht treaty is certainly not confined to Britain and Denmark. The political blood brothers of the right wing anti-federalist Tory back benchers are to be found among the anti-Maastricht foot soldiery of the neo-Gaullist and National Front-led Maastricht treaty rejection campaign in France. They also lead the cheerleaders for the — as yet — rather mystical but potentially dangerous D-mark nationalism celebrated by the Republican and the Christian Social Union right wing in Germany.

Protracted stagflation and mass unemployment will of course further strengthen this Euro-nationalist right. That is why the European Community desperately needs a strategy to rebuild the European economy so that it can put the unemployed back to work on the basis of long term, ecologically sustainable growth.

However, such a strategy has to start from the realities of European economic integration. Those who fear Euro-monetarist deflation for economic and monetary union have reason. But any attempt to recreate a world of largely separate national economies in which currency devaluation could act as a spur to unilateral export-led growth is doomed. Capitalism is no longer like that.

Those who want an EMU which serves the goal of growth, employment and defence of the environment should resist the dismantling of political union. Only in a strengthened political union can there be a credible strategy for ensuring that economic forces serve society's needs rather than the other way round. It is the only route to European economic recovery.

Discuss your selection of ideas and arguments with someone else and see if you can come to an agreement through exchanging views.

Let's now work on some essay titles.

* 'THE MIDDLE-CLASSES' ASSAULT ON CULTURE HAS GIVEN RISE TO THE CONCEPT OF CONSUMER ART'.

Imagine three people reacting very differently to this statement (because for example, they don't accept a common definition of 'culture', 'middle class', 'consumerism' or because they even dispute the relationship established here between social class and culture). According to the beliefs and values which you have attributed to your fictitious speakers try to identify among the statements below those which each one might make. Call your speakers A,B and C and mark the chart accordingly:

172

Statements	Speakers		
	A	B	C
* We live in a market economy where consumption is as important as production.			
* There is a reactionary elitism in the arts.			
* The imposition of middle-class values has led to the denigration of the privileges of enlightened amateurs.			
* The privileged classes resent sharing their possessions.			
* So-called advanced societies are dominated by commercialism.			
* It is an arrogance of upper social classes to assume that they alone have access to Culture.			
* This statement is elitist.			
* It is increasingly difficult, nowadays, to tell the difference between a work of art and a commercial product.			
* The media have produced a culture of uniformity.			
* With an increase in poverty, there has been an expansion of the moneyed classes. Whither the middle class?			
* The great works of the past have been classified and indexed but what we call contemporary art is often only a collection of objects which people would have us believe are of equal value.			
* The middle-classes are often of working-class origin.			
* Popular culture is often valued by intellectuals or theoreticians.			

Continued . . .

Statements	Speakers		
	A	B	C
* The upper middle classes have always been very active in the cultural sphere.			
* It would seem that the proletariat has always been excluded from culture.			
* Culture must not be confused with the possession of gadgets.			
* To survive, we have to consume. What is wrong then with speaking of culture in terms of consumption?			
* A work of art is to be admired not consumed!			
* The great profits that are made in the art world are utterly scandalous.			
* How can private individuals be allowed to buy works of art that are part of the national heritage?			
* Art has always needed patrons and it is to the wealthy of the past that we owe the existence of the treasures that we admire in museums or libraries.			
* The tragedy of our age is that people no longer have a scale of values: cartoons, rock music, design, gastronomy, advertising, Turner and Bach are all put together in the same basket.			

Compare your choice with someones else. Try to explain why and how you have attributed certain statements to a particular speaker and give a brief description of each one. Then imagine that your role is to try to establish a consensus in a group of people with opposing views on this question.

* IN SO-CALLED ADVANCED SOCIETIES, PEOPLE PREFER TO BECOME SHAREHOLDERS RATHER THAN TO JOIN A TRADE UNION

How would you discuss this statement? Select in the list below six 'ideas' which you find interesting and/or relevant.

1) Everyone dreams of becoming a shareholder.

2) The privatisation of large companies enables many people to dream of becoming rich.

3) Popular capitalism is a myth.

4) Small shareholders have no say in the running of the companies in which they have shares.

5) Those whose principal desire is to grow rich tend to feel less and less sympathetic towards the have-nots of our society.

6) In a democracy, it is acceptable for people to grow rich.

7) Union struggles have become archaic.

8) Each one for himself is the motto of liberal societies.

9) The influence of the unions on politics has diminished.

10) The era of great union struggles has passed.

11) Society is more divided than ever.

12) Unions are characterised by a sluggish bureaucracy.

13) Without individuals, a society cannot thrive.

14) An absence of solidarity is a potential threat to society.

15) Political stability is guaranteed if the government can convince everyone that they can be free.

Compare your choice with someone else.

* DO BANKS BEAR THE BRUNT OF THE RESPONSIBILITY FOR THIRD WORLD DEBT?

Choose five of the following statements to illustrate your answer:

1) Modern society is dependent on the smooth running of the banking system.

2) The banks are principally to blame for the debts of Third World Countries.

3) Countries whose economies are not developed are those with little or no credit system.

4) Interest rates set by the banks are too high.

5) Banks are not philanthropic societies. If they fail to make a profit, they go bankrupt.

6) Most governments seem to have very little power over banks.

7) The primary aim of the banks is to protect the interests of their shareholders.

8) There are many immoral practices in the international financial system.

9) It is not the banks who are responsible for the imbroglio of Third World debt but the corrupt political leaders of these countries themselves.

10) The debts of Third World countries do not concern us.

11) There is nothing immoral in making a profit with one's money.

12) Banking activities ought to be subject to a stricter control by the authorities.

13) Why blame the bankers? Bankers are ordinary people like everyone else.

14) There are no bad creditors. There are only bad debtors.

15) It is scandalous that banks make profits at the expense of poor countries.

* IS OUR AGE CHARACTERISED BY A LACK OF ORIGINAL THINKING?

Choose five of the following statements to illustrate your answer:

1) The entertainment industry is rapidly expanding.

2) People no longer have the time to think.

3) We live in an audio-visual civilisation.

4) We no longer have any models to guide our thinking.

5) There is a continual demand for production to become more and more efficient.

6) Wanting to assert our difference, whether it be ethnic or sexual, is to reject the universality of all true culture.

7) Nothing has any meaning anymore.

8) Standardised leisure activities turn people into morons.

9) A love of money has always existed.

10) People are not more stupid now than in the past.

11) Thought is more noble than action.

12) Each age should define its own lifestyle.

13) The number of educated people is increasing.

14) People sell books like packets of soap powder.

15) Creating is not thinking.

Compare your choice with someone else and discuss the points on which you agree or differ.

In the final section of this chapter you will find further essay titles: as most subjects have already been mentioned in previous chapters, working on them will also be useful revision.

Each essay title is followed by ideas for discussion; before reading them, try to do your own thinking and make sure you have dealt with the following:

- What is at stake here?

- What are the different issues raised by this statement?

- List those you perceive as being the most relevant.

- Establish the relationships that you see between them.

- Then identify clusters of ideas which you see as

    1. supporting the original statement of the essay title
    2. contradicting it
    3. coming to a compromise.

* UNEMPLOYMENT

Unemployment is one of the greatest challenges we now have to face.

1) In spite of declarations from the different parties, there is no political solution to the problem of unemployment.

2) Replacing men by machines increases both productivity and unemployment.

3) In an economy based on free competition, it is market forces alone that should determine employment.

4) The State has a duty to intervene to ensure that everyone has the right to work.

5) If we stopped importing goods that have been produced cheaply by the underpaid labour force of the Third World, there would be work for everyone in the industrial countries.

6) The present unemployment is only a temporary phenomenon; the introduction of radical changes in the economic system will soon resolve the problem.

7) Within a few years, part-time work will become the norm and few people will be employed full-time.

8) In a society of free individuals, nobody owes anyone anything.

9) If part-time work were to become widespread, the problem of remuneration would arise: should part-time workers receive half the salary or the full salary?

10) Society has a duty to ensure a decent existence to those to whom it cannot offer work.

*TAXES

In a modern society, a reduction in individual taxation is a sign of progress.

1) Reducing taxes means that individuals are able to use their money as they see fit.

2) The less assistance people receive from the State, the more responsibility they will take for themselves.

3) A low rate of taxation means less state control and more individual freedom.

4) Nowadays, a criticism of the State implies a criticism of the Welfare State. Those people who want a less powerful State, see only good in the free-market system.

5) To boost investment, there must be a reduction in taxes and income.

6) It is a myth to believe that reducing taxes encourages people to save more, or, better still, to invest more.

7) If we are to emerge from a recession, we must consume more and, therefore, be taxed less.

8) The State can reduce social inequality by imposing heavier taxes on the rich to help the poor.

9) Reducing taxes is a means of deluding people, since what the State does not receive in one area, it recoups in another.

10) A decrease in taxes can mean a deterioration in the quality of education and of public health.

*FREE TRADE

It is artificial to protect an economy from foreign competition.

1) Protectionist measures encourage domestic industries to be inefficient, whereas free trade forces them to be competitive.

2) It is more important to ensure full employment in our own country than to help provide work for the labour force of other countries by buying their products.

3) All the big industrial countries practise free trade.

4) No country practises free trade; it only exists in textbooks on economics and in the speeches of politicians.

5) The free circulation of goods encourages the expansion of the internal market.

6) The free circulation of goods goes hand in hand with that of people; an attack on either is an attack on the principle of freedom.

7) Why not control imports when we know that all the exporting countries break the rules of free trade by subsidising their products?

8) Tariff barriers and import quotas should only be used in exceptional cases.

9) Protectionism develops when the international market is unable to absorb the increase in production of manufactured goods.

10) It is ridiculous to see a country like Japan participate in the development of codes of conduct in international commerce when we know that it is practically impossible to export anything there.

*FREEDOM OF INFORMATION

To function properly, representative democracy requires the active participation of free, well-informed citizens.

1) The notion of State secrecy has been expanded to encompass an ever wider sphere of activity. This poses a threat to individual freedom and to our right to information.

2) To function properly, a democratic regime has to rely upon the indifference of most individuals. It is only personal dissatisfaction that stimulates action. Otherwise, people put their trust in their representatives.

3) How can people say that the citizens of democratic countries are not well-informed when they are being constantly bombarded by the media?

4) If we consider the various political and financial controls to which the press, radio and televison are subjected, we realise that freedom of information is a myth.

5) In our society, everyone is free to produce a newspaper if they so wish.

6) It is absurd to hear politicians claim that individual freedom is being protected through hands-off economic policies, when the State itself is acquiring an increasingly complex network of information on each individual.

7) Parliamentary debates are public.

8) Many societies suffer from the absence of an official forum where the hidden aspects of government action can be debated. No European country, for example, has the equivalent of the senatorial commissions of inquiry of the United States.

9) In a democracy, the State is the best judge of what should not be discussed in public: it must take into account the interests of national security and the stability of the social order.

10) We live in a world where the sinister visions of Kafka and Orwell should be taken seriously.

*THE ELECTORAL SYSTEM

A fundamental principle of representative democracy is that the party composition of the national Parliament should reflect as closely as possible the voting patterns of the electorate.

1) A Parliament cannot be truly representative of the people if there is an imbalance between the number of votes and the number of seats obtained by each political party.

2) Above all, an election must enable a strong majority to emerge in government and the single majority ballot is the best way of achieving this.

3) A two round majority ballot or, better still, proportional representation, makes it possible for a government majority to emerge that reflects as closely as possible the voting patterns of the electorate.

4) The political options available to our society are sufficiently clear-cut to be expressed in a two-party system. The arrival of new national parties on the political scene cannot, therefore, be justified.

5) Proportional representation leads to political instability.

6) To oppose proportional representation on the grounds that it can lead to unstable and weak governments is fallacious unless you consider that Holland, Germany and the Scandinavian countries all have weak governments.

7) Supporters of a single majority ballot are in reality opposed to a government of dialogue and compromise.

8) Voters need a simple choice on which to base their decision. Proportional representation is too complex a mechanism and it could mislead people.

9) Does saying that proportional representation or the majority ballot in two rounds presents voters with a choice that is too complicated, really mean that there are some countries where the electorate is capable of making such a choice and others where it is not?

*THE DOLLAR

The health of the dollar is a matter of universal concern.

1) Why is the dollar a privileged currency?

2) Does the international monetary system depend on the dollar?

3) Why is the North American economy the most important in the world?

4) How can the fall of the dollar since 1985 be explained?

5) One of the signs of a healthy economy is usually the low level of debt incurred by its public sector. Yet the level of debt of the North American economy is one of the highest in the world.

6) Most multinational companies are in fact North American.

7) What is the relationship between the yen and the dollar?

8) The balance of trade has become one of the major preoccupations of the North American administration. What effect does this have on the world economy?

9) Is the creation of a common European currency an effective means of combating the supremacy of the dollar?

10) Are we surprised to see the North American economy showing signs of weakness?

11) What do we mean by the imperialism of the dollar?

12) Almost the whole of the Third World debt is in dollars. Should the dollar be replaced by other currencies?

13) What could be the political consequences of the dollar invading the rouble area?

14) It is high time to find a more stable basis for the international monetary system. What solution do we suggest?

*POETRY

Poetry has become obsolete.

1) People no longer have the time to read.

2) Poetry demands a form of meditation.

3) The number of poetry-reading societies is increasing.

4) Everyone is secretly writing poetry.

5) Poetry is the source of truth.

6) Poetry sells badly.

7) Poets are not welcome in our mercenary and technocratic society.

8) Can you imagine a business man reading poetry between two very important meetings?

9) Poetry challenges generally accepted ideas.

10) Poetry is reserved for a minority.

11) We all have our moments of being a poet, whether we know it or not.

12) Can songs be considered poetry?

13) School often puts people off poetry.

14) A poem demands humility and patience from its reader.

15) Poets are not intellectuals.

16) Poetry is often obscure.

17) A poem is composed of sounds and images.

18) In our age, the qualities of sensitivity and of imagination are no longer appreciated and it is poetry that suffers.

19) Many people find poetry irrelevant.

20) Is the novelist also a poet?

*HISTORY AND THE NOVEL

'The rise of the novel in the Enlightenment period to become the dominant form of the nineteenth century is related to the declining authority of the 'providential plots' of revealed religion, History replacing Theology as the privileged discourse through which human life is to be understood'.

David Lodge, *Write On* (Penguin 1980) p. 198-9

1) History is a story.

2) History like the novel is subject to the constraints of the written word.

3) A novel is neither true nor false but relies upon the credulity of the reader.

4) The novel is essentially about truth and reality.

5) The novel is also a social text.

6) The novel is about conflict.

7) The history of ordinary people has yet to be written. The popular novel will help achieve this.

8) Like the novel, history must have its heroes.

9) The lessons of history are to be read in the novel.

10) Great novels can be compared to historical frescos.

11) The novel shuns historical anecdote and trivial detail.

12) The historian and the novelist have similar functions.

13) The historian is content with describing events, whereas the novelist analyses and projects into the future.

14) Although a novel and a history book may use the same material, they are not read in the same way because they do not have the same status.

15) The New History, like the New Novel, is concerned first and foremost with questions of language.

16) Time is the major preoccupation of historians and novelists.

17) It is naive to think that history can be objective.

18) The historian shrinks before the complexity of human behaviour, whereas the novelist revels in it.

19) The novelist does not have to justify himself in anyone's eyes, least of all in the eyes of history.

20) Both the historian and novelist are products of their age.

* ADVERTISING

A group of students working on this title "Advertising should be banned" organised their thoughts as follows:

By way of introduction:

What is advertising? Is it encouraging people to consume more? Is it a means of deception or seduction? Does it provide information or promote free competition?

* Advertising has always existed. It has simply taken a different form in our age and become more powerful.

* Advertising exists even in socialist countries.

* We will never be able to ban advertising completely, at least not in a democratic country.

* Why go so far as to say that advertising should be banned?

* Advertising is an unwelcome intrusion into our everyday lives.

* Is it possible to make an objective assessment of the influence that advertising has on us?

* Is the influence of advertising as harmful as it is often suggested?

* Is there a positive side to advertising?

To prove that there is no reason for advertising to be banned:

* Advertising promotes competition which is an essential component of a market economy.

* Advertising is a means of subsidising the media, allowing the price of newspapers, for example, to be maintained at a relatively low level.

* Advertising tells us about the choice of products available to the consumer.

* We do not need to look at advertisements if we do not want to.

* Advertisements can be artistic and amusing.

* If you know the tricks of advertising, you are not taken in by what you see.

* Advertising livens up grey urban landscapes.

* Advertising does not necessarily persuade you to buy a particular product but helps you decide between different brand names.

* Advertising is a major source of employment. It would therefore, be absurd to make so many people redundant.

* Great painters have produced posters which are considered to be true works of art.

To show that advertising should be controlled or even completely banned:

* Its influence over the young and uneducated is too strong.

* Advertising is often degrading and sexist.

* It reinforces stereotyped roles, in particular that of the male and female, and strengthens social inequality.

* It is immoral.

* It encourages people to smoke, drink and eat too much.

* It increases the profits of multinational companies and causes small businesses to go bankrupt.

* It deceives people.

* It is intrusive.

* Films are always being interrupted on television.

* The landscape of both city and country is spoilt by ugly and tasteless billboards.

* Advertising exists in every sphere of life. Even the universities need to sell themselves.

* It is dangerous.

* It has been proved that advertising manipulates us by appealing to our unconscious.

* It modifies our behaviour and the very fabric of society by attaching a special importance to the image and to play-acting at the expense of deeper values. Nowadays, politics is nothing more than showmanship.

To sum up:

* It may be an exaggeration to say that advertising should be completely banned as it does have some good points.

* Advertising is not, therefore, totally bad or totally good.

* Advertising could be subjected to a form of censorship or control.

Bearing in mind that:

* Censorship is not a democratic principle.

* Public opinion is the sole judge of what is an infringement to its freedom.

* We are not children who need protecting against everything.

* Advertising is a game; you must learn the rules so as not to lose.

In conclusion, therefore:

* Advertising should not be banned but should be subject to controls so that it does not completely take over our lives.

* Advertising brings a little gaiety, frivolity and spice to our lives, which would otherwise be rather dull.

* What kind of life would it be if we had no choice?

This is not yet a structured plan, and more work has to be done in order to produce an essay. Precise guidelines on drawing up a plan are to be found in chapter 10.

In this last example 'Advertising should be banned' the data has been provisionally organised in such a way that the argument is beginning to take shape; this could be called a draft plan. Some ideas and articulations are as yet ill-defined and irrelevant or redundant, but this attempt at organising the material is a necessary and unavoidable step in essay writing. (It is in fact the result of sorting out notes and ideas first written as random thoughts.)

Chapter 9

Choosing the right words and expressions

This chapter offers you a selection of activities designed to improve your proficiency in English. All exercises are short and self-contained - some more difficult than others. It's up to you to decide which ones you work on and in which order. Concentrate here on the actual wording and on building up your own stock of expressions according to your needs. (Remember that there's an index and a mini dictionary on pages 320 and 293).

* GRAPHIC PRESENTATION (I)

Study the following charts carefully:

Trade deliveries of LPs, cassettes, compact discs and singles

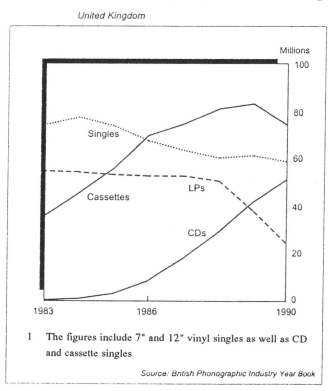

United Kingdom

1 The figures include 7" and 12" vinyl singles as well as CD and cassette singles

Source: British Phonographic Industry Year Book

Radio listening: by age

United Kingdom			Hours and minutes and percentages		
	1986	1987	1988	1989	1990
Age group					
(hours:minutes per week)					
4-15 years	2:12	2:07	2:13	2:21	2:26
16-34	11:24	11:18	11:14	12:07	12:28
35-64	9:56	10:16	10:33	11:10	11:42
65 years and over	8:27	8:44	8:49	9:00	9:18
All aged 4 years and over	8:40	8:52	9:12	9:46	10:12
Reach[1]					
(percentages)					
Daily	*43*	*43*	*43*	*44*	*45*
Weekly	*75*	*74*	*73*	*74*	*74*

[1] Percentage of UK population aged 4 and over who listened to radio for
at least half a programme a day

Source: British Broadcasting Corporation

Weekly radio listening, (percentage of population)

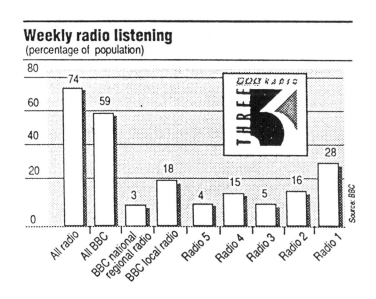

Weekly radio listening
(percentage of population)

Write down what strikes you most.

Which five of the following sentences do you consider to be most useful in expressing what you would say about this survey?

1) Between 1983 and 1989 the sales of cassettes rose.

2) In 1989, sales of compact discs (CDs) exceeded sales of long-play albums (LPs) for the first time.

3) By 1990, CD sales were more than double those of LPs.

4) Sales of cassettes continue to exceed sales of CDs.

5) Radio listening has increased by 18% between 1986 and 1990.

6) In all age groups there is an increase in radio listening.

7) In 1990, on average, people listened to the radio for just over 10 hours each week.

8) In 1990 those aged 16-34 spent the most time listening to the radio.

9) Those aged 4-15 spend the least time listening to the radio.

10) Since 1986 the proportion of people who listen to the radio has remained fairly constant at around 43%.

11) The weekly reach of Radio 3 is only 5%.

12) Radio 1 is more popular than BBC local radio.

13) A similar percentage of people listen to Radio 2 and Radio 4.

14) How do people arrive at these statistics? How is the market research carried out?

15) It would be interesting to know the age group and social background of the audience of individual radio stations.

Compare and discuss your choice with someone else.

Reading of national newspapers: by sex and age, 1971 and 1990

Great Britain

	Percentage of adults reading each paper in 1990			Percentage of each age group reading each paper in 1990			Readership[1] (millions)	
	Males	Females	All adults	25-44	45-64	65 & over	1971	1990
Daily newspapers								
The Sun	25	20	23	24	21	16	8.5	10.2
Daily Mirror	22	17	19	18	21	18	13.8	8.7
Daily Mail	10	9	9	8	11	11	4.8	4.2
Daily Express	10	8	9	7	10	11	9.7	3.9
Daily Star	8	5	6	8	5	3		2.8
Daily Telegraph	6	4	5	4	7	7	3.6	2.3
Today	5	3	4	5	3	1		1.7
The Guardian	4	2	3	4	3	1	1.1	1.3
The Times	3	2	3	3	3	2	1.1	1.2
The Independent	3	2	2	3	3	1		1.1
Financial Times	2	1	2	2	2		0.7	0.7
Any daily newspaper[2]	69	59	64	62	68	63		
Sunday newspapers								
News of the World	31	28	29	32	27	21	15.8	13.2
Sunday Mirror	22	19	21	21	21	17	13.5	9.3
The People	17	15	16	16	18	15	14.4	7.4
Mail on Sunday	13	11	12	14	13	7		5.6
Sunday Express	10	9	10	7	13	14	10.4	4.4
The Sunday Times	9	7	8	9	8	4	3.7	3.5
Sunday Telegraph	5	4	4	3	6	5	2.1	1.9
The Observer	5	4	4	5	4	3	2.4	1.8
Independent on Sunday[3]	3	2	3	3	2	1		1.2
Any Sunday newspaper[3]	74	69	71	70	75	67		

[1] Defined as the average issue readership and represents the number of people who claim to have read or looked at one or more copies of a given publication during a period equal to the interval at which the publication appears

[2] Includes the above newspapers plus the Daily Record

[3] Includes the above newspapers plus the Sunday Post, Sunday Mail, Scotland on Sunday and Sunday Sport

Source: National Readership Surveys, Joint Industry Committee for National Readership Surveys; Circulation Review; Audit Bureau of Circulation

Reading of the most popular magazines: by sex and age, 1971 and 1990

Great Britain

	Percentage of adults reading each magazine in 1990			Percentage of each age group reading each magazine in 1990				Readership[1] (millions)	
	Males	Females	All adults	15-24	25-44	45-64	65 & over	1971	1990
General magazines									
Radio Times	18	19	19	20	20	18	17	9.5	8.5
TV Times	18	19	19	21	19	18	15	9.9	8.4
Reader's Digest	14	13	13	8	13	17	14	9.2	6.1
What Car	7	1	4	6	5	3	1		1.8
National Geographic	5	3	4	4	4	4	2	1.1	1.7
Exchange & Mart	5	2	3	5	4	3	1		1.5
Women's magazines[2]									
Woman's Own	3	16	10	10	11	9	8	7.2	4.3
Bella	3	15	10	12	11	8	6		4.3
Woman's Weekly	2	11	7	4	5	9	10	4.7	3.1
Woman	2	11	7	6	8	6	5	8.0	3.0
Best	2	11	6	9	8	5	3		2.9
Prima	2	10	6	7	8	5	2		2.6

1 Defined as the average issue readership and represents the number of people who claim to have read, or looked at, one or more copies of a given publication during a period equal to the interval at which the publication appears.

2 The age analysis for women's magazines includes male readers

Source: National Readership Surveys, Joint Industry Committee for National Readership Surveys; Circulation Review; Audit Bureau of Circulation

Libraries: material on loan

United Kingdom   Thousands

	1980-81	1983-84	1986-87	1989-90[1]
Adult fiction	14,992	16,162	15,801	17,349
Adult non-fiction	7,580	8,332	8,652	9,824
Children's books	5,703	6,265	6,472	8,034
Sound & video recordings	633	1,048	997	2,088

[1] Figures for 1989-90 are not comparable with earlier years

*Source:*Public Library Statistics,
Chartered Institute for Public Finance and Accountancy

Methods of obtaining current books

Great Britain   Percentages

	1981	1984	1986	1988	1990
Bought (including book clubs)	31	35	34	37	38
Library	38	33	33	33	32
Borrowed from friend or relative	17	17	19	17	15
Gift	9	9	7	7	8
Already in home	4	4	4	4	4
Don't know	1	2	3	2	3

Source: The Book Report, *Euromonitor*

Analyse the four charts and note what strikes you most.
Compare your reactions with someone else.

Write a short article (500 words) on British reading habits (comparing them if possible with what you know about reading habits in another country); you may find the following expressions and remarks useful and even challenging:

* The English do not read very much.

* Television encourages people to read.

* The circulation of national newspapers is falling.

* The Radio and TV Times have the highest sales figures.

* Political issues are extensively covered in the press.

* Men are more likely to read newspapers than women.

* A higher proportion of people in the 45 - 64 age group read a daily newspaper than in any other age group.

* The readership of Sunday newspapers has fallen despite the introduction of larger newspapers and more colour supplements.

* In 1990 the most widely read newspaper in Great Britain was *The Sun* which was read by one quarter of all men and 1/5 of all women.

* In 1990 the most popular Sunday newspaper was *The News of the World* which had an average issue readership of 13.2 million.

* General monthly magazines are still very popular.

* People do not necessarily read the books they buy.

* The most popular method of obtaining a book is to buy it, either from a shop or through a book club rather than to borrow it or receive it as a gift.

* Many people use the public libraries.

* Women are more likely to visit a public library than men.

* In 1989-90 over 8 million children's books were borrowed from public libraries: 40% more than in 1980-81.

1) Nationalism

Which ten words and expressions would be most useful in writing an essay on this topic?

> to preserve one's national identity
> threat to democracy
> defence of freedom
> struggle for independence
> to demand autonomy
> protection of minorities
> devolution of power
> decentralisation
> national consciousness
> national pride
> territorial dispute
> self-governing state
> fear of totalitarianism
> denial of political rights
> sovereignty
> bureaucratic dictatorship
> ethnic communities
> nation-states
> greater integration
> federalism
> international trade and finance
> global capitalism
> monetary union
> political union
> technocrats
> modern technology
> multinationals
> European Union
> standardisation
> Big Brother

2) Tragedy

Which twenty words would be most useful were you to write an essay on this subject?

act	error	misunderstanding
action	failure	mystery
anguish	fate	obstacle
battle	fear	paradox
condemnation	fight	passion
confession	God	power
conflict	greatness	promise
confusion	grief	reason
crime	guilt	separation
curse	helplessness	sorrow
death	honour	spectacle
despair	hope	struggle
destiny	horror	triumph
disaster	injustice	violence
dispute	judgement	virtue
drama	justice	vocation
enemy	love	will

3) Town and Country

The sentences below would be useful in an essay or discussion on the relative advantages and disadvantages of living in a town or in the country. Complete the gaps:

1) Nature is the great provider but it .... be harnesssed by human effort.

2) Whatever tourists might ...., nature is not hospitable.

3) We need only .... storms, tempests and earthquakes to be convinced of this.

4) It is amusing to .... that the word "city" is often used in conjunction with the adjective "inhuman".

5) Nothing is .... human than an urban conglomeration.

6) It is after all .... and .... who have created cities.

7) City dwellers .... to think that rural life is healthy and relaxing.

8) .... have been completely spoilt by the tents and weekend cottages of the city dweller.

9) The attitude of city dwellers towards the country is ....

10) The more built-up the countryside is, the more city dwellers .... it.

Suggested answers in Appendix 1.

4) Leisure activities

Were you to write an essay on this topic, which word(s) would you eliminate in each of the sentences below?

1) What are organised *leisure/rest* activities?

2) All *spontaneity/sadness* is destroyed when we let other people *plan/create* our free time for us.

3) Our professional life is frequently very *restrictive/amusing*; it leaves no room for the *imagination/ugliness*. Are we going to apply the same *restraints/coercion* to our leisure activities?

4) The *worst/best* type of wastage is not that of *money/sleep* but of time.

5) The aim of leisure activities should be to restore our *vitality/boredom*.

6) Fashionable leisure activities are frequently very *dull/flawed*.

7) We should devote a large proportion of our spare time to the *contemplation/admiration* of beauty.

8) Many people nowadays are *obsessed/bored* with physical fitness.

   Justify your choice to someone else.

* MAKE YOUR CHOICE

Eliminate one or two words in each sentence in order to produce a meaningful and correct statement:

1) We are presented here with a Marxist *analysis/example* of the situation.

2) This *practice/definition* is much *too concise/vague*.

3) The *strategy/discussion* to be adopted seems quite *straightforward/rosy*.

4) The *question/attitude* raised is particularly *complex/neat*.

5) We shall *lately/first of all* examine the possible consequences of such a *course of action/progress*.

6) We shall then ask ourselves *whether/because* this attitude can be justified.

7) *Why not/so,* in this case, begin with the end?

8) *In due course/by way of summary*, we shall conclude with a quotation from the Prime Minister.

9) This list is *inevitable/incomplete*.

10) How can we *talk/discuss* such a subject?

Justify your choice to someone else.

* PROSODY: A FEW EXAMPLES:

Complete the following sentences, using the words provided:

rhythm - alexandrine - rhymes - feet - line - stanzas - caesura -sonnet - poem - tercet - enjambements - ode - quatrains - hemistich - ballad

1) Youth ....with truth

2) An .... is a .... of twelve ....

3) Learn the first three .... of this ....

4) A .... is composed of two .... and of two ....

5) I'm out of breath because of the ....

6) Is the .... half of any line or only of an alexandrine?

7) Pay attention to the ....! Don't forget the ....
at the hemistich.

8) What are the differences between an .... and a ....?

Suggested answers in Appendix 1.

* THE OPPOSITE

How would you say the exact opposite to each of the following statements?

1) Reading is a waste of time.

2) Culture is a luxury.

3) Violence is inevitable.

4) Justice is an illusion.

5) People go to the theatre/cinema to laugh and to relax.

6) Contemporary art is a failure.

7) We live in an egalitarian world.

8) Poetry is reserved for an elite.

9) Artists should be servants of their age.

10) Men and women are equal in theory and in reality.

Discuss your answers with someone else.

* ON MEANING

Write ten correct and meaningful sentences by matching beginnings from Column 1 with endings from Column 2.

Column 1		Column 2
1. How is it possible to read a novel with	a)	is speaking the truth
2. It is difficult to know who	b)	consumer habits in the two countries
3. To conclude, I shall compare	c)	the underlying causes of the problem
4. I shall now focus on	d)	no characters?
5. But this is really	e)	another question
6. I have the impression that	f)	this course of action
7. The author has clearly not succeeded in	g)	both sides of the question
8. We must consider	h)	this discussion is leading nowhere
9. Her prolific output	i)	overcoming his prejudices
10. We have no choice but to take	j)	never ceases to astonish us

Suggested answers in Appendix 1.

* WORDS AND EXPRESSIONS

Complete the following sentences by using an appropriate word from the list below:

consider - agree - interpretation - point out - shall begin -attitude - is meant by - sentence - reasons - define - examples - weaknesses - focus on - support - issues - argument.

1) Without precise ...., I cannot follow the logic of this ....

2) We must first of all .... whether there is any justification for this ....

3) We still have to .... on what .... the word 'freedom'.

4) I .... by explaining the .... for adopting this position.

5) Next, I shall try to .... the .... in his argument.

6) I cannot agree with his .... of the situation.

7) Before proceeding with the discussion, it will be necessary to .... our terms.

8) I shall then go on to .... my argument with examples.

9) The .... can be interpreted in a number of different ways.

10) I would now like to .... the key .... raised in the initial statement.

Suggested answers in Appendix 1.

* WORDS AND EXPRESSIONS: SPEAKING AND WRITING

Re-read the article on Europe on page 170 and write ten full sentences (all dealing with Europe) using the words and expressions given:

defence - strategy - adopted - ebb - confined - national - unemployment - suffused - needs - integration - serves - rebuild - features - Euro-nationalist - dismantling - Maastricht - world - stagnation - questioning - attempt - undemocratic

1) Some people think that the high tide of European .... is beginning to ....

2) Much of the debate on European political union is .... with hypocrisy and ignorance.

3) There are those who claim that the ...... treaty is essentially ....

4) Most of the undemocratic .... of the treaty were
........................at the specific demand of the British.

5) The .... of European union is not .... to
Britain and Denmark.

6) Protracted .... and mass .... will
strengthen the .... right.

7) The European community needs a .... to ....
the European economy.

8) Any .... to recreate a .... of largely
separate .... economies is doomed.

9) Those who want an EMU which .... the goal of
growth, employment and .... of the environment
should resist the .... of political union.

10) Economic forces should serve society's .... rather
than the other way round.

Answers in Appendix 1.

* WHICH WORDS WOULD YOU FIND MOST USEFUL:

1 When discussing a play and/or a novel?

2 In assessing a political broadcast and/or government policies on education?

3 In discussing the marketing potential of a new product with colleagues within the same multinational corporation?

4 When expressing your views on Twentieth Century writers and/or philosophers?

5 When writing a short article on either the Middle East or the Eurotunnel?

6 As a social worker in discussion with somebody who has just committed a petty crime?

7 When trying to convince somebody that s/he ought to read more and/or know more about history and/or art?

8 In the summing up of a criminal case?

Compare your choice with someone else.

accent	composition	diversity
account	concession	doctrine
accusation	conclusion	doubt
age	confirmation	drama
alternative	conflict	dream
analysis	consciousness	duty
appliance	constraint	effort
argument	context	emergence
art criticism	convention	error
(minor) art	conversation	essay
article	criticism	evidence
attack	culture	evolution
attitude	current events	example
awareness	debate	excess
background	decade	existence
balance	decision	expression
battle	defect	extract
burlesque	defence	fact
calculation	definition	farce
century	degree	fashion in clothes
challenge	desire	feeling
change	deterioration	field
cliché	development	fight
clue	dialogue	followers
code	difficulty	form
comedy	discussion	function
commonplace	disparity	guide
complex	distribution	habit

hour	myth	proposal
hypothesis	nature	public
identity	norm	quantity
ideology	novel	quest
illogicality	novelty	question
impression	number	quotation
impropriety	obligation	reason
improvement	observation	reform
indication	opinion	relationship
interest	opposition	remark
introduction	organisation	research
investigation	page	result
irony	panorama	revision
judgment	paradox	route
knowledge	part	rule
lack	party	sarcasm
language	passage	schedule
law	period	scruples
lesson	perspective	seat
letter	philosophy	selection
level	place	sentence
link	plan	sequel
lot	plan of action	series
management	poem	share
meaning	point	situation
means	point of view	sketch
measure	politics	society
meeting	possibility	state
merit	power	statement
metaphor	prevision	story
method	problem	strategy
mind	process	study
mistake	programme	style
moment	progress	summary
motion	prohibition	superficial view
movement	propaganda	superiority
multiplicity	proportion	surprise

symbol	text	upheaval
system	thought	vocabulary
system of government	time	war
taboo	together	way
taste	tragedy	way of life
technique	transformation	wisdom
tendency	transition	work
tension	truth	world
term	turn of phrase	writer
testimony	unit	

* ON LITERATURE.

Here is a list of words frequently used in essays on contemporary literature.

absurd	freedom	prejudice
allegory	humanism	presupposition
anachronism	ideology	quest
appeal	immanence	realism
argument	incitement	reality
belief	irony	rhetoric
brilliance	language	romanticism
burlesque	legend	scepticism
challenge	metaphor	story
code	metonymy	strategy
collectivity	morality	surrealism
comedy	myth	symbol
conflict	narrative	symbolism
conviction	narrator	technique
credibility	naturalism	tragedy
demonstration	optimism	trait
decision	parody	transcendence
digression	pessimism	vigour
distinction	plot	vision
elegance	philosophy	writing
expression	point of view	
focus	power	

1. Find a definition for words you're not sure about; compare your definition(s) with someone else.

2. Use as many words as possible to write a short text (100 to 150 words) on one of the following topics:

    2.1   *Can the novel do without characters?*
    2.2   *Contemporary literature is profoundly boring.*
    2.3   *Literature has nothing to do with politics.*
    2.4   *What makes a fictional character interesting?*
    2.5   *How can literary texts challenge the social order?*
    2.6   *What is existentialism?*

Discuss your text with someone else.

* YES/NO/WHY?

Read these utterances carefully.
Note what strikes you about them in the way they are formulated.
Discuss your assessment/choice with someone else.
Re-read them and try to see whether you could use them in an essay. If not, why not?

1) We must be careful not to kid ourselves.

2) The most important aspect is the humorous dimension of the text.

3) The argument cannot be faulted - it's just the examples.

4) Is this text comprehensible? You must be joking!

5) I don't fancy the way the writer plays around with language.

6) Metonymy and metaphor are the very lifeblood of poetry.

7) What exactly does the expression, "the materiality of language", mean?

8) Empson discovered the ambiguities of narratology.

9) Well, I think I can stop here even though I haven't said everything.

10) Political and religious issues are not to be discussed. That's all there is to it. To me it's as clear as daylight!

* FROM ORAL TO WRITTEN (1)

The role of trade unions today

This is an extract from a transcription of a debate between a sociogist and a politician on trade unions today; read it carefully first and then re-write it as if you wanted to incorporate it in an essay on the same topic. Leave out what seems to you irrelevant, i.e. the marks of the spoken code such as repetitions, exclamations etc.

- *I think it's true to say that unions nowadays have lost their credibility.*

- *Instead of talking about credibility, let's be blunt; they have lost their members.*

- *Would you go as far as to say, though, that unions are a thing of the past?*

- *No, but I would say that they are definitely on the decline. People have better things to do with their time than to be union activists. With all the different forms of entertainment at their disposal they would be mad to opt for political struggle.*

- *But you seem to think that everything is for the best in the best of all possible worlds. You completely ignore the problem of unemployment.*

- *No, this is a very serious matter. Have the unions any solution to the problem of unemployment? It is they who are avoiding the issue.*

- *I don't think you are being absolutely fair on this point.*

- *Give me some examples, then. Tell me which trade unions have come up with any concrete proposals to solve the question.*

- *First of all, unions should be given the opportunity to voice their opinions on the subject. This might lead to a definite programme of action.*

- *Excuse me but we are living in a democracy where unions have complete freedom of speech, indeed, they are allocated a considerable amount of media space. You know as well as I that some union leaders have become television stars.*

- *That's not really the issue.*

- *That's precisely the issue! If union leaders were less preoccupied with their media performance, they would give more thought to the real problems of our society.*

- *Do you think then, that this is one of the reasons why unions have lost their appeal?*

- *What exactly do you mean?*

- *Do you think that union leaders are responsible for this decline in popularity?*

- *Of course they are. They are a bunch of clowns and pompous idiots.*

- *I think you're going a bit far!*

- *We have to recognise the facts. The primary ambition of union leaders is to become television stars. People no longer take them seriously.*

- *As television stars are enjoying enormous prestige at the moment your argument is none too convincing. Leaving that aside, do you think that there are fundamental changes in society that could account for this decline in the influence of trade unions?*

- *Of course there are. It's obvious.*

- *Can you give me some examples?*

- *Of course. As a sociologist, you are probably more familiar with the problem than I am. The fact is that there is no longer any proletariat.*

- *But there's still a working class, isn't there?*

- *I'm not so sure about that. The working classes have become bourgeois. They have a house of their own, they go on holiday by the sea and in the mountains. Their children even go to university.*

- *Really? Well I never!*

- *It's true. The working class no longer identifies with trade union causes - it's all a lot of old hat. Are you a member of a trade union, by the way?*

After this last question the debate got really heated ... You don't have to be in such a passionate frame of mind to discuss this question, so select from this exchange what seems to you interesting or relevant in order to write down ideas, in a coherent way, on *'the role of trade unions.'*

Compare your text with someone else.

* FROM ORAL TO WRITTEN (2)

What makes you laugh?

Ask people around you the same question.
Write down your ideas.

212

Now read the text below, which is a transcription of a discussion on the same topic recorded at the end of a dinner party (the speakers were not aware at the time that they were being recorded ... and were quite surprised when they heard what they had said!).

- *What do you expect? People never laugh nowadays.*

- *What do you mean 'never laugh'? There's no need to exaggerate.*

- *Just look at young people in the street, they're all dressed in black with long faces!*

- *You have to admit, there's nothing funny about the age in which we live.*

- *There's always something: war, poverty.*

- *Now it's Aids, unemployment.*

- *What makes you laugh anyway?*

- *A good joke.*

- *Can you give me some examples?*

- *No, that's the problem, people daren't tell jokes nowadays.*

- *Why not?*

- *Because they're immediately accused of being racist, chauvinist or anti-semitic. You know, the other day, I began to tell an Irish joke; you know, the one about the Irish labourer.*

- *No, which one?*

- *An Irish labourer leaps off the top of a scaffolding and lands in a heap. One of his friends says to the old man who has been talking to the labourer: 'Why do you suppose he jumped off the* *scaffolding like that?' The old man replies 'Perhaps it was because I told him I used to fly in Wellingtons* in the war'!*

- *That's a good one!*

- *Luckily we have the Irish.*

- *The Irish don't always like being made fun of by the English.*

- *That's right. It always happens that whenever I begin to tell the joke, someone in the audience pops up and says in a dignified tone: "I am Irish and proud of the fact".*

- *Really?*

- *Yes, mind you, I do understand their feelings. There's no particular reason for picking on the Irish. It's just a myth, a caricature.*

- *That's true, there always has to be a scapegoat. It happens in all cultures.*

- *The Scots are said to be stingy, the Bretons stubborn, the Normans indecisive.*

- *It doesn't make me laugh anyway!*

- *What makes you laugh then?*

- *Well, I don't really know - funny, unforeseen situations, puns, witticisms.*

- *Spoonerisms?*

- *Yes, but they are often rather smutty.*

- *That's only natural, laughter always has something to do with sex.*

* name of bomber planes/rubber boots

- *Everything does!*

- *No, I'm being serious, people have produced studies on the subject.*

- *Really?*

- *I assure you it's true.*

We had to stop the transcription here as the discussion explored a subject-matter for laughter which was, we felt, beyond the scope of this book! But there are expressions here that you may find useful.

Make your choice and write an answer to the question: 'what makes you laugh?' Compare yours with someone else.

* TURNS OF PHRASE

The time has come to give you a list of useful turns of phrase to help you organise a discussion or write an essay.

Go through the list below and note those with which you are already familiar (most, if not all, have been used in previous chapters).

Compare your list with someone else.

Then, working with a partner, select turns of phrase which would enable you to:

A. *Introduce a subject.*

B. *Classify your ideas.*

C. *Enumerate different aspects of a problem.*

D. *Express an opinion (agreeing or disagreeing, violently or mildly).*

E. *Present an idea and/or an example.*

F. *Link and compare two ideas (show their similarities or differences, or assess their respective values).*

G. *Make a point convincingly.*

H. *Question a viewpoint.*

I. *Argue in a subtle, undogmatic and concessionary manner.*

J. *Refute and/or shift the argument (by raising other questions).*

K. *Conclude (bring the discussion to an end).*

- **The question raised here is** (whether we should impose sanctions)

- **The central issue is** (whether we shall leave the EMU)

- **We are confronted here with** (a categorical statement)

- **First of all,** (I shall try to define the key words)

- **I shall begin** (by attempting to prove that equality is a myth)

- **I shall argue that** (political union is an absolute necessity)

- **Our discussion will focus on** (the nuclear safety problem)

- **I shall conclude by saying** (that it is only by adopting such a course of action that the planet can be saved)

- **It may be concluded that** (there is no simple answer to this problem)

- **In conclusion, we may say that** (more public expenditure is required)

- **To draw** (this debate, this discussion) **to a conclusion**

- **By way of conclusion,** (I shall quote this sentence of Bernard Shaw ...)

- **To arrive at** (a clearer understanding of the question)

- **In short,** (I believe that this point of view is out-dated)

- **I suggest, therefore,** (that we adopt a different course of action)

- **It is impossible** (to do full justice to the question)

- **We should be careful not** (to make generalisations)

- **To what extent** (is this a question of religion?)

- **If it is true that** (trade unions have lost their popularity) **we shall nevertheless not forget** (the role of government in this decline)

- **It would be more relevant to look at the question of** (individual privacy) **from the point of view of ...**

- **To be** (less dogmatic)

- **I find the argument** (weak, biased) **and** (indefensible)

- **This position is** (untenable)

- **As in** (a particular text/author/century) **the** (moral, political, religious) **question is being completely** (ignored, disregarded)

- **To finish, I shall compare** (Mr Y's attitude/technique/viewpoint) **with that of** (Mrs Y)

- **Not only** (is this idea false) **but it is also** (dangerous)

- **The same applies to** (the death penalty)

- **The same is true of** (developing countries)

- **The same idea can be found in** (a particular author/text/century)

- **Note that** (this idea is not new)

- **Far from** (diminishing the influence of television, a scandal like this strengthens it)

- **This means that** (the concept of justice is not universal)

- **What** (people want) **is** (to earn more money)

- **I would like to make it clear that** (I am limiting my definition of art to literature)

- **It could be that** (I am wrong)

- **If we consider** (the facts) **we must conclude that** (this statement has no foundation in reality)

- **How is it possible** (to make such a stupid remark)!

- **Similarly,** (the whole world is concerned about the health of the dollar)

- **By way of example, I shall take the case of** (Shakespearian tragedy)

- **It is possible that** (my attitude may seem a little harsh) **but** (I can justify myself)

- **It would appear that** (my hypothesis is now confirmed)

- **It is correct to say that** (the number of single parent families in England has increased)

- **It would be surprising to** (discover) **that** (the opposite is equally true)

- **To take an example**, (I shall quote Malcolm Lowry's *Under the Volcano*)

- **Contrary to what is generally believed**, (the creation of the Booker Prize has not helped to produce better novels)

- **Firstly**, (I shall analyse the relations between the political parties and trade unions)
Secondly,
Thirdly,

- **It is true that** (all the problems have not yet been resolved)

- **It goes without saying** (that there is no simple solution to the problem)

- **There is no doubt that** (the Channel Tunnel has had many opponents)

- **As for** (the American government, its role should be closely examined)

- **Admittedly**, (most people prefer the novel to poetry)

- **We must accept the fact that** (we all have our weaknesses)

- **My intention is not** (to present a detailed analysis of the constitution of the country)

- **My point is this**, (how can we possibly deny these people their basic human rights?)

- **Clearly,** (this is not a matter to be taken lightly)

- **I shall confine myself** (to asking which of the two countries is the more democratic)

- **My argument has shown that** (the position is untenable)

- **When all is said and done,** (the question has been badly put)

- **Undoubtedly,** (the development of tourism is a good thing) **but** (at the same time, we must recognise its dangers)

- **As far as I am concerned,** (the media exert a dangerous influence)

- **The more** (we study the question), **the more** (aware we become of the difficulties)

- **However,** (the question is not so simple)

- **Nonetheless,** (I am willing to accept the validity of his argument)

- **Nevertheless,** (I would like to express my reservations)

- **Finally,** (I cannot agree with the underlying suppositions)

- (These examples) **prove, therefore, that** (the question is more complex than it first appeared)

Remember that an essay is a demonstration and what matters is not to learn all these expressions but to feel that you have a battery of verbal tools at your disposal which will enable you to express what you want to say or write on a particular subject.

Should you feel more secure armed with a more complete list than this one, we would advise you to re-read the previous chapters and make your own selection of useful (and recurrent) turns of phrase.

Hopefully, the preceeding exercises have stressed the importance of an adequate manipulation of linguistic tools when writing in English. The important points you should keep in mind are to:

1. master the vocabulary, however simple, you are most likely to use again and again, e.g. example, problem, exercise etc.

2. make sure that you have at your disposal words and expressions which do not have an obvious equivalent in your own language.

3. understand that the production of meaning doesn't rest entirely on lexical items (vocabulary), for syntax also comes into play. You should be able at this stage to use complex sentence structures to express strong or conciliatory views, contradictions, implications, causes and consequences, to illustrate and convince, to draw up parallels between different situations, to compare and evaluate attitudes etc.

This is not a grammar book but we hope that in giving you so many utterances in English, you will have picked up turns of phrases which will enable you to communicate efficiently.

If some examples seem to you too convoluted or remote and far from your usual way of saying things, don't forget that social communication (as practised in the media, in schools, by politicians etc.) does not produce 'simple messages'; it presupposes a certain knowledge or set of common values on the part of the receiver. Therefore, to fully understand what is going on and to be able to challenge the various discourses which are imposed upon us, we have to explore and practise the resources (tricks and traps) of language.

Hopefully, this book will enable you not only to write an essay in English, but also teach you *How to do things with words!*

Chapter 10

How to begin?

It may seem odd to give guidelines on how to write an introduction, be it to an essay or to a debate, almost at the end of such a book. This is not due to misjudgment on our part, but is in fact logical. It is often argued that some people start writing before knowing what they are going to say and that it is the very process of writing which makes them think and hopefully write coherently. This may happen, but it seems to us just as fallacious to pretend that this is the 'normal' way of writing an essay, as it is to suggest that essay writing is an art which you possess or not. A frequent belief is that if you do, things come naturally; if you don't, you have to work hard to acquire a skill you can only hope to develop to a limited extent(!).

Let's be more realistic and admit that we all have to make an effort to organise our thoughts and ideas and to work on how best to make a point (let alone convince somebody ...).

So when you're thinking about an introduction you have to know:

- what ideas you already have on a given subject

- how these ideas differ from other people's

- how they compare with the views expressed on the same subject by authors or journalists you are familiar with.

In the previous chapters we invited you to explore your own ideas and to discuss them; so we assume that you are now ready to come to terms with what is in our experience one of the main hurdles of essay writing: the introduction. The aim of this chapter is thus to help you to write an introduction.

The first step in writing an essay is to read the title carefully so as to avoid embarking on the wrong path; it will either ask a specific question or present a comment on some particular problem or issue. You have to identify what is at stake and what you are being asked to do.

To misinterpret the subject of an essay title is a frequent error which is usually the result of careless reading.

All too often people think that by starting to write as soon as possible they will be able to write more and thus improve their chances of doing well. More often than not, this is a miscalculation. You need some time to think about the particular light thrown onto the subject. If you pay attention to the way the title is phrased, you will not always succeed in interpreting correctly the meaning of the question but you will considerably reduce your chances of going off track. Once you have identified the problem(s) raised in the essay title, you're in a position to demonstrate your understanding of the issue or issues involved. An essay is primarily a demonstration and you will have succeeded if you feel satisfied at the end of your essay that you have demonstrated your own viewpoint on the subject by presenting your argument in a coherent and logical way.

Naturally, your essay will begin with an introduction; but you should not write that introduction before you have:

1) thought about the subject

2) decided what your plan is going to be.

As you have already seen in chapter 6, drawing up a plan requires selecting from the several ideas you may have on a particular subject.

You should first write down all the ideas which come to your mind concerning the subject and you should do so without bothering about the order in which you write them down.

Once you have a few ideas on paper, you should then begin to look for what some of them have in common, e.g. some ideas may put forward a particular point of view either for or against. This phase is often overlooked by students who tend to assume that their ideas are disjointed and that it is pointless to look for any relationship between them. Yet this is very unlikely.

Such a relationship may not be apparent at first, but the ideas and points of view have been chosen and expressed by you, and even though you may feel that they are not original, they have somehow become part of your own frame of mind. What you have to do is establish the link that must exist between those apparently unrelated ideas. Such an exercise is not necessarily easy, particularly if you are used to writing at random without giving too much thought to the logical order of your argument. However, by practising with the help of a few guidelines, you should soon be able to improve your skills until it becomes a pleasurable routine. You will eventually discover that your natural reaction to an essay title is to:

1) look for keywords and their meaning.

2) presume that the articulation of those keywords holds the key to a correct understanding of the essay title.

3) identify the question asked on the issue(s) raised, i.e.: 'what is at stake here'?

4) write at random all your thoughts on the subject.

5) establish the relationships (by implication or contradiction) that you can detect between these apparently disjointed ideas.

6) use them to draw up your own plan.

When you have achieved this, you will be well prepared for writing an essay and you will no longer need our book.

Let's take an example to illustrate what we mean. Consider the following title:

'doctrines have the advantage that they allow one not to have ideas..'
Edouard Herriot

The keywords here are:

doctrines   advantage   allow one not   ideas

1) The first keyword is apparently less easy to define than the other three. According to the dictionary:

- an 'idea' is a 'belief' or 'viewpoint' or 'opinion'

- 'advantage' means 'benefit' or 'profit'

- 'allow one not to' is 'to permit one not to'

- a 'doctrine' is a 1) 'creed' or body of teachings of a religious, political or philosophical group; dogma 2) a principle or body of principles that is taught or advocated.

2) Articulation between keywords: The two concepts of 'doctrines' and 'ideas' are presented here as being opposed to each other and the articulation of that opposition is built around the other two keywords in the title: doctrines have the advantage that they allow one not to have ideas. Does it mean that ideas are a hindrance or, more so, that there is no place for ideas (i.e. for individual opinions) in doctrines?

To adopt a particular doctrine means to adopt it uncritically. By juxtaposing a positive notion ('advantage') and a negative one ('allows one not'), the essay title introduces in a fairly ironical way a profound criticism of the impact of doctrines on an essential component of individual freedom, the 'freedom of thought'.

3) What is at stake here is therefore a denunciation of 'doctrinal' systems of thought, which limit our individual right to think for ourselves by telling us what we must hold as true and unquestionable. It is also a criticism of those people who endorse doctrines and give up their right to have opinions of their own, almost a relief for some as the essay title ironically suggests. What you are asked to do here is to develop an argument for or against this statement.

4) Let us now assume that you have written at random 20 ideas or questions on this topic:

* DOCTRINES HAVE THE ADVANTAGE THAT THEY ALLOW ONE NOT TO HAVE IDEAS

1) At first sight, this statement seems to present a paradox.

2) What is a doctrine?

3) What do doctrines contain if not ideas?

4) The adjective 'doctrinaire' derived from doctrine, describes someone who is intolerant and lacking in critical awareness.

5) How can you tell if someone has an idea?

6) Can doctrine be taken to mean ideology?

7) The persuasive power of doctrines lies in their claim to represent an absolute and unique truth.

8) People support a doctrine in which they believe; the stronger the belief, the less likely they are to think for themselves.

9) How does a doctrine differ from a religion?

10) Does this statement express contempt for all forms of commitment?

11) Can we describe the 'advantage' that ideas have over doctrines?

12) Ideas are only important insofar as they lead to action.

13) This statement is condemnatory.

14) Without doctrines, the masses can be easily manipulated.

15) It is undoubtedly easier to condemn someone with whom you do not agree if you know you are expressing the orthodox views of a particular doctrine.

16) Are all forms of political organisation 'doctrinaire'?

17) Can we draw up a list of all the doctrines prevalent at a particular moment of history?

18) Is the role of every government to 'indoctrinate' its citizens?

19) Is intolerance a characteristic of all doctrines?

20) Why do we need doctrines?

5) Read these viewpoints/questions carefully and try to establish clusters of points which have something in common. Would you agree that:

a) some of the above points are reactions to what seems at first to be a rather provocative statement (1-10-13)

b) certain other points rightly concentrate on the meaning of 'doctrine' (2-3-4-6-9-17), some of the questions here being more specific than others (6-9).

c) other questions are even more specific in the sense that they already imply a certain definition of 'doctrine' and build upon the implications of such a definition (7-16-18-19-20). Note that these implications all have a negative connotation.

d) other points concern the keyword 'ideas' and further explore some issues related to the opposition between doctrines and ideas alleged in the title in a way that either

   i) reinforces the negative connotation noted under c) ie: 8-15.
or

   ii) introduces doctrines in a less negative way, ie: 3-14.
or

   iii) presents a hitherto entirely positive concept of ideas in a more qualified manner, i.e.: 5-11-12.

This is just one way of linking together the various points made at random earlier. Many more ways could be devised and you may have already noticed other clusters, grouped around different relationships and connections.

6) *The plan*: Let us now see how these connections could lead to a plan and therefore eventually help you to write an introduction. What emerges from the above is:

a) a series of questions concerning the keywords of the subject title as well as an initial reaction of surprise vis-à-vis the title itself (see 5(a) and 5(b)). It is with this material that you will later write your introduction.

b) an opposition between 'doctrine' and 'ideas', which gives an almost self-evident negative connotation to the first (see 5(c) and 5 (d) (i)), and by opposition, a positive one to the second. This could be the first argument of your essay.

c) a questioning of the absolute value of the previous argument. This could be the second main argument of your essay. It would consist in qualifying your first argument by exploring the view that, for example, not all 'doctrines' necessarily demand blind following and some might even positively encourage discussion and individual opinions. A 'doctrine' is not to be systematically confused with religion. There is always an element of absolute irrationality in the latter, i.e. a belief in something or somebody that is by definition supernatural and thus cannot be proved. Some 'doctrines' are equally based on notions that cannot be demonstrated (such as the supremacy of one race over all others), but this does not apply to all 'doctrines' (see 5(d)ii)). Similarly, 'ideas' should not be regarded as something godlike, e.g. 'ideas' that do not lead to action might be stale. (see 5(d)(iii)).

This is just one idea of a plan on this subject. There are in fact a variety of plans which can be drawn on any subject. What differentiates a good plan from a bad one is the logic of the connections established between its different parts and ideas. This does not mean to say that there is no originality and creativity going into the organisation of your data; a display of such qualities makes the difference between a good and a very good essay. But contrary to what many people say, these qualities are not innate, they have to be developed through practice and it would be irresponsible to pretend otherwise.

To illustrate the point that a variety of plans can be drawn, let us take another essay title as an example:

* OUR SOCIETIES ARE FOUNDED ON THE BELIEF THAT ALL CITIZENS ARE EQUAL BEFORE THE LAW

1) Keywords: founded
                 belief
                 are equal before the law

2) What do they mean?

3) What is at stake here?

The title does not so much state that all citizens are equal before the law, but that our societies are founded on the belief that all citizens are equal before the law.

This introduces a certain ambiguity on the subject. What counts as a foundation to our societies is the belief that such equality exists. Whether it does or not is thus open to question. You might believe that men/women are equal before the law or on the contrary, that they are not. Whichever way you approach this question, your ideas and statements will show that you share that belief, that you don't share it at all, or perhaps that you think the issue lies elsewhere, for example that this is just one instance of inequality and that, while recognising that it matters, you think it cannot be understood separately from other forms of inequality.

In this as in any other essay, you can with equal validity defend any one of these positions. It is not the position you adopt that matters but the way in which you present the argument to defend that position. There is no such thing as right or wrong here; only good or bad arguments.

In other words you could argue equally well here for or against the belief. By definition, to argue that this is not a question of belief but of fact - i.e. that all men/women are equal - is in itself an indication that you agree with the essay title but that you do so in a doctrinaire manner, which does not usually help to produce the best arguments(!).

Now carefully read some random ideas on this topic:

1) Many people find the system of justice mystifying.

2) Most people think that justice is the same for all, but once they become involved with the law, they change their minds.

3) It is ridiculous to say that resorting to justice is too expensive for many people. Those who cannot afford to do so can receive free legal aid.

4) Justice is created in the image of man, that is, it is imperfect.

5) Isn't justice always portrayed by a blindfolded woman, holding a sword in one hand and a pair of scales in the other?

6) Justice is always class-bound.

7) Magistrates, like doctors, often hide behind jargon which is incomprehensible to ordinary mortals.

8) Not all societies have the same conception of justice.

9) There are some crimes which governments choose to leave unpunished.

10) The incomprehensibility of legal language contributes to the process of mystification.

11) The law is powerless in the face of international terrorism.

12) It is a myth perpetrated by democracies that all citizens are equal before the law.

'Our societies are founded on the belief that all citizens are equal before the law'...

Let's see how you could proceed to write your essay:

1) if you share this belief

2) if you don't

3) if you think the issue is elsewhere

1) *if you share this belief:*
Clearly, among the ideas presented here, those which you would endorse would probably be (1-3-5). These are all arguments that you could advance and develop to make the point of what could thus be the first part of your essay. If you have read the title carefully, however, you will have noticed that it refers to a belief.

If something is obvious or can be demonstrated, there is no need to believe in it; you can only accept that it exists. So, belief introduces a certain questioning of this alleged equality. The fact that you share this belief does not and should not prevent your seeing that there is an issue raised here and that others may see it differently from the way you do. How can this be? What can misguide people into thinking that all men/women are not equal before the law? To some extent, you have to anticipate their arguments and try to refute them. This could be the second part of your essay.

2. *if you don't share this belief:*
The ideas with which you could identify, might be 2-6-7-9-10-12.

3. *if you think the issue is elsewhere:*
The relevant points here are 4-8-11-12.

Some guidelines have been given above for a plan for the first position. Now try and draw up plans for the second and third positions along the same lines.

When you have decided on the plan you wish to adopt, you are then ready to write the introduction to your essay.

The purpose of an introduction is to introduce the essay, and this is less tautological than it may seem. What it means is that, after reading your introduction, your reader should:

1) know what you are talking about (what is the subject matter of your discussion).

2) be able to assess your understanding of the subject title.

3) see how you define the keywords that you have identified.

4) understand clearly how you are going to proceed to discuss them.

This means that it is in your introduction and nowhere else that you will:

1) say what you understand the subject to be about.

2) define the keywords.

3) indicate what are the key issues which the subject raises.

4) announce what ideas you are going to develop, in which order and why.

You could test the guidelines in this chapter by applying them to the previous essay title:

'Our societies are founded on the belief that all citizens are equal before the law'.

- Think about the title (underline the keywords, identify the key concepts and issues)

- Write down your ideas and discuss them with someone else.

- Mix them with the following:

231

1) The aim of the law is to sanction a particular social order and that of justice is to protect it.

2) Our system of justice prides itself on its independance and neutrality.

3) In a democratic society, can you imagine anyone escaping the authority of the law?

4) According to John Stuart Mill, anyone in a society must be permitted to express his or her opinion, however pernicious that opinion is believed to be.

5) By persuading people that it is unreasonable not to obey the law, you convince them that the law is the most perfect expression of reason.

6) The replacement of divine right by the rule of law marked an important stage in the evolution of society.

7) The law is the best mechanism there is for social domination.

8) The law is the best guarantee of individual freedom.

9) The development of laws and the administration of justice have become so ritualised that only a minority of citizens are in a position to understand them.

10) Justice is expensive.

11) In actual fact, this statement is a definition of justice.

12) Equality is a myth.

13) 'Liberty, equality, fraternity' is the motto for a Utopian state.

14) Who has not, at some time, experienced injustice?

15) We would all like to live in a just world but it is only human to

make mistakes. It is impossible to imagine, let alone put in practice, a perfect system of justice.

16) It would be wrong to believe that the fall of the aristocracy put an end to privilege.

17) Miscarriages of justice are inevitable.

18) There will always be liars and cheats.

19) Those whose task it is to interpret the law are not infallible.

20) The law can never anticipate all the possible aberrations of human behaviour.

Select the material which will enable you to draw a plan and to write an introduction (you will be well advised to follow the guidelines given in the previous pages).

Then compare your text with someone else.

Bear in mind that this is a topic which could be treated in a technical way by law or social science students who would then be asked to display a specialised knowledge of the issues involved. In a general essay, such specialist knowledge is not expected and students are instead required to use their own judgement and experience.

Here is one example of an introduction to such an essay written by a student whose background was mainly literary:

'Our societies are founded on the belief that all citizens are equal before the law'.

Although our planet has become smaller with the advent of modern methods of transport, this does not mean that the differences between cultures have been eradicated. Indeed, I am suspicious of any statement that seems to ignore the diversity of human behaviour and to reflect the attitudes of the European colonialist. In actual fact, there is a great variety of human societies with widely differing value systems. I shall begin by considering the term 'belief' with its religious connotations. I shall then examine the notion of equality, and I shall focus on the principles underlying the secular state. I shall go on to argue that, however admirable the quest for 'Utopia' may be, unfortunately experience shows that all citizens do not possess equal rights.

Here is an example, written by a student in management studies:

It is undoubtedly true that without wealth, a society cannot flourish and this inevitably produces a certain degree of social inequality. However, we cannot afford to ignore the claims of morality and, in particular, the issue of human rights. I shall begin by analysing the present-day social and economic situation in the light of these two conflicting claims. I shall then proceed to suggest ways of curbing the excesses of wealth and of closing the gap between rich and poor or between the powerful and the weak.

Here is yet another example, written this time by a social sciences student:

Equality before the law is one of the fundamental principles of every democratic society. It emerged at a time when the rule of divine right was being replaced by a more rational, individualistic social order. From the end of the eighteenth century onwards, the existence of a neutral and impartial law was supposed to give rise to an egalitarian society where the administration of justice would be the best guarantee against the eventual excesses of power.

As the ultimate sanction of power and of social structure, the law represented for everyone the most perfect expression of democracy. This explains why the popular belief that we are all equal before the law is so strongly rooted in our societies.

But, like all beliefs, is this belief justified? Has privilege really disappeared? Isn't equality before the law a myth? By replacing obedience to God by obedience to the law, haven't we simply substituted one illusion of equality for another? This is what my study will attempt to prove: I shall begin by stressing the conservative nature of law and of justice and then I shall go on to examine the mechanisms and rituals that enable the myth of equality before the law to be perpetrated.

Finally apply the method you have just been practising to another example:

'the right to strike is a fundamental freedom which every society should recognise'.

- Think about it first.

- Write down your ideas.

- Compare and/or mix them with the following:

1) The right to strike is a test of the democratic nature of a society: when it is not recognised, other human rights are also absent.

2) Because they possess a monopoly on the right to strike, unions are more powerful than the political bodies who have been elected to govern a country.

3) Recent history has shown that it is in the interest of society to place strict controls on the right to strike.

4) All democratic societies should be capable of establishing a social pact between the State, the employers and the unions.

5) The right to strike is often used for political ends.

6) The unions are becoming less and less representative of the interests of the majority of workers.

7) How can we claim the right to strike in a society where we no longer have the right to work?

8) Is it acceptable nowadays for strikes to paralyse a country?

9) Trade union groups are the first to reject the only practice that is truly democratic: taking a secret ballot of their members on all the important issues.

10) There are close links between the unions and the political parties.
11) In our age the risk of unemployment has split the ranks of the workers.

12) 'Everyman for himself and God for us all' seems to be everyone's motto nowadays and only a small proportion of workers are protected by the unions.

13) Can employers prevent their employees from going on strike?

14) Do priests and doctors go on strike?

- Organise your data.

- Write an introduction.

- Compare your text with someone else.

Remember, the introduction is probably the most difficult part of the essay, so get as much practice as you can and select to start with three essay titles (from previous chapters or from chapter 12), of graded difficulty (one easy, one less easy, one difficult). **Work** on them. We are confident that, if you take some time over this, you will be in a much better position to write an introduction and an essay.

Remember that an essay is a DEMONSTRATION and that the introduction plays a vital part as it indicates the process of your reasoning, working towards establishing a coherent argument.

Chapter 11

To conclude

In an essay the conclusion should be shorter than the introduction and - this may surprise you - you would be well advised to spend less time on it than on your introduction. Very often students repeat some sentences of their essay in the conclusion; this should be avoided, as should the repetition of the essay title in full in the introduction.

A conclusion may be seen as an artificial ending to a debate which could go on; this is not entirely false as most essays have to be ended because time and space are limited, not because all possible and plausible paths have been explored in the discussion. One easy 'way out' in finishing an essay is to write a sentence like: 'I would like to conclude by again stressing that the point of view expressed in the essay title is extremely limited as it fails to take into account an important aspect of the question. This aspect was briefly discussed in the latter half of the essay. The relationship between ... and ... could be further developed but this would constitute another debate'.

This would indicate that you have written a coherent argument but without taking into consideration every aspect of the issues raised by the subject; and you suggest in your conclusion yet another avenue which could be explored if time allowed.

In Chapter 9 you will find useful turns of phrase for composing your conclusion.

Let's take an example:

* **THE RELATIONSHIP BETWEEN THE RICHER COUNTRIES OF THE NORTH AND THE POORER ONES OF THE SOUTH IS DETERMINED BY THE NORTH. AT THE SAME TIME, THE NORTH REMAINS ESSENTIALLY INDIFFERENT TO THE WELFARE OF POOR COUNTRIES.**

The keywords are: *relationship, countries of the North, countries of the South, determined, indifferent.*

The question raised here is a relatively straightforward one. After presenting the main issues, you will then be expected to argue for or against the statement, either totally or in a qualified manner.

Here are a few examples of random thoughts on the subject:

1) The vast majority of poor countries only export raw materials and the price of these materials on the international market, with a few exceptions, is always determined by the countries who are doing the buying.

2) Poor countries are often in debt and their creditors are frequently powerful Western companies.

3) It is wrong to say that the terms of exchange are never in the interest of the countries exporting the raw materials. Prices fluctuate on the international market, sometimes in favour of the importing countries, sometimes in favour of the exporting countries.

4) Many poor countries are providing a cheap labour force for the multinational companies of the rich countries.

5) Without the technical advances introduced by the multinationals, most of the poor countries would be even poorer.

6) Multinational companies exploit the Third World and make enormous profits.

7) Poor countries make a minimal contribution to the international exchange; international commerce is mainly between rich countries.

8) Industrial countries have - and always have had - the loudest voice in the control of international economic relations as is evidenced in the GATT agreements.

9) Why should the rich countries increase their aid to the poorer ones when they have so much difficulty in providing for their own needs?

10) Leaving aside all moral considerations, the lack of interest in the Third World shown by the rich countries is extremely short-sighted: we should consider the crisis of over-production which now permanently threatens industrial nations.

Since the main objective of this chapter is to help you to write a conclusion to an essay, we will leave it to you to test the previous guidelines on the links that you could establish between the various statements as well as the plan that could be derived from the exercise, and we will thus concentrate on the conclusion.

Let's assume that your essay has tended to agree with the essay title, either in an unqualified or in a qualified way.

Now, recall our earlier advice in this chapter, namely that your conclusion can be used to raise issues directly related to your argument (or indeed derived from it), but which you cannot explore fully, either because of a lack of time or space, or because of the way in which you have constructed your plan. If you have agreed with the original statement of the essay here, it means that you are probably not satisfied with a state of affairs that penalises the South. You are likely to have developed the moral argument involved as part of your essay. In your conclusion, you might decide to go further and to suggest that the loser of such a policy is not only the South since, paradoxically, the North too will - sooner or later - pay a price for it. With technological progress constantly pushing up productivity in the industrial countries, their markets will find it increasingly difficult to absorb the goods supplied by industry. Would it not make economic sense to help the poorer countries to be less poor and to consume more so that they - in turn - can help to solve a crisis of over-production at world level? This is the argument of point no. 10 and it could be used in your conclusion as a relevant avenue which you are suggesting could be explored further.

It might often be the case that one or two of the random ideas which you have written before drawing your plan will in fact be the sort of material which you might want to save for your conclusion.

This will not always happen of course, since the process of developing your argument may make you aware of some important issues which you had overlooked at the beginning.

* Are these rough conclusions presented below acceptable to you? *Yes? No? Maybe?*

1) How can literature be defined?

Aristotle in the 4th century BC tried to answer this question in the *Poetics* and the debate still continues. At a time when the death of the book is being frequently discussed, it is more important to defend literature than to try to define it. What use, anyway, is a definition of literature to the reader?

2) Are the arts and science compatible?

As has been pointed out, men and women of letters have frequently been scientists. The encyclopaedists of the eighteenth century have been mentioned and Stephen Hawkins' book *A Brief History of Time* is an expression of a modern scientist's desire to get across his findings in a palatable literary form. Novelists such as H.G. Wells and J. Huxley - and these are by no means the only ones - were certainly aware of the importance of science. Indeed, one writer was supposed to have said 'Art must go beyond personal feeling. Through the appplication of rigorous methods, it must become as precise as the physical sciences'. At the same time, scientists themselves are not completely cut off from the world of arts. On the contrary, if science is to include the social sciences, together with the human sciences, then the area it covers is immense. What we are really concerned with, here, is a desire for knowledge: science and the arts can simply be regarded as two different ways of arriving at the same goal.

3) The media provide us with information but at what cost?

One point of view is that a price must be paid for everything. This is true of the media, where our tolerance (putting up with idiotic programmes and advertising) is the price we pay for the luxury of being able to travel in a few seconds from one end of the planet to the other. No system of information is perfect. The media are no more to blame than our own propensity to let others do the talking and acting. Indeed, the media are simply a reflection of ourselves and they should remind us that we are all victims of laziness.

4) What is happiness?

We may all ponder on the reasons for our unhappiness. I have tried to show how our experience of happiness is so fleeting and so insubstantial that it is quickly transformed into memory. Indeed, one might ask the question: is happiness ever anything other than a memory? What is really important, however, is not to define happiness but to try to help those in mental anguish and who have lost what can be considered life's essential ingredient: hope.

5) The goal of science is to acquire foresight.

To conclude, I have tried to show that without the qualities of the imagination, the scientist remains an average run-of-the-mill worker, incapable of participating in any of the great discoveries of the human mind. I would like to suggest that the ultimate aim of science is progress and that, to achieve this goal, reason alone is inadequate: a 'few grains of madness' are also necessary.

Discuss your comments, remarks and suggestions with someone else.

* LITERATURE

Read these short extracts from Eric Landowski's book on French essay writing. Then try to assess for each of them what has been argued. Choose among these statements those which would be 'your line' - the type of argument you could have developed.
Discuss your choice with someone else.

1) Reading, conceived as the 'meeting of minds', increases our understanding of the world and of ourselves; it teaches us how to live. It also possesses a moral function.

2) Reading is an inner adventure, a dialogue (or a form of psychoanalysis) whose object is to 'find ourselves' or 'to know ourselves'.

3) The best way to understand the problems of literary and aesthetic theory is to make a practical attempt at literary interpretation.

4) It would be asking too much of writers to expect them to change the world: they begin with the much more modest aim of entertaining the reader.

5) Writers have a key role to play in society. We need only refer to our recent past for confirmation. Writers, artists, intellectuals and creative people in general have always been amongst those who 'unhesitantly promote the great values of the human mind.'

6) Through reading we become closer to 'reality'; we discover the world around us and in us.

7) Reading, especially the reading of novels, deepens our knowledge of an age.

8) A discourse that is essentially prescriptive and concerned with the aims of literature (education? entertainment? information?) should be replaced by one that is descriptive and that attempts to define the actual process of literary creation.

* THE 'BRILLIANT' ESSAY

Read this definition carefully.

> The 'brilliant essay' is not simply an essay that can play with paradox or that shows signs of original thought. It is also one that reflects a sound general knowledge. Without demanding that we become specialists, the essay does require a minimum of knowledge concerning the 'great human problems'.
>
> Eric Landowski

- What is meant by 'a sound general knowledge'?

- What are, in your view, 'the great human problems'?

- Discuss your understanding of these questions with someone else.

- Draw up a list of issues you now feel confident to discuss.

- Exchange views with someone else on your respective lists.

* THE REAL CONCLUSION . . .

We cannot guarantee that you will be able to produce a brilliant essay after reading this book, but we hope we have succeeded in providing you with some stimulation and useful guidelines.

We hope that you will now feel more confident in debating issues in English and that you will enjoy for many years to come the game-playing approach that we have adopted here.

We would also like to feel that we have not only given you the opportunity to practise and improve your communication skills in English but that by introducing you to some of the important issues of our day, we have helped to sharpen the way you see things around you and in the world at large.

Chapter 12

On the other hand

In this final chapter you will find a selection of topics for discussion - and essay titles - presented in two broad categories:

1 SOCIETY

2 CULTURE

This division is arbitrary since, as you now know, culture and society are closely intertwined.

But it may help you to see the type of topics which are fairly frequent or which appear regularly in examinations.

Moreover, this book has shown that discussing issues and writing an essay in most cases leads you to cross the boundaries of various disciplines (e.g. sociology, politics, languages, literature, aesthetics, business studies etc.)

When debating a subject, one good strategy - which we have illustrated - consists in stressing the relationships (of implication, inclusion, similarity etc.) between viewpoints which apparently diverge in their presuppositions and subject matter (e.g. a title with a keyword such as 'culture' - usually perceived as belonging to the realm of Humanities - Art, Philosophy, History etc. - could be discussed and commented on from a political, or a social, or a commercial viewpoint).

The selection of texts (on pages 252-281) further explores subjects which have been discussed throughout the book and this choice of material will help you to acquire the general knowledge which is assessed in an examination, and provide you with facts and figures on certain issues.

1) SOCIETY

1) Money is power

2) The extent to which a government should intervene in the economic sector has always been a matter of dispute.

3) Public opinion can be manipulated.

4) Social cohesion is only a superficial phenonemon.

5) Wage-earners have only one weapon at their disposal: the power to strike.

6) A position of inferiority at work creates a rebellious attitude.

7) State secrecy allows the powers-that-be to do as they please.

8) Both scientists and private companies have closely-guarded secrets.

9) The law, like political power, is the property of the few.

10) Human life is made up of conflict.

11) It is those people who claim to be 'apolitical' who are always talking about national unity.

12) There is no such thing as international law: might is always right.

13) The power of the State decreases in inverse proportion to that of multinationals.

14) Receiving a pension will soon be considered a luxury.

15) The right to self-determination is the prerogative of rich countries.

16) Consumer credit creates the illusion of wealth.

17) We only lend money to the rich.

18) The business world should be self-regulatory.

19) In the East as in the West, too many people have a vested interest in the arms race for it to stop.

20) In politics the notions of right and left are outmoded concepts.

21) A public service should not be concerned with making profits.

22) By intervening in the affairs of other countries, the two superpowers succeeded in prolonging their conflict.

23) A United Europe will never be a reality as long as European leaders are primarily concerned with their popularity in national elections.

24) It is scandalous that in our age people are still starving.

25) People are both attracted and intimidated by novelty.

26) A radical opposition is always short-lived.

27) We become famous through what we destroy, not through what we create.

28) Living entails making compromises.

29) Revolutionaries are above pity.

30) Disciples cannot remain true to themselves or to others.

31) Statistics can give a veneer of scientific truth to almost anything.

32) Individualism and egotism often go hand in hand.

33) Certain societies are more tolerant of eccentricity than others.

34) Racism is a disgrace to the human race.

35) In a democracy, there should be a balance between the freedom of the individual and the wishes of the majority.

36) It was the two superpowers who were responsible for maintaining world peace.

37) In countries where communists are in the minority, the parties of the left denounce extremism and put forward policies that are 'rational' and 'progressive'.

38) Amnesia affects societies as well as individuals.

39) Ingratitude is a collective 'virtue'; all social classes claim at some time or other, to be unfairly treated.

40) An absence of solidarity suggests that a society is in decline.

41) How can tax inequality still exist in a society where everyone has the vote?

42) Virtue is seldom untainted by vice.

43) Learning to share duties should first be taught in the family.

44) Sports competitions have completely altered the nature of sport.

45) Few people succeed in overcoming their prejudices.

46) Honesty is the greatest virtue.

47) People are not fundamentally evil.

48) Cruelty towards animals should be more severely punished.

49) Should bringing up children be the prerogative of women?

50) The number of religious sects is greater now than it ever was.

2) CULTURE

1) Culture is what we have in common with others.

2) What we call culture is the collusion of a select few.

3) The greatest ambition of parents is to have children who are intellectuals.

4) What should be the role of a minister of culture?

5) Culture will henceforth be judged in terms of consumption.

6) It is inconceivable that history should not play an important part in general culture.

7) Whatever we may say, all the key positions in present-day society are held by people of culture.

8) In every society, some cultural practices are valued more highly than others.

9) Efficiency is the keyword in our age and it is incompatible with culture.

10) The very word, culture, is intimidating.

2.1 Mass Communication

1) There are fewer and fewer daily newspapers.

2) The stories of our age have their origin in the media.

3) Our way of life has been drastically altered by television.

4) Television like advertising exploits cultural myths.

5) Mass communication leads to conformity in human behaviour.

6) The media determine what is acceptable standard English.

7) Television and the cinema use the same techniques.

8) Are we well-informed?

9) Media-culture is not a third-rate culture.

10) Schools and universities should attach special importance to the study of mass communication.

2.2 Language and Literature

1) Is language a means of communication?

2) Every writer is a prisoner of ideology.

3) Reading sharpens our powers of reasoning and therefore of judgment.

4) We are conditioned by language.

5) Our use of language is determined by power relations.

6) What is meant by reading?

7) Books should not be a form of escapism.

8) Like the poem, the novel enacts a quest.

9) A fundamental question underlies all fiction: how can 'reality' be represented?

10) Poetry presents human life as an enigma.

11) The theatre appeals to our senses and not to our intellect.

12) Modern theatre is no longer a theatre of the sublime or a theatre of illusion.

13) It is paradoxically in the theatre that we become aware of the importance of silence.

14) Great literary works demolish national frontiers.

15) Can a feminist reading of a literary text be defended?

16) Critics are so vain as to believe - and to make others believe - that they alone have understood the work in question.

17) Critics and writers have the annoying tendency of taking themselves seriously.

18) What are the criteria for defining literary genres?

19) Is it necessary to study the language of a literary text?

20) Has literature suffered or benefited from audiovisual developments?

21) Why do people make a rigid distinction between form and content (or style and ideas) in the study of a literary text?

22) How do we recognise a literary text?

23) Do you agree that it is the work that deepens our understanding of an author's life and not vice versa?

24) Our best literary tradition is that of the aphorism or maxim.

25) The novel should express the multiplicity of relations that exist between the visible and the invisible.

2.3 Art

1) There is an increasing tendency to denigrate, and contemporary art is an example of this.

2) Despair is not an excuse for attaching undue value to the mediocre works of art displayed in our galleries.

3) Artists are completely free: they do not owe anyone anything.

4) Art does not represent reality, it produces it.

5) Why are we so interested in the 'sincerity' of the artist?

6) Beauty cannot be explained.

7) In art the rational coexists with the irrational.

8) Ugliness is transfigured by great artists.

9) Great art is also the expression of violence in the world..

10) What type of freedom does art express?

The use you will make of this material will of course be dictated by **your needs** and objectives, whether you decide to illustrate a point you are in the process of making in an essay, and are therefore looking for 'quotations', or whether you are seeking information (facts, figures, reports) on a particular topic, e.g. War in Europe, Trade and Industry in Contemporary Britain, Immigration in the West, Poets and Writers etc.

Throughout the book we have illustrated various strategies and exercises based on texts; you should then be familiar with various ways of exploring this type of source material, but it may be appropriate to reiterate in broad terms the various ways of processing these data.

You may use a text as a 'pretext', that is as a display of linguistic and discursive resources. You will pick up in the text words and expressions you wish to learn and/or use for a particular purpose (say or write something, express an opinion, contradict somebody or a viewpoint etc.).

You may use a text as a piece of information. You will then select items of information from it that you need on a particular subject; this will enable you to sustain an argument with some evidence and to quote, if need be, your sources. By collecting and comparing several texts on the same question or issue you could build up a fairly complete 'file' or 'dossier' on one particular point (e.g: urban development, the unions etc.).

You may alternatively use a text as the expression of an opinion, that you try to understand first (by a careful reading of what is said explicitly and implied) and then contradict or dispute (calling upon your own reading of the same question); the text becomes then a stimulus to your own analysis of an issue, in other words, a pretext to express your personal viewpoints. Some texts are so structured that you may find it useful to go back to the guidelines we spelled out in chapter 10 in order to get the most from them in terms of information and strategies.

A final remark: it may not always be practical to read a text in pairs or collectively, but we would advise you to try and share your reactions about a particular piece with someone else. This is a method we have been strongly advocating in the belief that meaning must come from somewhere; initially inscribed in the text, meaning is produced by words set in a network of relations.

If a text is to be understood, these relations have to be perceived and identified, be they approved or disapproved of, by the reader. Therefore the more you manipulate the text, the more you care to listen to someone else's understanding of it, the more you will feel at ease in debating and essay writing.

These skills will eventually enable you to become as active as possible in the process which has been the objective of this book: the production of meaning.

* World 'is failing to curb Aids spread'

World 'is failing to curb Aids spread'

Chris Mihill in Amsterdam

NATIONS are failing to keep up with the spread of Aids as the gap between the progress of the disease and the global response widens dangerously, a conference heard yesterday.

Wide-ranging changes in society to combat poverty and discrimination would be needed as well as a scientific search for a vaccine, researchers warned.

The opening session of the eighth world conference on Aids in Amsterdam, attended by 11,000 delegates from 133 countries, heard that science alone would not defeat Aids.

Dr Jonathan Mann, conference chairman, said previous efforts against the virus had failed to stem its spread because they had not considered wider social issues.

"The gap between the intensifying pace of the pandemic and the lagging national and global response is widening, rapidly and dangerously. Global vulnerability to Aids is increasing."

He said 13 million people were infected with HIV and by 1995 this would reach 20 million. By 2000 the number could range between 38 million and 110 million. Dr Mann, director of the International Aids Centre at Harvard University, said: "The response to the epidemic at national and global levels has reached a plateau and in some cases is declining, at the very time the epidemic is expanding and intensifying."

He added: "The course of the pandemic is not yet being influenced in any substantial manner by current efforts."

The knowledge existed to slow the epidemic through health education, but was not implemented in many countries because of lack of resources. Poverty, discrimination, and the role and status of women must be taken into account.

Dr Michael Merson, director of the global Aids programme for the World Health Organisation, said: "People are made vulnerable to HIV by social factors: poverty, discrimination, and the subordinate status of women among them. Without equality and partnership between the sexes, women will continue to be socially vulnerable to infection particularly through sexual transmission.

"With every passing week over 15,000 women become infected with HIV. In more and more parts of the world the infection rate in women is drawing close to or even surpassing that in men."

Dr Eka Esu-Williams, president of the Society for Women and Aids in Africa, said: "Knowledge about Aids does little good if women do not have the economic and social status to negotiate sexual relationships with their partners."

Aids activists demonstrated at the conference against the high price of drugs preventing some getting treatment, while another group paraded through the city delivering coffins to consulates of countries that restrict visitors with HIV.

AIDS in the World Estimate and Projections 1992 and 1995

	HIV INFECTIONS			AIDS	
	All Adults 1992 estimate	Women 1992 estimate	All Adults 1995 projection	Adults 1992 estimate	Adults 1995 projection
1 North America	1,167,000	128,500	1,495,000	257,500	534,000
2 Western Europe	718,000	122,000	1,186,000	99,000	279,500
3 Australia/Oceania	28,000	3,500	40,000	4,500	11,500
4 Latin America	995,000	199,000	1,407,000	173,000	417,500
5 Sub-Saharan Africa	7,803,000	3,901,500	11,449,000	1,367,00	3,277,500
6 Caribbean	310,000	124,000	474,000	43,000	121,000
7 Eastern Europe	27,000	2,500	44,000	2,500	9,500
8 Southeast Mediterranean	35,000	6,000	59,000	3,500	12,500
9 North East Asia	41,000	7,000	80,000	3,500	14,500
10 Southeast Asia	675,000	223,000	1,220,000	65,000	240,500
TOTAL	11,799,00	4,717,000	17,454,000	2,018,500	4,918,000

Proportion of Global Adult HIV Infections by Mode of Transmissions January 1992

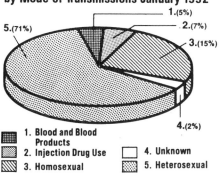

1.(5%)
2.(7%)
5.(71%)
3.(15%)
4.(2%)

1. Blood and Blood Products
2. Injection Drug Use
3. Homosexual
4. Unknown
5. Heterosexual

THE WORLD'S HEAVIEST SMOKERS

Annual cigarette consumption per country (millions). All figures are for 1991

China	1,617,000
USA	516,500
CIS and the Baltic States	456,000
Japan	328,300
Brazil	156,400
Indonesia	146,511
Germany	145,500
Poland –	102,100
France	97,100
United Kingdom	96,838

Daily cigarette consumption per man, woman and child. All figures are for 1991

Greece	7.8
Japan	7.3
Poland	7.3
Hungary	7.0
Switzerland	6.5
Bulgaria	6.1
South Korea	6.0
Spain	5.9
Australia	5.6
USA	5.6

United Kingdom = 4.6

SOURCE: E.R.C. STATISTICS INTERNATIONAL PLC, 'THE WORLD CIGARETTE MARKET. THE 1992 INTERNATIONAL SURVEY'

'Frontier of freedom' vital to preserve democracy

Press watchdog bites privacy law

Georgina Henry
Media Editor

BRITISH democracy will be imperilled and freedom of expression put at risk if the Government decides self-regulation of the press has failed and legislates to control it, the Press Complaints Commission warned yesterday.

In a long submission to Sir David Calcutt, QC, who is reviewing press regulation, the commission said it was vital "to draw a frontier of freedom between the Government and the press." It added: "Pluralism requires that the press be subject, like all citizens, to the law but never the state.

"As a working rule, there is considerable merit in Tom Paine's view that all governments tend to tyranny. An independent press is the most powerful of all constraints upon that evil in a democracy."

The commission, made up of lay and press members, which operates a code of practice drawn up by editors, is fighting to persuade the Government that self-regulation can work after months of criticism over the way newspapers have reported the marriage difficulties of the Prince and Princess of Wales and the private lives of politicians like David Mellor, Paddy Ashdown and Virginia Bottomley. Sir David is due to make his recommendations early next year, at the same time as Clive Soley, Labour MP for Hammersmith, will bring forward a private member's bill for freedom and responsibility of the press.

Newspapers fear the Government could decide to bring in a privacy law, or new criminal offences for journalist trespass, or turn the voluntary commission into a statutory tribunal with the power to put injunctions on stories and fine the press.

The commission argues that statutory control by the press will lead to self-censorship and maintains that self-regulation under the commission, set up in January 1991 after it was recommended by Sir David's first investigation, has demonstrably succeeded.

The written code of practice has proved to be a "Highway Code, a set of rules to help [journalists] drive more safely and responsibly through the legal, moral and ethical obstacles that face them every day". It points out that there are few complaints about privacy and harassment, the two main areas of criticism.

Kelvin MacKenzie, editor of the Sun, is quoted as saying that in the 18 months of the commission there have been 50 complaints against his newspaper, of which nine were upheld, seven rejected and 34 resolved after conciliation — out of 61,000 published stories. "In our view the code of practice has been an outstanding success. Its principles have become an integral part of the warp and weft of the professional lives of our journalists."

Paul Dacre, editor of the Daily Mail, says the press is showing a growing commitment to the need for self-regulation … "privacy legislation would inevitably mean the guilty would conceal the crimes behind laws designed to protect the innocent. One man's privacy is another man's public interest."

The main contention, the commission says, is over the balance drawn between the right of privacy and the public interest in publication. "The commission takes the firm view that the same measure should be applied whether it is the privacy of a private citizen or of a public figure and they apply this principle at every adjudication.

"Public figures may make the headlines but the privacy of other people is just as cherished a liberty."

The wider argument, it says, is of the benefits of a free press. "Newspapers and periodicals are public watchdogs, scrutinising those who exercise power. A democratic press will never be a nice press."

Children of 8 see TV fiction as fact

MORE than half of all eight-year-olds are unable to understand that the characters of Grange Hill, Neighbours and EastEnders are fictions created by actors, the British Association was told yesterday.

Dr Barrie Gunter, head of research for the Independent Television Commission, said 26 per cent partly understood the distinction between fabricated characters and situations and reality, but 29 per cent were confused.

The remaining 45 per cent understood the difference. At the age of 12, 65 per cent understood the difference.

Even so, he argued, children could learn a lot about such things as courtrooms, operating theatres, company boardrooms and jails from contemporary drama, and even young children had no serious trouble identifying those situations which distorted reality. But research on either side of the Atlantic created different pictures.

One American finding suggested that people who watched a great deal of television were more afraid of crime and violence than others.

The British finding was that perception of crime had more to do with social background and real experience than viewing habits.

British viewers who watched US crime dramas might form the opinion that the US was a dangerous place. They did not feel the same way about Britain. And watching The Bill or Juliet Bravo did not shape children's views about the police in any specific direction.

Dr Gunter also examined the way in which viewers absorbed news. "Research has shown that the more an item is covered in the news, the more salient it becomes in the public consciousness." He added: "Unfortunately, increased salience does not invariably lead to greater understanding of what the item is about."

He had asked 500 Londoners about eight political figures and three stories prominent in the news the previous week and found that the average memory score was 50 per cent.

However, one study in San Francisco, made by telephone shortly after the evening's main news bulletin, found that 51 per cent could not recall anything at all.

On average of those who could remember something, it was likely to be just one story out of the usual 19.

Dr Gunter had bad news for those who claimed they watched television to keep informed. Research showed that even they did not score much better on memory of news than those who claimed to watch only for entertainment.

Neo-Nazi growth worries Bonn

Anna Tomforde in Bonn

THE German government said yesterday it was concerned at the rapid rise of xenophobic attacks and the simultaneous growth of the neo-Nazi movement.

The interior minister, Rudolf Seiters, presenting a report on internal security, said there were 40,000 neo-Nazi activists in Germany in 1991, compared with 32,300 registered members of extreme rightwing organisations in 1990.

Racist attacks on foreigners, mainly refugees from third world countries and from eastern Europe, increased five-fold in 1991, to over 1,300.

Mr Seiters said he was concerned at the "growing brutality" of the neo-Nazi movement. In 1991, three foreigners — all Africans — died in attacks. One was stabbed, the other died in a fire and the third was thrown off a moving tram.

In the first seven months of this year police have recorded 650 racist attacks and seven people have died as a result of xenophobic violence.

Of the 40,000 neo-Nazi activists, 4,200 were "extremely violent skinheads" said the report.

The report showed that 30 per cent of the almost daily attacks on foreigners took place in the former East Germany.

The statistics — showing a rise in attacks from 270 in 1990 to 1,300 last year — reflect routine reports every weekend of attacks on asylum hostels, discotheques and camping sites.

Last weekend, 11 people were injured in three attacks in eastern Germany which involved skinheads armed with baseball bats, storming hostels, destroying the interior and throwing petrol bombs at inmates.

The report said three people were killed in xenophobic attacks in 1991 and 449 were injured in physical assaults. There were 383 cases of arson caused by petrol bombings and other explosions.

Meanwhile, thousands of neo-Nazis, their number reinforced by rightwing extremists from Britain, France, Holland, Denmark, Greece and South Africa, are expected to march to the Bavarian town of Wunsiedel tomorrow to mark the fifth anniversary of the death of Rudolf Hess, Hitler's deputy.

Make sure your car is a green machine!

RECYCLING all those old cans, saving water and planting trees are all good deeds for the world. But nothing will do more for the environment than the responsible care and driving of your car.

Here's a check list of green tips for car drivers:

Check your exhaust pipe. Want a clue to your engine's health? Rub a finger round the inside of your exhaust pipe. Ideally, your finger should come out coated with a light grey-brown powder. If it's any other colour, something may be wrong with the engine or, if you have one, the catalytic converter.

Keep your tyres firm. Adding air to your tyres is one of the kindest things you can do for the air outside them. Correctly inflated tyres mean better petrol mileage and less pollution. Tyre pressure should be checked at least once every two weeks when the tyres are cold.

By DAVID ANTHONY

Check your choke. A major hazard is too-rich automatic choke, with unburnt hydrocarbons coming out of the exhaust. If the choke is set too lean, it won't permit enough petrol into the cold engine, and the car labours to start; if set too rich, the choke stays closed longer, flooding the engine with petrol and causing it to run rich, even when warm. Choke adjustment is an easy job for a mechanic.

Stay tuned. Dirty carburettors or fuel injectors, clogged air filters, worn points and plugs and an ignored ignition system not only waste fuel and lower engine performance, they cause increased emissions. A tune-up should include a thorough examination, and repair if necessary, of the exhaust emissions and evaporative-control emissions systems.

Drive in the "economy range". On open roads maintain speeds as close as possible to the economical 55-70mph range. It takes less petrol and produces fewer emissions to travel at this than at 30mph.

Recap speedily. A large proportion of emissions from the evaporating petrol are released into the atmosphere when we refuel. After you've filled your tank, replace the petrol cap fast and close it tightly. Even from a surface the size of your filler cap, volumes of petrol vapour can escape in seconds. Multiply that amount by more than 19 million cars, refuelling frequently, and you get the point!

Most people think there is nothing they can do to change the car's impact on the environment - that the problem lies at the door of the government or the motor and oil industries.

This attitude could not be more wrong. Each one of us can do something the very next time we drive a car.

Islington Chronicle, 19 August, 1992, p.7

259

Privatisation dream 'a sham'

Michael Simmons

THREE years after their anti-communist revolutions, the countries of eastern Europe face economic catastrophe, mass unemployment and social and political breakdown as their remaining state enterprises fall deeper into debt, in many cases terminally, according to a report on their economies published today.

Hopes that privatisation would be achieved in four or five years have turned out to be "wildly optimistic", according to the authors, Paul Reynolds and Peter Young. At the present rate, they say, it will take Poland, Czechoslovakia and Hungary an average of 28 years to privatise only half of the state companies still on their hands.

The report, entitled Eastern Promise and published by the Adam Smith Institute in London, is one of the most thorough and pessimistic appraisals of eastern Europe since the collapse of communism in 1989. It is sure to raise concern in Western capitals about the efficacy of World Bank policies, and of bodies such as the British expertise fund set up by Margaret Thatcher three years ago to help promote free-market economics.

"The existence of Western advisers has not led to a general reassessment of privatisation and reform programmes," the report says. "In effect, there is a serious mismatch between the need for advice and the supply of advice available.

"In this, foreign aid fund providers must share the blame . . . Many tens of millions of dollars have been spent in each country. But still East European governments are unable to put together any kind of [privatisation] strategies and programmes," the report says.

Western advice, the authors suggest, should not necessarily be taken. Rather, the example of east Asian enterprises should be examined for ways of competing successfully in international markets.

With every passing year, the authors warn, radical reform is made more difficult. After two years, living standards are still declining for most people. "If it hasn't worked after five years, they will turn to other solutions."

In Poland and Hungary, the state-owned sector represents two-thirds of the economy, and in other countries as much as 90 per cent. Up to two-thirds of state enterprises in each country are on the brink of collapse.

The Polish privatisation minister, Janusz Lewandowski, has written a foreword endorsing the report.

"The reform process will become politically and socially unsustainable and will be abandoned," the authors predict, "causing major economic and political destabilisation."

Eastern Promise, £65, from the Adam Smith Institute, 23 Great Smith Street, London SW1P 3BL.

Women beware, British man about the house

EUROPE'S legion of working women who long for a caring "new man" to share their duvet and the household chores would be ill-advised to start searching in the United Kingdom.

Researchers dispatched by Brussels to far corners of the European Community have found that few husbands are quite so disinclined to lift a finger round the house as the British. Even the stereotyped chauvinists of France and Italy emerge as better disposed to visit the supermarket or escort children to playschool.

Challenged with a list of six common domestic tasks, three out of four fathers in Britain claimed not to be in charge of any of them — a proportion larger than for the European Community as a whole. They left it to women to take the lead in shopping, washing-up, cooking, cleaning, transporting children or helping them to dress.

Ex-Communist eastern Germany, the Netherlands and Greece emerge as the only places where a majority of fathers, interviewed about the years before their children went to school, agreed they were responsible for at least one of the items. In the case of Greek men it emerged that their burst of domesticity was overwhelmingly confined to visiting shops.

Spanish husbands, meanwhile,

By David Utting

topped the league for all-round household hopelessness, with almost 8 out of 10 admitting to no responsibilities at all — an assessment which was more than confirmed by the views of Spanish wives and partners who took part in the survey.

The strangest results were from Ireland, where 84 per cent of men stoutly maintain that they take no responsibility whatsoever for shopping, cleaning, cooking, washing-up, and dressing the children or driving them to school.

Yet the Irishmen's view of themselves as devil-may-care, unliberated, macho sort of fellows appears to be sheer fantasy. According to their wives and partners, nearly 70 per cent of their menfolk take responsibility for at least one household task, putting them among the most domesticated men in Europe.

The "Family and Work" survey, one of a series commissioned by the European Commission's Employment and Social Affairs Directorate, was based on almost 17,000 interviews in the 12 member states. The results are due for publication in Britain this summer.

Looking at the domestic tasks where European men — albeit the minority — are prepared to

Percentage of men who will NOT take responsibility for chores		
Country	They say	Partners say
Belgium	60.8	61.0
Denmark	51.1	47.5
W Ger	60.7	71.1
E Ger	42.7	62.7
Greece	47.2	49.8
Spain	76.6	79.7
France	58.4	60.7
Ireland	84.0	31.9
Italy	55.6	60.2
L'bourg	58.9	64.9
N'lands	45.7	46.2
Portugal	69.3	71.9
UK	74.2	70.6
EC average	61.6	65.4

average enthusiasm.

Those British husbands who do anything are at their best when clutching a dishcloth or tea towel at the kitchen sink, although their willingness to act as family chef is greater even than Frenchmen's.

The survey authors, Marianne Kempeneers of Montreal University and Eva Lelièvre of the London School of Economics, found that British women were unusual in Europe because of the extensive availability of part-time jobs. Their working lives were marked by interruptions to care for children and they were more prone to feel that promotion had been sacrificed as a consequence.

West German, Dutch and Irish women were more likely to mark motherhood with a prolonged or permanent exit from the labour force. But women living in Denmark and southern Europe found less difficulty reconciling work with their family responsibilities — possibly because childcare was easier to obtain.

take a lead, the survey identifies a North-South divide. Men in Portugal and the Mediterranean countries appear more concerned with the "public" duties of shopping or dressing and driving their children; further north it is the "private" chores such as dishwashing, cooking and cleaning which are treated with above-

Of those men who DO take responsibility for at least one chore, what percentage* are willing to do which task?						
Country	Shop	Dishes	Drive children	Dress children	Cook	Clean
Belgium	49	55	35	26	29	29
Denmark	39	55	23	32	36	26
W Ger	70	46	30	21	22	34
E Ger	64	53	48	27	23	27
Greece	91	16	16	22	20	13
Spain	48	25	42	57	30	29
France	48	48	49	38	37	35
Ireland	16	18	72	14	10	7
Italy	69	5	39	30	23	12
N'lands	53	66	6	28	28	34
Portugal	75	37	36	35	39	26
UK	51	72	26	37	48	42
EC average	59	42	35	31	30	29

*According to wives/partners. *Source: Eurobarometer 34*

Ministry admits that 'Japanese disease' is killing worn-out workers

Kevin Rafferty in Tokyo

JAPAN'S labour ministry has finally admitted the danger of a Japanese disease called *karoshi* which is said to kill up to 10,000 people a year in the prime of life.

Karoshi means death by exhaustion or overwork and in some jobs it is regarded as virtually an occupational hazard, although doctors may list the cause of death as a heart attack or stroke.

Officials said this week that they would compile a manual with a checklist to catch cases that normal medical examinations miss. Lawyers for victims claim that some of those who succumb are only in their early twenties. But the ministry admits to just a handful of cases a year, and then only after legal argument and long delays.

Japan is a nation of workaholics where working hours are longer: more than 2,150 a year at the last count against 1,989 in Britain, 1,957 in the US and 1,638 in Germany. More overtime is worked and holidays are shorter than in any other industrial country: nine paid days of holiday a year, half that of the US and just over a third of Britain.

On top, come after-hours drinking and smoking with the boys, regarded as part of the job, and sardine-packed journeys home.

The difficulty has been in getting recognition that white-collar workers can die of *karoshi*. Last month, in a landmark case, Tokyo labour courts recognised that Jun Ishii, an executive at Mitsui who had died of a heart attack two years before aged 47, had died from overwork.

Akio Koiso, a Fuji Bank clerk who protested against long hours, calculated that in the mid-1980s about 40 per cent of his fellow employees got home after midnight.

Japan's labour standards law says that employers may not force employees to work more than eight hours a day or 40 a week. But a judge recently upheld a decision by a large electrical company to sack an employee who refused to work overtime.

Some Japanese regard the possibility of *karoshi* as part of the job. A survey by a Tokyo university found one in four students starting work this year were prepared to accept the risk of *karoshi* for a job with a favoured company.

263

Rent fears of single mothers

By ANNA KING MURDOCH

SINGLE mothers who are renting private accommodation in Victoria are in danger of being made homeless at some time in the future, according to the results of a two-day phone-in.

About 114 women responded to the phone-in, which was organised by the Council of Single Mothers and Their Children, and the resulting picture is of certain discrimination against single mothers in the private rental market.

The phone-in report found that many women faced high rental costs, lack of repairs and maintenance, harassment from landlords and real-estate agents, and lack of long-term housing options.

Up to 80 per cent of the women were paying more than $100 per week rent, which represented 37 per cent of total income for the 70 per cent who relied solely on the sole parent pension ($264.40 for a woman with two children, including maximum rent assistance).

The council says the report shows that most single mothers who are renting are consistently "rent poor".

Many of the women said the housing they were renting was in appalling disrepair, but they did not ask for repairs and maintenance for fear of rent rises or eviction. One woman said: "Too many hassles, no repairs being done, no stove and no hot water."

About 44 per cent of women had suffered from some form of harassment, either invasion of privacy (23 per cent), being threatened with eviction (13 per cent), or sexual harassment (seven per cent). Two women had been sexually assaulted by their landlords.

Some form of discrimination had affected 69 per cent of the women. One Koori woman said: "I can't get into the private rental market on my own because I am a woman, I am a single parent and I'm black."

The report recommends that rent assistance be increased for sole-parent families, and that the Federal Government adopt the Australian Council of Social Services recommendation to add $930 million for the housing needs of low-income earners.

The report also recommends tax incentives for domestic property investors to encourage them to provide long-term tenure to sole-parent families, and that the Ministry of Housing set a up a private rental housing maintenance program.

It recommends harsher penalties against real-estate agents who discriminate against single parents, that low-income people be given priority access to low-cost private rental housing and a community education program to create a more positive attitude to single mothers and their children.

How hidden persuasion makes shoppers spend

Counter culture: In the second of a series on supermarkets, James Erlichman looks at the subtle psychology gearing soft sell to big profits

ENTERING a supermarket is like taking a seat in the psychiatrist's chair — the food shopper's deepest desires will be laid open and explored.

In-store cameras backed up by discreet human surveillance measure when and where we are tempted to pause and drop that*unneccessary little luxury into the trolley.

The laser beam at the checkout records whether more mozzarella cheese is being sold after it was moved to an eye-catching display or featured in the supermarket's latest TV advertisement.

Everything is geared to increased sales and profits, which means getting consumers to buy things they don't really need, but cannot resist.

Supermarkets don't like talking openly about tactics. They wish to appear the friendly grocer who helps wash our salads, not our brains.

However, it is hard to disguise that virtually every new superstore has its primary doors on the left so the shopping is done clockwise, to the right. "Nine out of 10 people are right handed and they prefer turning to the right," said Wendy Godfrey, a spokeswoman for Sainsbury's.

She denies, however, that the smell of fresh bread from the in-store bakery is drawn by

265

ventilation ducts to be wafted at customers as they enter the store. "We used to do that, but now we don't need to because we bake throughout the day and the smell naturally pervades the store."

Sainsbury's believes customers associate it with high quality fresh produce. That is why fruit and vegetables greet the shopper first at newer stores.

Profits from the store's own label products are normally higher than those from the big manufacturers. So own label baked beans are usually placed to the left of the Heinz display because the eye reads left to right and will spot the store's brand first.

The big manufacturers can rectify this by paying a premium for better display. How much they pay — especially when they may well be making the own brand version for the supermarket — is a closely guarded secret.

Of the 16,000 items of food which a superstore displays, only about 200 are KVIs — known value items — essentials such as tea, butter and coffee, the price of which will be known by most customers. Two rules apply here. Firstly, keep the cost competitive, which means halving gross profit margins to 15 per cent. Second, dot the KVIs around the store, so customers will have to hunt them out and walk past the frozen black forest gateau, or mange tout peas — items they do not really need.

Sainsbury's second largest superstore, at Hampton in south-west London, covers 42,000 square feet, has 41 checkouts, a vast delicatessen, in-store bakery, coffee shop, a one-hour dry cleaning service and a bank of petrol pumps outside. Can a store be too big, threatening and confusing the customer? Current thinking is that abundance sells. A well-stocked 20-foot display of tomato ketchup sells more sauce than a depleted shelf 15 feet long.

"I don't think there is a maximum size unless it is how fast the average customer can get round without the frozen food defrosting," said John Davidson, a lecturer in retail marketing at the University of Surrey.

"The jury is out on lighting," he said. "It is kept soft in the wine section to encourage browsing, but it is sharp and bright at the cosmetics counter to suggest cleanliness."

Width of aisles is also a factor. "If they move too fast they are missing buying opportunities," said Andy Mitchell, research officer with the Institute of Grocery Distribution. "They also try to bounce you back and forth across the aisle by putting the best-selling digestive biscuit on one side and the most popular chocolate one on the other."

Diversification into non-food products can also boost sales. Discount petrol often attracts people who end up filling a trolley as well as their fuel tank.

Convenience and cost are also behind Sunday trading. Round-the-clock running of freezer and chill cabinets means supermarkets cost a lot to operate after closing. Many perishables thrown away on Saturday afternoon could be sold on Sunday. Just as important, however, is the psychology of leisure shopping. Internal studies show that people buy more expensive, discretionary items when they are relaxed and browsing.

It is not only how much one buys, but what one buys. A supermarket makes more profit from its own brand, microwave cook-chill chicken kiev than it does from the ingredients needed to make it at home.

Many consumers appear willing to pay almost any price to avoid preparing food. Grated carrots wrapped in a nice plastic bag sell briskly for £1.18 a pound at Sainsbury's. Whole carrots, a few feet *a way, cost just 19p a pound.

* unnecessary   * away

Income equality gap widens for minorities

By Margaret L. Usdansky
USA TODAY

Black children are three times as likely to be poor as white children.

Half of Native American households earn less than $20,000 annually.

Fewer than half of Hispanic adults 25 and over have a high school diploma.

Even Asians, the USA's most economically successful minority group, saw poverty rise during the 1980s — to almost 17% for children.

These grim statistics, to be released today by the Census Bureau, underscore one of the central economic trends of the 1980s: income inequality rose and, as it did, minorities often were hit the hardest.

"The poor are doing worse and the rich are doing better, and it shows up in these populations to a greater degree," says University of Chicago sociologist Douglas Massey.

The reason: They are disproportionately likely to be poor.

The Census figures show that socio-economic positions of the different groups shifted little in relation to each other.

Blacks and Native Americans remain worst off, with the lowest median household in-comes and the highest poverty and unemployment rates.

Hispanics of all races continue to lag behind non-Hispanic whites in employment and income and remain at the bottom in education — partly because of the wave of Hispanic immigrants who came to the USA in the 1980s from countries where schooling often ends before high school.

And Asians continue to lead every group, including whites, in median household income and college education, even though their poverty rates are higher than those of whites.

Experts say the statistics appear contradictory for Asians because they have become the USA's most diverse minority group. Many of the 3.8 million Asian immigrants arriving here in the 1980s were less well off than earlier immigrants.

"Much of that increase (in Asian poverty) is probably due to refugees turned immigrants, the Vietnamese, the Cambodians, the Hmong, the Laotians," says Texas Christian University sociologist Morrison Wong.

At the same time, Asians' high median income reflects higher educational attainment and professional careers common in groups such as Asian Indians, Japanese and Filipinos.

267

Almost 37% of Asians 25 and older have a bachelor's degree, compared with 22% of whites, 11% of blacks and 9% of Hispanics and Native Americans.

But the income statistics can be misleading. On average, Asian households are larger than white households, so even though Asian household income is higher, that income supports more people.

"If you have four household members working, even if the poorest is only earning ten or twelve thousand a year, that's a substantial household income," says Brookings Institution economist Gary Burtless.

Experts disagree on why blacks and Native Americans trail so far behind. One theory: They are hampered by residential segregation.

Native Americans "are in some sense a conquered people, forced onto reservations. Blacks came over here as slaves. But the common thread . . . is that they are segregated," says Massey.

"When problems start to multiply in a segregated environment, their effect is magnified because you get a concentration of poverty, you get a concentration of social problems that you don't get with the other groups. And then they become norms," he says.

Income, poverty rise

Asians have maintained their lead in median household income over the last decade, but also have seen a 5% increase in children in poverty:

☐ 1980[1] ☐ 1990

1 – Adjusted for inflation

Blacks, Native Americans trail in income . . .
Median household income

White	$29,632 / $31,435
Black	$18,340 / $19,758
Native American	$20,541 / $20,025
Asian	$33,463 / $36,784
Hispanic[2]	$22,629 / $24,156

2 – Hispanics can be of any race.

. . . lead in poverty statistics . . .
Percentage below poverty line

White	9.4% / 9.8%
Black	29.9% / 29.5%
Native American	27.5% / 30.9%
Asian	13.1% / 14.1%
Hispanic	23.5% / 25.3%

. . . and children are affected
Children below poverty line

White	11% / 12.3%
Black	37.8% / 38.8%
Native American	32.5% / 37.6%
Asian	14.9% / 16.6%
Hispanic	29.1% / 31%

Source: Census Bureau

By Marty Baumann, USA TODAY

268

More China-backed broking firms set up in Hongkong

HONGKONG — Stock broking houses backed by China are opening in Hongkong, much to the resentment of established players who envy their political and corporate connections in the mainland.

Three new houses have emerged to bring the number of Chinese stock brokerages to about 10, many of which are big players in the Hongkong bourse and are set to compete well against US and British broking concerns dominant here.

The moves coincide with heightened Chinese participation in the Hongkong property market and with the upcoming listing of nine mainland companies — debuts which will boost Hongkong's market capitalisation, which stood at US$177 billion at the end of November.

Established brokers realise the Chinese will be tough competitors because they have valuable political and corporate links.

"We do not resent their presence," one US broker here said. "One cannot avoid insider trading elsewhere in the world either."

He said Chinese involvement was a natural development of the economic boom in China, the popularity of China plays — Hongkong-based companies active in Chinese market — in the Hongkong market, and the fact that Hongkong was reverting to Chinese rule in 1997.

An assistant sales director of a leading British house said Chinese money was capable of moving the market.

"I would not rule out the possibility that they would use whatever political or corporate information to play the market," he said. "Anybody else would. But it is difficult to analyse insider information about politics."

Recent attacks by Beijing on Hongkong Governor Chris Patten's proposed political reforms have sliced one sixth off Hongkong's Hang Seng index. China has also undermined individual stocks, namely the Jardine group, for backing Mr Patten.

A sales director with a US brokerage said there would be bigger insider traders than the Chinese, such as the majority shareholders of the listed companies or those close to the British colonial government.

"(Majority shareholders) are the ones who move the share prices up and down for their convenience," he said.

He welcomed the new Chinese brokerages because they would generate more turnover. — AFP

269

Credit-Card Issuers Battle in Singapore

Giveaways Escalate as New Curbs and Saturation Tighten Market

By G. Pierre Goad
Staff Reporter

SINGAPORE – American Express offered a Porsche. Visa International countered with a more expensive Mercedes. Then American Express put a three-bedroom condominium up for grabs.

Special giveaways are old hat in the credit- and charge-card industry. But Singapore's card marketers are setting new standards for such marketing efforts with their splashy promotions.

With growth in the number of credit and charge cards issued slowing down, card issuers are concentrating their marketing firepower on getting cardholders to use the plastic in their wallets more often. While card use is on the rise, card issuers say, cash is still by far the dominant method of payment. Charge and credit cards account for about 10% of consumer purchases in Singapore, compared with 20% in the U.S.

The number of charge and credit cards issued in Singapore doubled to just over one million, or about one card for every three Singaporeans, between 1988 and 1991. In November 1991 the Monetary Authority of Singapore, the central bank, raised the minimum annual income required to use a card to S$30,000 (US$18,337) from S$24,000, cutting the number of potential cardholders. The central bank also capped credit limits on credit cards at two months' salary. Some issuing banks had allowed credit limits to widen to five months' salary.

The central bank was worried about the rapid growth in the number and use of credit and charge cards. The new rules had the desired effect. After growing nearly 30% in 1991 the number of cards issued grew just 6% in the first nine months of 1992 from a year earlier.

Credit cards allow users to roll over their outstanding balances by paying interest, while balances on charge cards must be paid in full at the end of each billing period. Credit- and charge-card issuers earn money from annual fees charged to cardholders and from fees charged to merchants, usually a fixed percentage of each sale using a card. In addition credit-card issuers earn money from the interest payments by cardholders on their outstanding balances.

The business is highly competitive, and with card numbers nearing a plateau in Singapore, issuers are pushing hard to increase card usage and their individual share of total usage.

American Express International Inc., a unit of American Express Co., opened the contest bidding in July with a Porsche 968 sports car valued at S$320,000, including tax. Coupled with less-valuable prizes and gifts, the promotion ran from July to September.

Visa International replied last month with a Mercedes-Benz 300SL valued at S$370,000 in a sweepstakes that runs until Feb. 28. Visa's program was barely out of the garage when American Express, which has 170,000 cards issued in Singapore, unveiled its condo contest. The charge-card concern will give away a new, furnished apartment valued at about S$700,000 to S$800,000. Holders of Singapore-dollar American Express cards get one number for the "lucky draw" for each S$100 billed to the card between Nov. 15 and May. 15. The Visa contest operates in a similar manner.

Africa's sham democracy

Barry Crawford on how Africa is being recolonised and ruined under the banners of multi-party democracy

Over the past two years dictatorial presidents in more than 20 African states have been overthrown, voted out of power, or forced to agree to elections. The pace of change is unprecedented in the post-colonial era, and there seems to be no stopping the multi-party bandwagon. But this is not Africa's second liberation, nor is it real democratisation. In effect, Africa is being recolonised.

The West has initiated the reform process. The transition to multi-party politics is a top-down affair with the masses either indifferent or quietly applauding from the sidelines. For example, the celebrated electoral defeat of Zambia's president Kenneth Kaunda took place after the participation of only half the electorate. The same apathy was evident more recently in Alpha Oumar Konare's election as president of Mali. The new political agenda has been drafted in the West, adopted by a new African elite schooled in the economics of the International Monetary Fund (IMF), and presented to the masses for rubber stamping.

Notice of the West's new agenda for Africa was given last July by the World Bank's outgoing chairman, Barber Conable. He told the heads of state at the Organisation of African Unity summit in Nigeria that Western decisions about debt rescheduling and aid would now be based on the criteria of 'good governance' and 'transparency'. In other words, if you want Western support, open your country up to Western supervision.

The twin weapons of aid suspension and debt repayment have forced through reforms with remarkable ease. On 28 November last year the aid donors' meeting in Paris, chaired by the World Bank, suspended all new assistance to Kenya. It then took president Moi all of five days to lift the ban on opposition parties. This follows the precedent the West set in Zambia, and Moi seems destined to go the same way as Kaunda. So too are Malawi's president Banda and Congo's president Mobutu.

The Western financiers justify stopping aid by saying that they cannot stand by while African regimes abuse human rights. The idea that the West has become squeamish after decades of underwriting corrupt despots and sponsoring terrorist groups like Unita stretches all credibility. This new-found affection for human rights and democracy is a cover for an agenda which promotes neither. The old guard of Africa is being swept aside because its function was specific to the Cold War. The West no longer requires the corrupt old client regimes that it sponsored to contain Soviet influence and wage war against African liberation movements.

Instead, what is demanded today is the removal of all barriers to Western economic penetration. The Western bankers are imposing programmes of privatisation, currency devaluation and the abolition of state subsidies, supposedly to attract foreign investment and stimulate competition. But in the middle of a slump, Africa is just about the last place Western capitalists will invest in. All that these 'structural adjustment' programmes have produced is mass redundancies and immiseration. Eight years of structural adjustment have halved Ghana's gross domestic product. Nigeria's per capita income has fallen by two thirds over the past decade. The IMF now has similar agreements with 23 African governments. Not one has been carried through to completion and economic take-off.

This failure and the resulting human misery have not deterred the West. Instead, the programmes are moving into higher gear, using multi-party democracy to smooth the way. As the *Economist* cynically put it, 'people tend to accept painful policies more readily from elected governments than from dictators'. Zambia is a case in point. Violent food riots thwarted Kaunda's attempts to cut the maize subsidy in 1986 and 1990; the 100 per cent price hike following Chiluba's election produced no protests. The subsidy is now likely to be ended altogether.

By making a break with its old stooges and sponsoring the democracy debate, the West seeks to key into the popular revulsion against corruption and nepotism. The collapse of Stalinism has brought down with it all ideological barriers to Western domination. Since a Western solution is now accepted on all sides, at least by default, so too is the idea of African blame. Instead of exposing Western responsibility for Africa's crisis, the democracy debate is putting Africa in the dock.

All kinds of theories are being advanced as to why democracy has had such a bad time in Africa. The *Economist* suggests that democracy is alien to African culture, arguing that there isn't 'any African language whose political lexicon includes the concept of a leader of the loyal opposition. Instead there is a clear concept of a political enemy' (22 February 1992). *Newsweek* asks whether democracy in Africa is 'just an alien spell that is bound to wear off?' and adds that 'making the leap from the palaver tree to multi-party politics is made harder by the often volatile ethnic mix of African states' (9 December 1991).

The Western-defined terms of the democracy debate have been accepted by the African intelligentsia. They promote the image of the 1990s as the era of Africa's second liberation. The argument is that Africa's marginalisation in the New World Order is indicative of a loosening of Western control, giving Africans the breathing space to build their own political and economic institutions. This is turning reality on its head. Africa's lowly international status is the result of firmer Western domination in the post-Cold War world.

Instead of fantasising about liberation, the evidence of recolonisation needs to be honestly examined. Ghana has had World Bank officials sitting in on its cabinet meetings; an ex-World Bank technocrat is prime minister of Cameroon; Benin's IMF representative is now caretaker prime minister; Angola is looking into compensating Portuguese farmers for having seized land from them 17 years ago; Mozambique is inviting them back to their old sugar estates; South Africa controls the sales of Angolan and Botswanan diamonds. And so it goes on.

The current preoccupation with dictatorship and corruption is misplaced. African governments implementing Western strategies all have these attributes. The overriding issue in Africa today should be the obscenity of imposing austerity economics upon a starving continent. The democracy debate obscures this criminal process. Worse, it endows those who are responsible for it with legitimacy. Let us have no more of this sham debate about democracy. ●

LIVING MARXISM

Rough justice for women

A.C. Grayling welcomes a book which demonstrates the shortcomings of the law when dealing with minority groups

DO WOMEN get a fair deal at the hands of the criminal justice system in Britain? That is Helena Kennedy's central question. Her answer is an unequivocal "no". Her book is a sober and sobering explanation of why this is so. She puts her case, and suggests remedies, with compelling clarity. This is an important book; if it gets the wide readership it deserves it will make a substantial difference to public debate about Britain's legal system.

Kennedy practises at the criminal Bar. There are more lucrative and mannerly regions of the law, but Kennedy's choice is governed by the fact that in criminal proceedings the liberty of the subject is at stake. Her achievements are not restricted to the courts; she is an active campaigner for penal and constitutional reform, and television has made her widely known.

Women have to struggle to succeed in any of the professions, the Bar not least among them. But that is not Kennedy's main point. Her concern is with those who are at the receiving end of criminal justice, especially women. Practising as a barrister has given her ample opportunity to experience the failure of the system to treat women and other disadvantaged groups fairly.

It is a mere commonplace to say that the legal system was created by men for men. Relatively few women commit serious offences, and the assumptions and practices of the courts reflect this fact. They show it also when women come before the courts as victims of crime. In a host of ways the courts fail to recognise the reality of women's lives, with unjust results. The same applies to members of ethnic minorities. Kennedy uses a wide range of cases to show how women are disadvantaged, whether as victims of rape and domestic violence, or as defendants on charges ranging in seriousness from prostitution to murder. Even though in a recent instance a woman was exonerated from a murder charge, the cases make grim but profoundly instructive reading.

A salient example is that of battered women who appear before the courts either as accessories to the killing of a child, or because they killed their partners. There are widespread misconceptions about such women among judges and juries, who cannot understand why

---

EVE WAS FRAMED: WOMEN AND BRITISH JUSTICE
by Helena Kennedy
Chatto and Windus £16.99, 285 pages

---

they stay with their battering partners. Do they take perverse enjoyment in beatings – or are the beatings not really so bad after all (as if there were an acceptable minimum of domestic violence)? In the US the behaviour of abused women has been recognised as a species of stress disorder, now called "Battered Woman's Syndrome". Research shows its devastating effects: victims come to be oppressed and controlled by the mere threat of violence, and find themselves frozen into an inability either to escape or resist – even, in some cases, into inability to protect children at risk, as in the Hedda Nussbaum case in New York.

Battered women mask the physical and mental effects of their suffering, and in court seem emotionally detached. Profound misperceptions result. One concerns the crucial matter of provocation. A defence can attempt to reduce a murder charge to one of manslaughter by pleading provocation, but courts will only comply if the provocation was immediate – as when someone discovers his wife's infidelity, and kills her in a rage. There have been cases of women killing partners not in blind anger, but when the men were unawares, perhaps in drunken sleep. The cumulative effects on women of years of persistent beatings and fear are still not understood by courts, who apply the standard provocation test, with resulting injustice.

These misunderstandings parallel many

assumptions about women which distort the law's treatment of them. Whereas "fragrant" examples of femininity like Mary Archer prompt lyricism from judges, the case is otherwise for prostitutes, lesbians, and women with children in care, who risk condemnation as much for what they are as for the crime they have committed. Barristers learn to urge women clients to dress and behave demurely in court; anything that challenges acceptable stereotypings runs a risk. This applies as much to the rape victim as to the alleged murderess, and deeply affects the justice either can hope to receive.

Kennedy describes case after case where these considerations apply. Her sober language cannot hide their shocking nature, and as they accumulate one has the sense that the law is truly a foreign country for women who find themselves in its toils. But the story is not entirely negative. Kennedy applauds the improvements – few and slow though they are – which are taking place, and suggests further reforms. These include public scrutiny of judicial appointments, training for judges, and positive action to increase the number of women judges. As her book eloquently testifies, reform is long overdue.

HARMONY WITH A HOLE IN THE MIDDLE

Standpunkt

Andrew Lavender

A FEW years ago, an early spate of Euro-drama on television cele-brated a kind of post-yuppy existence where you could drink espresso at a pavement café, talk about French films and keep an eye on your BMW — a scene set in any (western) European country of your choice. The BBC's new soap opera, Eldorado, set in a Spanish resort, prom-ises to be much more down-market but its much-publi-cised recipe of sun, sea, sangria and sex puts it in the same upbeat category.

There's a promised land awaiting across the Channel, a world of fabulous cosmo-politan opportunity. This fits the Europhile vision of a happily federated continent — but something has gone sour. A more sceptical brand of drama on stage and screen finds nothing to savour when it comes to notions of Euro-pean harmony.

This is certainly the case in several new British plays which take contemporary Europe as their setting but find scant cause for celebra-tion. In Howard Brenton's Berlin Bertie, it is Bertie, the ex-Stasi agent, who provides all the grits. "The grand world views are collapsing

into rubble — what will there be that we can rely on?" he muses. In Dusty Hughes's A Slip Of The Tongue, John Malkovich plays a dissident writer whose womanising is a metaphor for the fresh res-ponsibilities of a democratic age: you can't indulge your desires, Hughes sug-gests, without hurting some-one along the way.

Both plays are in part cau-tionary tales about the cal-lous grip of capitalism — an empire, it is suggested, at least as insidious as any-thing that has just been overthrown.

This is hardly a new sensi-bility. More telling is the work of British playwrights who have seen the European future and found the sight almost too awful. Harold Pinter and Howard Barker both set their most recent plays in a generalised Euro-pean no man's land. Pinter's Party Time has a group of well-heeled party animals swapping conversational barbs while an armed upris-ing takes place outside. Barker's A Hard Heart is even more bleak. "My son is the product of a single night of love," says the central character (a woman around whom a country is collaps-ing), "if love it is when strangers collide in chaos."

I F THESE plays share a theme, it is the lack of communication between people, an impasse more profound than a simple difference of class or culture. Caught in a changing world, the characters find it impossible to relate to each other. But their sense of alienation goes deeper still. "All relationships will be tainted now," suggests Berlin Bertie. "The 'pure in heart' will never have any influence in the re-united Germany." Nor, the play suggests, anywhere else on the continent.

The playwrights home in less on the social and political turmoil of the past few years than on Europe as a place of emotional and even moral crisis, where there are no values left, nothing in which to believe any more.

It would be easy to dismiss this as a peculiarly British impression, the result of our customary half-cock engagement with events across the Channel, but Europe has become the setting for films from farther afield which explore the disturbing links between place and person. Woody Allen, the master chronicler of paranoia, has set his new film Shadows And Fog in Mitteleuropa, while Steven Soderbergh goes to Prague for Kafka.

One breathtaking recent film, Europa by Danish director Lars Von Trier, is also partly about alienation.

Amid its technical bravado — the film boasts a bagful of camera and editing trickery — Europa has sophisticated things to say about a continent putting itself back together.

Its setting is Germany in 1945. Max, a young German-American, returns to his homeland after the war and takes a job as a sleeping car attendant, which allows Von Trier to shift him rapidly across a blitzed and smouldering landscape, and to examine a more personal kind of journey. Max finds himself surrounded by bureaucratic pedants and is ultimately betrayed by just about everyone he meets.

Europa may be set nearly 50 years in the past but, as the title expansively implies, there is something mythic about its subject matter. The old order is in ruins, but the new one is built on half-truths, evasions and treachery. For all the film's irony this is a deeply pessimistic and contemporary vision.

In the wake of recent events in eastern and central Europe, artists are searching for the place — literal or metaphorical — where one feels most secure. But it's no comfort for either federalists or nationalists that they can't find it anywhere.

Sugar and spice, a vice

Lorna Sage

OUR TREACHEROUS
HEARTS
Why Women Let Men
Get Their Way
by Ros Coward
Faber £14.99

A FEMINIST generation ago, veteran American radical Tillie Olsen wrote (in a book called *Silences*) about motherhood as 'the least understood, least and last explored, tormentingly complex *core* of women's oppression'. Motherhood is so entangled with love, with needs and satisfactions, that it remains stubbornly sanctified. Ironically enough, now that childbearing is more or less voluntary for women — anyone who (like me) grew up in the 1950s remembers contraception being denied to the unmarried, abortion to everyone — motherhood has become more and more the focus for guilt, mystification and competitive anxiety.

Ros Coward's new book looks with polite, but actually quite savage scepticism at late twentieth-century woman's romance with reproduction. And she comes to the conclusion that unless we can untangle our motives and recognise that our private choices add up to a pattern, we are going to stay trapped in the 'caring' roles, *plus* jobs (but without careers), *plus* the obligation to stay slim and sexy, without the prestige of public achievement etc.

Women, she says, are in effect underwriting a public world of macho struggle, institutionalised selfishness and amoral greed, by sustaining private spaces where altruism, creativity and unpaid work are still supposed to be 'naturally' the rule. There's nothing very natural about it, she wants to argue, even though many women — including professional women — will shrug and say that their maternal instincts just took over. She has talked to around 150 of them, and knows from her own experience what she's talking about, since she herself gave up a university job to go freelance and look after her children.

Laying her own complicity on the line in this confiding way makes her tone confusing to start with. Is she simply inviting us around for a companionable moan (Oh dear, look what we've done, *again*. Comic, guilty grimaces and wry smirks all round)? Actually no, or not most of the time. Many of her sample women confess, for instance, that they didn't exactly sacrifice their careers, their careers weren't working out the way they wanted them to *before* the babies. So that this becomes a question about why women — for better or worse — 'seem to regard work and a career as dispensable'; and whether family life may not sometimes provide 'a good excuse' for giving up the struggle. (Just imagine a world in which eyebrows were raised when a woman said she was resigning to spend more time with her family, and you'll get the drift. It's just not done to regard a woman who says this as copping out.)

The notion that benign Nature is behind it — women are by nature caring, hate competition — also looks increasingly implausible if you consider the competitive ethos *within* the culture of child-rearing these days. Coward has some blackly funny anecdotal stuff about mothers' aggressions on behalf of their offspring, and some more sober evidence of the way in which well-meaning women secretly enjoy and encourage their small sons' violence, thus piling up problems for their daughters (who are being taught to suppress their own vices).

All in all it amounts to a cruel but convincing picture of women's supposed 'niceness' as grossly collusive. Women are horribly obliging, they have adjusted to the contradictions of the times — at once independent, worldly and ambitious and at the same time 'internalising a much clearer sense of the "moral" agenda than men do.' Hence, she says bleakly, 'the widely shared delusion that women are nicer and more moral than men'. Hence, too, the pervasive sense she reports in herself and her sample of unease, anxiety, exhaustion, and guilt, guilt, guilt. At one point I felt as though I would never hear about anything else.

It's this guilt, she thinks, that mothers lay on their daughters, generation after generation. More honesty and we may begin to unravel the tangle of possessiveness, disappointment and self-doubt. There's a virtue too, perhaps in sharing the guilt out. Coward says 'we' a lot, and she's transparently nostalgic for the old days, in the 1970s, in the Women's Movement, so different from the privatised world of the family. Sisterhood *versus* bitter home truths. For her, and her generation, the profession of 'settling down' has acquired added irony in a political climate which privileges private-enterprise solutions.

So it's back to the barricades for proper crèches, communal child care, a really new new man, feminisation of the workplace, another crack at feminist solidarity, even: so that how you manage mothering can really be a choice. But first — she has to be right — you need an assault on the mystique of motherhood, which is still much the best means for getting women to do the work, DIY oppression.

Once upon a time . . . began a story starring a brave young boy. **Justine Hankins** reflects on the one feminine exception to the fairy-tale rule

What Dorothy did best

HAVING CHILDREN as main characters in films is a popular way of appealing to a child audience. Children identify with the character, who is usually presented as just a normal kid, and through them experience the fantasy of independence from parents and adventure. However, it seems that girls do not have adventures or fantasies, or if they do, they are not interesting enough to be made into films.

Countless features have been made in which a male child or teenager is faced with a challenge to which he ultimately rises. Think of Back To The Future or Home Alone. Michael J Fox, for example, is not presented as a glamorous star but as just an ordinary American boy who has an extraordinary experience. Boys are involved in the action and girls, if they're lucky, may be allowed to tag along. Adventure requires robust and brave boys, and is no place for delicate and cowardly girls.

The problem is that adventure is itself a masculine concept: the domestic and passive characteristics deemed as feminine are antithetical to the daring adventurous spirit. If a girl becomes an active participant, she becomes a tomboy.

Virtually the only exception to this — as well as being one of the most well-known and

best-loved films of all time — is The Wizard Of Oz. Just as with boys' adventure stories, the opening scenes encourage the child audience to identify with this ordinary girl. They identify with her boredom and what child has not felt at times misunderstood or ignored by busy parents or relatives?

Dorothy's arrival in Munchkinland marks the beginning of the adventure but, more significantly, marks the feminisation of that adventure, the scenery full of pretty flowers and delicate pastel shades. Even though she becomes assertive and active, Dorothy never stops being the quintessential girl, a fact signified by her gingham frock and hair bows. And how many boy-heroes take time out of their mission for a session in the beauty parlour?

The film constantly maintains a specific and idealised image of girlhood, and in the Land of Oz, it is never threatened by the encroachment of masculinity. The two most important figures are women, representing good and evil. The exaggerated and simpering femininity of the good witch is presented not as passivity but as power. Qualities stereotyped as feminine — such as kindness, sympathy and sentiment — are deeply ingrained in the narrative. Dorothy befriends and helps a collection of pathetic and incompetent male characters, and rapidly develops from an uninspired schoolgirl to someone who organises and precipitates action.

THE journey down the yellow brick road is a quest for the great, all-knowing patriarch. Masculinity, however, proves to be ineffective and foolish. The great wizard is revealed (by the dog, Toto, in fact) to be a useless old man who has preserved power through deception. Ultimately, as the good witch kindly informs us, Dorothy had the power all the time.

Of course it is easy to get carried away with this "patriarchy revealed" interpretation of The Wizard Of Oz and it must be remembered that the intention behind it was basically reactionary. The proposed moral of the tale is, after all, "There's no place like home" — in other words, make the most of your lovely conventional home-life because once a Kansas farm girl, always a Kansas farm girl.

Yet while this is the film's intended message, is it the message most people (especially girls) take away from it? The film manages inadvertently to challenge the very values it claims to hold so dear. The drab black and white world in which Dorothy is just another kid cannot compete in appeal to the opulent and happy Land of Oz where an ordinary girl can become a national heroine.

James Wood

Something To Remember Me By: Three Tales
by SAUL BELLOW
£13.99 222pp
Secker and Warburg

NEARING the end of his banquet, Saul Bellow might have good reason to be filling up, hoarding, piling it on. Instead, he has been divesting. Since *The Dean's December* (1982) his fiction has been slimmer, with a quick tension, and a new, somewhat aerated levity. Bellow has not become gloomier, as the usual charge has it. He has become funnier about gloomier things (the mass-confusion we find ourselves in, the heartlessness of contemporary America).

Brevity — Chicago-brevity, vernacular-brevity — has always been his style, though he is famous for his large novels and his plenitude. Consider his characteristic metaphors: "You had to study Mason to find the humanity in him. It was as hard to see as the thin line of mercury in some thermometers." (*The Dean's December*). Or this: "He walked on a wooden leg, gracefully bending and straightening like a gondolier" (*Herzog*); "One eye was set a little closer to the nose than the other, giving a touch of Jewish pathos to his look" (*The Bellarosa Connection*). The wit is lizard-quick: it darts out but recoils almost as quickly. The image is finished promptly, sternly. No wasted words.

So it is no surprise that this collection of recent short fiction (two of the book's three stories, *A Theft* and *The Bellarosa Connection*, have already been published in paperback) should begin with an introduction in praise of shortness. The reasons are familiar enough. The writer must compete with a storm of distractions — newspapers, television, advertising, celebrities. These engines of triviality are on overdrive. Bellow finds a brilliant image, at once hilarious and sinister: "Vast organisations exist to get our attention. They make cunning plans . . . Think of our consciousness as a territory just opening to settlement and exploitation, something like an Oklahoma land rush." So the writer may have to make adjustments, shorten, reduce. Bellow admits that he has hardly been exemplary, but quotes with approval a sentence of Chekhov's: "Odd, I have now a mania for shortness. Whatever I read — my own or other people's works — it all seems to me not short enough."

Bellow's introduction proposes, but also enacts, a kind of summary brevity, a final prayer or collect. All the themes of his work are contained in it, in particular the plea for clearer private space amidst public, post-modernist frenzy (though Bellow's emphasis on the importance of *resisting* rather than accommodating this "landrush" on the mind, marks him as high modernist or even pre-modernist). Obsessed readers will consider these six pages enough cause to buy this attractive book; the floating reader may want to consider the only previously unpublished story, which gives the book its valedictory title.

The title-story returns us to Bellow's memory-source, the Chicago of the 1930s. A teenage boy is delivering flowers — "the package had the shape of a padded kite" — in wintry February: "The temperature a few degrees above zero, botanical frost shapes on the windowpane, the snow swept up in heaps . . . " This is the world of one of Bellow's greatest short stories, *A Silver Dish*, in which a young boy travels with his father to the end of the Chicago tramline, in freezing weather and during the Depression, to beg for a loan from a prominent church elder. (Once inside the elder's house, the sly father gets other ideas, and steals a silver dish on display.) The narrator of *Something To Remember Me By* notices everything: "When I came to the boulevard on the edge of the park, two small men rushed out of a doorway with rifles, wheeled around aiming upward, and fired at pigeons near the roof-top. Several birds fell straight down, and the men scooped up the soft bodies and ran indoors, dark litle guys in fluttering white shirts. Depression hunters and their city game."

The boyish narrator delivers his flowers, and is then tempted by a prostitute into a nearby room. He sheds his clothes, only to find that a practical joke has been played. The woman throws his clothes out of the window, and the boy, clad only in a sheet and a dress makes his way back home, fearful of the punishment that awaits him from his strict father. Without money for his tram-fair, he agrees to help an old drunk, McKern, home for a fee. The drunk's daughters lay their father on his couch and undress him. The narrator casts a Bello-vian eye over his ruined nakedness: "I looked in at McKern . . . The parboiled face, the short nose pointed sharply, the life signs in the throat, the broken look of his neck, the black hair of his belly, tne short cylinder between his legs ending in a spiral of loose skin, the white shine of the shins, the tragic expression of his feet." This marvellous passage returns us to the style of Bellow's first novel *Dangling Man* (1944) — the helpless observation, the eccentric precision of that observation, its sympathy and wily simplicity. As Bellow nears the end, he returns to his beginning. If this is "writing short," let it be an art lawful as eating.

Appendix 1

Suggested Answers

Chapter 2

Page 11

dream - amusing - pay - reduced - reserved for men - poem - pleasure - game - idea - bet

were the words to be eliminated

Page 12

1 research - 2 freedom - 3 proposals - 4 subject - 5 issues - 6 limit - 7 quality - 8 carried out

Page 15

1 - c / 2 - a / 3 - b / 4 - f / 5 - d / 6 - g / 7 - e / 8 - i / 9 - h / 10 - 1 / 11 - j / 12 - k.

Page 23

SPARKS FLY OVER JEANS AD'S 'RISK' TO MACHO MEN

The phenomenally successful Levis 501 advertisement campaign, which took buttoned-fly jeans from costume museum back to high fashion, has been attacked as sexist, ageist and sizeist - but yesterday it was denounced as dangerous, writes Maev Kennedy.

James Tye, director general of the British Safety Council, said the latest ad was "totally mindless and highly dangerous" and is writing to the Independent Broadcasting Authority demanding that it be banned.

The story line is a role-reversed Cinderella, as a young woman with a pair of jeans goes in search of the man with narrow enough hips.

She finds her perfect fit in a workshop, a young mechanic already conveniently half out of his .boiler suit

Instead of a fairy tale Mr Tye saw a death trap "in which the Prince Charming character is seen to have total disregard for Health and Safety laws" with the "semi-naked macho mechanic standing in a shower of sparks". It would incite dangerous copy-cat exploits among apprentices.

Stef Tiratelli of Bartle Bogle Hegarty, the agency that .devised the campaign, said: "When we launched Launderette (their first Levis ad) we didn't expect people would start taking all their clothes off in public, and we would not expect people to start copying this one."

1. primarily (1)
2. played (3)
3. consistent (5)
4. concerned (8)

bled (2)
spread (4)
barons (6) run (7)
insomuch as (9)

Chapter 6

Page 112

1 - c / 2 - d / 3 - a / 4 - b / 5 - f / 6 - e / 7 - g / 8 - h / 9 - j / 10 - i

Chapter 9

Page 199

1. must
2. say
3. think of
4. note
5. more
6. men ... women
7. are wrong
8. Beauty spots
9. ambiguous
10. like

Page 201

1. - rhymes/ 2. - alexandrine - line - feet/ 3. - stanzas - poem/ 4. - sonnet - quatrains - tercets/ 5. - enjambement/ 6. - hemistich/ 7 - rhythm - caesura/ 8 - ode - ballad/

Page 203

1 - d; 2 - a; 3 - b; 4 - c; 5 - e; 6 - h, 7 - i; 8 - g; 9 - j; 10 - f.

1.	examples	argument
2.	consider	attitude
3.	agree	is meant by
4.	shall begin	reasons
5.	point out	weaknesses
6.	interpretation	
7.	define	
8.	support	
9.	sentence	
10.	focus on	issues

1.	integration	ebb	
2.	suffused		
3.	Maastricht	undemocratic	
4.	features	adopted	
5.	questioning	confined	
6.	stagnation	unemployment	Euro-nationalist
7.	strategy	rebuild	
8.	attempt	world	national
9.	serves	defence	dismantling
10.	needs		

Appendix 2

Sources and notes

Chapter 2

Well-being means never feeling dependent on your children.
Sunday Times, 15 November, 1992.

We're here to make life easier.
Evening Standard Magazine, December, 1992, no. 132.

She can't eat, she can't sleep, she's stopped wanting to care.
Evening Standard Magazine, December, 1992, no. 132.

Debts of honour.
Guardian, 26 June, 1992, p.29.

Professor: Care in community can be success.
Hampstead and Highgate Express, 17 July, 1992, p.19.

Soaps show blacks as underclass.
Times Higher Education Supplement, 19 June, 1992, p.4.

Sparks fly over jeans ad's "risk" to macho men.
Guardian, 28 August, 1992.

Women's work remains undervalued report claims.
Guardian, 7 September, 1992, p.11.

Life should not be so sweet ...
Islington Chronicle, 19 August, 1992, p.7.

Data "posing grave threat to privacy".
Guardian, 16 July, 1992, p.4.

Noisy frogs.
Sunday Times, 15 November, 1992.

Treaty with Aborigines "threatens safety".
Sunday Age, 26 July, 1992, p.5.

Heritage is crumbling !
Islington Chronicle, 18 November, 1992.

Just as young as you yoga !
Islington Chronicle, 18 November, 1992.

Police chief says justice is "a game".
Guardian, 16 October, 1992, p.8.

Aids study group vows to fight fear.
Hampstead and Highgate Express, 17 July, 1992, p.15.

It's mer-arculous !
National Examiner, 28 July, 1992.

Riotous rage of the have-nots.
Independent on Sunday, 19 July, 1992, p.24.

Mystery of the "missing" royal car.
Sunday Times, 15 December, 1992.

The Gallic symbol of failure.
Mail on Sunday, 12 July, 1992, p.21.

Boards' linguistic silence speaks volumes.
Financial Times, 9 July, 1992, p.10.

Prisoners of corporate culture.
Independent on Sunday, 2 August, 1992.

Can't pay, must pay.
Living Marxism, September, 1992, p.37.

Votes of disabled "denied".
Hampstead and Highgate Express, 17 July, 1992, p.20.

Pub regulars.
Islington Chronicle, 19 August, 1992, p.2.

Friends indeed.
Islington Chronicle, 19 August, 1992, p.3.

Pond plan intended to enhance environment.
Hampstead and Highgate Express, 17 July, 1992, p.22.

Superior persons.
Times Literary Supplement, 17 July, 1992, p.5.

Forlorn sameness of naturalism.
Guardian, 16 July, 1992, p.22.

The creative critic.
Guardian, 30 April, 1992, p.24.

Chapter 6

BT looks to EuroTV satellite links.
Guardian, 15 October, 1992, p.15.

Schools go international.
Independent on Sunday, 2 August, 1992, p.21.

Britain lags further behind competitors, study shows.
Guardian, 22 June, 1992.

Paperless dreams buried by office reams.
Guardian, 7 October, 1992, p.15.

International news causes Dow to fall 4 points.
Oakland Tribune, 25 July, 1992, B-4.

The hyperpoem.
Guardian, 17 September, 1992, p.3

Chapter 7

Union calls for pupil's charter.
Guardian, 28 July, 1992, p.6.

Court refuses plea for the right to die.
Guardian, 25 July, 1992, p.8.

Deny homosexuals some privileges, Vatican tells us.
International Herald Tribune, 18-19 July, 1992, p.5.

Animal rights fellowship for priest who says their souls are immortal.
Guardian, 14 July, 1992, p.4.

Methodists embrace concept of a god without sexual bias.
Guardian, 30 June, 1992.

Quotation: 'Life is . . . . short'
            'The condition . . . . body' Hobbes Leviathan. Ch.14

Chapter 8

A lot of soap but not much froth.
Guardian, 9 September, 1992, p.36.

Proportions of all families with dependent children headed by lone mothers and lone fathers.
Social trends 22, 1992, p.39.

Employees and self-employed: by sex and occupation, 1990.
Social trends 22, 1992, p.74.

Unemployment and vacancies.
Social trends 22, 1992, p.80.

Percentage entitled to annual paid holidays of duration.
Social trends 22, 1992, p.176.

Holidays taken by Great Britain residents: by destination.
Social trends 22, 1992, p.185.

United we prosper.
Guardian, 3 July, 1992, p.21.

Quotation: 'The rise of the novel . . . to be understood' D. Lodge,
Write on, Penguin 1980, p.198-9

Chapter 9

Trade deliveries of LPs, cassettes, compact discs and singles.
Social trends 22, 1992, p.179.

Radio listening: by age.
Social trends 22, 1992, p.178.

Weekly radio listening. (percentage of population).
Guardian, 30 June, 1992, p.3.

Reading of national newspapers: by sex and age, 1971 and 1991.
Social trends 22, 1992, p.180.

Reading of the most popular magazines: by sex and age, 1971 and
1991.
Social trends 22, 1992, p.179.

Libraries: material on loan.
Social trends 22, 1992, p.181.

Methods of obtaining current book.
Social trends 22, 1992, p.181.

Quotation: 'How to do things with words', I Austin,
Clarendon Press, Oxford, 1962

British reading habits: Information from
Social Trends, 1992, p.197.

Chapter 11

Eric Landowski: *Le devoir de français*, Editions Pédagogie Moderne, Paris, 1980, p.198.

Chapter 12

World "is failing to curb Aids spread".
Guardian, 19 October, 1992, p.4.

AIDS in the World Estimate and Projections 1992 and 1995.
Times Higher Education Supplement, 3 July, 1992, p.15.

The world's heaviest smokers
The Observer Magazine, November 1992

Press watchdog bites privacy law.
Guardian, 19 October, 1992, p.4.

Children of 8 see TV fiction as fact.
Guardian, 26 August, 1992, p.4.

Neo-Nazi growth worries Bonn.
Guardian, 14 August, 1992, p.6.

Make sure your car is a green machine !
Islington Chronicle, 19 August, 1992, p.7.

Privatisation dream "a sham".
Guardian, 19 October, 1992, p.6.

Women beware, British man about the house.
Guardian, 28 June, 1992.

Ministry admits that "Japanese disease "is killing worn-out workers.
Guardian, 26 August, 1992,p.7.

Rent fears of single mothers.
The Age, 15 July, 1992, p.16.

How hidden persuasion makes shoppers spend.
Guardian, 11 August, 1992.

Income equality gap widens for minorities.
USA Today, 24 July, 1992, p.36.

More China-backed broking firms set up in Hong Kong
Business Times, The Business Paper for South East Asia 31 December, 1992, p.4.

Credit-Card Issuers Battle in Singapore
The Asian Wall Street Journal 29 December, 1992, p.1.

Africa's sham democracy.
Living Marxism, September, 1992, p.36.

Rough justice for women.
Financial Times, 14-15 November 1992.

Harmony with a hole in the middle.
Guardian, 13 July, 1992, p.26.

Sugar and spice, a vice.
Observer, 21 June, 1992, p.58.

What Dorothy did best.
Guardian, 7 June, 1992.

Something to remember me by: Three tales.
Guardian, 10 November, 1992, p.14-15.

Mini dictionary

A

aberration	n.	departure from what is normal, expected, usual
abolish	vb.	to do away with; put an end to
access	n.	the right to enter or to use something
accessible	adj.	easy to approach or use; available
accessory	n.	1) additional/subsidiary 2) a small accompanying item of dress
account	vb.	to take into consideration; allow for
accountable	adj.	responsible to someone or for some action
acquire	vb.	to get or gain (something)
advent	n.	an arrival or coming
adversary	n.	an opposing contestant
affectation	n.	an assumed manner of speech, dress or behaviour
aggravate	vb.	to make worse
akin	adj.	similar
alexandrine	n.	a line of verse having six iambic feet, usually with a caesura after the third foot
allocate	vb.	to give or assign for a specific purpose
altruism	n.	the practice of unselfish concern for the welfare of others
amnesia	n.	a partial or total loss of memory; forgetfulness
analogy	n.	agreement or similarity
anguish	n.	extreme pain or misery
antithetical	adj.	directly contrasted
aphorism	n.	a short saying expressing a general truth; maxim
appal	vb.	to fill with horror; shock or dismay
appeal	n.	the power to attract or interest
appease	vb.	to soothe or calm
appliance	n.	a machine or device
appreciate	vb.	to value highly
archaic	adj.	out of date
arena	n.	a platform or stage
aside	n.	1) any confidential statement spoken in undertones 2) a digression
aspiration	n.	strong desire to achieve something
assault	n.	a violent attack
assess	vb.	to estimate the value of something
assign	vb.	to give or allocate
atrocities	n.	acts of extreme cruelty

audit	n.	an inspection, correction and verification of business (accounts) by a qualified person (accountant)
austerity	n.	a reduced availability of luxuries and consumer goods e.g. *an austerity budget*
autonomy	n.	the right or state of self-government
avert	vb.	to prevent from happening
awash	adj.	full or flooded

B

bail out	vb.	(informal) to help (a person, organisation, etc) out of a predicament
ballad	n.	a narrative poem in short stanzas of popular origin, originally sung to a repeated tune
ballot	n.	the democratic practice of selecting a representative, or a course of action by submitting the options to a vote of all qualified persons
ban	vb.	to prohibit or forbid
barely	adv.	scarcely; only just
behaviour	n.	1) manner of conducting oneself 2) the action of a machine etc. under normal or specified circumstances
bemoan	vb.	to mourn or lament; deplore
benefit	n.	a payment or series of payments made by an institution to a person who is ill, unemployed etc.
benign	adj.	gentle or kind
berate	vb.	to scold harshly, criticize
Big Brother	n.	a person, organization etc. that exercises total dictatorial control (originally used in G, Orwell's *1984*)
binary	adj.	composed of two parts or dual
black	adj.	pessimistic or macabre
blame	n.	responsibility for something that is wrong
blank	adj.	showing no interest e.g. *a line of blank faces*
blunt	adj.	direct or straightforward
blunt	vb.	to make dull; to diminish the sensitivity or perception of
blunder	n.	a stupid mistake
bombard	vb.	to attack with vigour
boom	vb.	to prosper or cause to prosper vigorously and rapidly e.g. *business boomed*
boost	vb.	to encourage or improve
bowl over	vb.	(informal) to surprise
brand	n.	a trade name identifying a manufacturer or a product

brandish	vb.	to wave or flourish
bring to bear	vb.	to bring into operation or effect
brunt	n.	the main force or shock of a blow, attack etc. e.g. *bear the brunt of*
buffer	n.	a person or thing that lessens shock or protects from damaging impact, circumstances, etc.
burlesque	n.	an artistic work, esp. literary or dramatic, satirizing a subject by caricaturing it
bureaucracy	n.	any administration in which action is impeded by unnecessary official procedures

C

caesura	n.	1) (in classical prosody) a break between words within a metrical foot, usually in the third or fourth foot of the line 2) (in modern prosody) a pause, esp. for sense usually near the middle of a verse line
callousness	n.	insensitivity to other people's suffering
campaign	n.	a series of co-ordinated activities designed to achieve a social, political or commercial goal
caricature	n.	the exaggeration of characteristic traits for comic effect
cavalierly	adv.	in an offhand, condescending manner
charitable	adj.	kindly; tolerant or compassionate
chassis	n.	the steel frame, wheels, engine, and mechanical parts of a motor vehicle
choreography	n.	the composition of dance steps and sequences for ballet and stage dancing
circumscribe	vb.	to restrict within limits
clamour	vb.	to make a public demand; make a loud noise or outcry
clear as daylight	adj.	very clear
cloud	vb.	to make or become gloomy or depressed
coercion	n.	the application of force or pressure
cohesion	n.	the tendency to unite
collaborate	vb.	to work with others on a joint project
collusion	n.	conspiracy
come to terms	vb.	to accept
common ground	n.	an agreed basis for identifying issues in an argument
compatible	adj.	able to exist together harmoniously; reconcilable
component	n.	a part or ingredient
conciliatory	adj.	intended to bring together two conflicting things; intended to reconcile
confiscate	n.	to seize

congestion	n.	overcrowding
conglomeration	n.	mass
connote	vb.	to imply or suggest (associations or ideas) other than the literal meaning
consign to the trashcan	vb.	to throw away
constraint	n.	restraint; something that serves to constrain; restrictive condition
contaminate	vb.	to make impure or pollute
continuing education	n.	adult education
contravene	vb.	to break the law or to infringe (rules, laws etc)
convention	n.	the most widely accepted view of what is thought to be proper behaviour, good taste etc.
cop-out	vb.	(slang) to fail to assume responsibility or to commit oneself
copulation	n.	sexual intercourse
coupé	n.	a four-seater car with a fixed roof, a sloping back, and usually two doors
coy	adj.	shy; modest
crack	n.	an attempt e.g. *a crack at feminist solidarity*
cram	vb.	to fill to superfluity; to stuff
crèche	n.	a day nursery for very young children
credible	adj.	capable of being believed
creditor	n.	a person or commercial entreprise to whom money is owed
credulity	n.	tendency to believe
crippling	adj.	very damaging e.g. *crippling debts*
croak	vb.	(informal) to make a low, hoarse cry
cry off	vb.	(informal) to withdraw from or cancel (an agreement or arrangement)
curb	vb.	to control or restrain
cut off	vb.	to separate

D

data	n.	1) a series of observations or facts
		2) the information operated on by a computer programme
database	n.	systematized collection of data that can be accessed immediately and manipulated by a data-processing system for a specific purpose
divine right of kings	n.	the concept that the right to rule derives from God and that kings are answerable for their actions to God alone
debase	vb.	to lower in quality or to degrade
debtor	n.	a person or commercial enterprise that owes money

deception	n.	trickery or deceit
decry	vb.	to express open disapproval of, disparage
deem	vb.	to consider or judge
degenerate	vb.	to become worse or deteriorate
delinquency	n.	offence or misdeed committed by a young person
delude	vb.	to deceive or mislead
delusion	n.	mistaken opinion or belief
demise	n.	the death or end
demolish	vb.	to destroy
denigrate	vb.	to criticise, blacken or belittle
denote	vb.	to have as a literal or obvious meaning
deplorable	adj.	very bad
depress	vb.	to make gloomy, or lower in spirits
derisory	adj.	ridiculous
despoil	vb.	to rob or plunder
deteriorate	vb.	to become worse
devastate	vb.	to destroy or lay waste
devise	vb.	to work out or plan
devolution		
of power	n.	the transfer of authority
dire	adj.	urgent or disastrous
directive	n.	instruction or order
disadvantaged	adj.	socially or economically deprived or discriminated against
discourse	n.	ensemble of discursive practices including language
discrimination	n.	unfair treatment of a person, racial group, minority etc.
disenfranchise	vb.	to deprive (a person) of the right to vote
disgrace	n.	a shameful state of affairs
dismantling	n.	the taking apart or destruction
disparity	n.	inequality or difference, as in age, rank, wages etc.
dispassionate	adj.	objective or free of emotion
displace	vb.	to remove from the usual location
display	vb.	to show or make visible
dissension	n.	disagreement
dissociate	vb.	to detach or distance
diversity	n.	the state of being different or varied
divest	vb.	to take away from or deprive
doctrine	n.	a body of principles that is taught or advocated
donate	vb.	to give (money etc.) esp. to a charity
doomed	adj.	condemned to fail
doughty	adj.	bold, or resolute
drab	adj.	dull or shabby

drastic	adj.	extreme or severe
drift	n.	the meaning
duplicity	n.	deception

E

ebb	vb.	to fall back or decline
EC	n.	European Community
eccentric	adj.	not normal or unconventional
egalitarian	adj.	relating to the doctrine of the equality of humankind
electorate	n.	the body of all qualifed voters
eliminate	vb.	to remove, get rid of
elitism	n.	awareness of being one of a select group
embed	vb.	to fix firmly in a surrounding solid mass
emergence	n.	an appearance
empiricism	n.	the doctrine that all knowledge derives from experience
EMU	n.	European Monetary Union
enact	vb.	to represent or perform
encroach	vb.	to advance beyond the usual limits; intrude
engender	vb.	to produce or cause
enhance	vb.	to increase in quality, value; improve
enlightened	adj.	informed
ensemble	n.	the cast of a play other than the principals; supporting players
ensure	vb.	to make certain; guarantee
entail	vb.	to bring about; have as a necessary consequence
enthuse	vb.	to feel or show enthusiasm
epicentre	n.	the heart
epitomise	vb.	to illustrate or typify
eradicate	vb.	to stamp out or get rid of
erode	vb.	to eat or wear away; destroy
escapism	n.	the inclination to retreat from an unpleasant reality
ethnic	adj.	relating to a human group having racial, religious, linguistic, and certain other traits in common
ethos	n.	the distinctive attitudes of a culture
evolution	n.	a gradual change
exacerbate	vb.	to make more intense; aggravate
exceed	vb.	to go beyond the limit
excess	adj.	an amount that is too much or beyond the normal quantity
existentialism	n.	a modern philosophical movement stressing the importance of personal experience and responsibility
exorcise	vb.	to expel or get rid of evil spirits by prayers and religious rites
experiment	n.	a test or investigation

exploit	vb.	to take advantage of
extent	n.	1) an area or volume 2) scope
extract	n.	a passage from a larger text
extremism	n.	fanaticism or immoderate opinions and actions
extrovert	n.	a person concerned more with external reality than inner feelings

F

fallacious	adj.	wrong or erroneous
fanciful	adj.	imaginary
fancy	vb.	(informal) to like
farce	n.	a humorous play based on improbable situations
feature	vb.	to have prominence in a film or programme
federal	adj.	relating to any association of parties or groups that retain some autonomy
field	n.	an area of knowledge
first and foremost	adv.	before all else
fit	adj.	appropriate or suitable
flagrant	adj.	outrageous, glaring or enormous
flaw	n.	an imperfection
flexible	adj.	adaptable or variable e.g. *flexible working hours*
flourish	vb.	to thrive or prosper
fluctuate	vb.	to constantly change
focus	n.	a point upon which attention, activity etc. is directed or concentrated
focus	vb.	to direct attention
foresight	n.	the act of looking forward or insight into future problems
forlorn	adj.	miserable
formulate	vb.	to express in systematic terms
forte	n.	strong point; something at which a person excels
forthcoming	adj.	1) approaching in time 2) about to appear 3) available 4) welcoming, sociable
foster	vb.	to develop or promote
fraught	adj.	worrying
free trade	n.	international trade that is free of such government interference as import quotas, export subsidies etc.
freelance	n.	a self-employed person, esp. a writer or an artist who is hired to do specific assignments
frenzied	adj.	wild or frantic
fresco	n.	wall-painting using watercolours on plaster
frivolous	adj.	unworthy of serious treatment; unimportant
fuel	vb.	to nourish

fuss	n.	a complaint or objection

G

gadget	n.	1) any object that is interesting for its novelty
		2) small mechanical appliance
gazelle	n.	a graceful antelope
gem	n.	a person or thing held to be a perfect example; treasure e.g. *the hall is regarded as an architectural gem*
generate	vb.	to produce or create
get underway	vb.	to start
ghetto	n.	a densely populated slum area of a city inhabited by a socially and economically deprived minority
gingham	n.	a cotton fabric in a checked or striped design
go hand in hand	vb.	to go together
grapple	vb.	to come to grips with or confront
grimace	n.	an ugly or distorted facial expression
groom	vb.	to make or keep (clothes, appearance etc.) clean and tidy
grovel	vb.	to humble or abase oneself

H

habitat	n.	the place in which a person, group, class etc. is normally found
hand down	vb.	to leave to a later generation; bequeath
harass	vb.	to trouble or torment by continual attacks
harbour	vb.	to think secretly
harness	vb.	to control so as to employ the energy or potential power of
harsh	adj.	severe or cruel
have-nots	n.	the poor
hectic	adj.	characterized by extreme activity or excitement
hegemonism	n.	the tendency for one state to dominate another
hellbent	adj.	strongly or rashly determined
hemistich	n.	a half line of verse
high time	adj.	a time that is almost too late eg. *it's high time you mended this shelf*
highlight	n.	the most exciting part of an event or period of time
hold in high regard	vb.	to respect highly
hold dear	vb.	to value highly
hooligan	n.	a rough lawless young person
hospitable	adj.	welcoming
hostel	n.	a supervised lodging house
hula-hoop	n.	a light hoop that is whirled around the body by movements of the waist and hips

humdrum	adj.	ordinary or dull
hyper-inflation	n.	inflation that is very high
hypothesis	n.	a suggested explanation for a group of facts or phenomena

I

iamb	n.	a metrical foot consisting of two syllables, a short one followed by a long one
ideology	n.	a body of ideas that reflects the beliefs and interests of a nation, political system etc.
idiotic	adj.	foolish, senseless
illogical	adj.	senseless, unreasonable
illogicality	n.	something that is not logical
imbroglio	n.	confused situation
immanence	n.	existence or presence
impact	n.	the impression made by an idea, cultural movement etc.
impair	vb.	to reduce the quality of, damage
impart	vb.	to communicate, give
imperialism	n.	1) the policy or practice of extending a state's rule over other territories; 2) the extension of authority, influence by any person, country etc.
imperil	vb.	to place in danger, endanger
implausible	adj.	unlikely; provoking disbelief
implement	vb.	to put into action
impropriety	n.	an indecency, an improper act or use
impulse	n.	an instinctive drive or urge
inadequate	adj.	insufficient
incessant	adj.	continual
incite	vb.	to stir up, provoke to action
incitement	n.	a provocation, encouragement, stimulus
incompatible	adj.	conflicting or antagonistic
incomprehensible	adj.	incapable of being understood
inconceivable	adj.	incapable of being imagined, unthinkable
inculcate	vb.	to teach by forceful repetition or drill into
incur	vb.	to run into, encounter, bring upon oneself
inadvertently	adv.	unintentionally
index	vb.	to put in order, catalogue
indication	n.	a sign
indigenous	adj.	native
indispensable	adj.	absolutely necessary; essential
indulge	vb.	to take to excess, or wallow in

ineffective	adj.	useless, having no effect
inextricable	adj.	not able to be separated or disentangled
infallible	adj.	a person or thing that is incapable of error or failure
inflation	n.	a progressive increase in the general level of prices brought about by an expansion in demand or the money supply
infringe	vb.	to break or violate (a law, agreement, etc.)
ingrained	adj.	deep-rooted, fixed
inquisitorial	adj.	denoting criminal procedure in which one party is both prosecutor and judge
insight	n.	the ability to perceive clearly or deeply
insofar	adv.	to the extent
insubstantial	adj.	thin, slight, weak
integrate	vb.	to mix with an existing community
integration	n.	the act of combining to make a unified whole
intervene	vb.	to disturb or hinder a course of action
intimidate	vb.	to frighten or alarm
intrinsic	adj.	relating to the essential nature of a thing, inherent
intrusion	n.	an unwelcome visit
inverse	adj.	opposite, contrary
irony	n.	the humorous or mildly sarcastic use of words to imply the opposite of what they normally mean
issue	n.	subject or topic of discussion

J

jeopardy	n.	danger, risk, peril
job-centre	n.	government office concerned with advertising jobs
join ranks	vb.	to unite

K

keep an eye on	vb.	to watch with special attention
keep at bay	vb.	to keep at a distance e.g. *Yoga keeps arthritis at bay*
kept woman	n.	a woman maintained by a man as his mistress
key	adj.	of great importance
keyword	n.	a significant word
kid oneself	vb.	(informal) to deceive oneself

L

laissez-faire	n.	the doctrine of unrestricted freedom in commerce
lay bare	vb.	to reveal, expose
layman	n.	a person who does not have specialized or professional knowledge
leave of absence	n.	permission to be absent from a place of work

let off steam	vb.	(informal) to release pent-up energy, feelings etc.
liquidate	vb.	1) to terminate the operations of a firm/ompany 2) to kill
listed building	n.	a building officially recognised as having special historical or architectural interest and therefore protected from demolition or alteration
live up to	vb.	to fulfil (an expectation, obligation, etc.)
lobby	n.	a group of persons who attempt to influence legislators on behalf of a particular interest
loch	n.	a Scottish word for lake
long-winded	adj.	too long
lot	n.	destiny, fortune
ludic	adj.	relating to play
ludicrous	adj.	silly or absurd
lump	vb.	to consider as a single group

M

macho	adj.	(informal) conventionally masculine
magnate	n.	a person of power and rank
malicious	adj.	evil-minded
mandate	n.	contract (permission) to act in a certain manner; authority to govern
manipulate	vb.	to control or influence (something/somebody) cleverly or skilfully
manpower	n.	power supplied by men; labour force
massive	adj.	large
materiality	n.	material or physical nature
matter	n.	a thing, question, affair
maw	n.	the stomach of a ferocious animal
maxim	n.	a brief expression of a general truth
mercenary	adj.	influenced by greed or gain
metaphor	n.	a figure of speech in which a word or phrase is applied to an object or action that it does not literally denote in order to imply a resemblance, for example: *'he is a lion in battle'*.
metonymy	n.	the substitution of a word referring to an attribute for the thing that is meant, as for example the use 'the crown' to refer to a monarch
mews	n.	buildings originally used as stables but now converted into homes
mimetic	adj.	relating to an imitative representation of nature or human behaviour
mindless	adj.	stupid or careless
minimal	adj.	smallest possible
minimise	vb.	to reduce or estimate at the least possible degree or amount

miscarriage	n.	an act of mismanagement or failure e.g. *a miscarriage of justice*
monolingual	adj.	knowing only one language
moonlight	vb.	to earn money on the side
moron	n.	a foolish or stupid person
multilingual	adj.	able to speak more than two languages
multiplicity	n.	a large number or great variety
murky	adj.	gloomy, dark
musty	adj.	stale or mouldy
muzzle	vb	to prevent from being heard or noticed
mystify	adj.	to confuse or to make mysterious or obscure
mystique	n.	an aura of mystery or power that surrounds a person or thing

N

name-dropping	n.	the practice of referring frequently to famous or fashionable people esp. as though they were intimate friends
narcissistic	adj.	directed towards oneself
narcotics	n.	drugs
narrator	n.	the teller of a story
nation state	n.	an independent state inhabited by all the people of one nation only
naturalism	n.	a movement esp. in art and literature, advocating detailed realistic and factual description
negotiation	n.	a discussion intended to produce a settlement or agreement
nexus	n.	central link or strand
norm	n.	an established standard of behaviour shared by members of a social group
novel	n.	an extended work in prose, either fictitious or partly so, dealing with character, action, throught etc. esp. in a form of a story
novelty	n.	the quality of being new, fresh and interesting
nutrient	n.	any substance that is nourishing, good for one's health

O

obligation	n.	a duty or a moral or legal requirement
obsolete	adj.	unfashionable or out of use/outmoded
ode	n.	a lyric poem addressed to a particular subject, with lines of varying lengths and complex rhythms
offspring	n.	1) the result 2) the immediate descendant of a person
ombudsman	n.	an official who investigates citizens' complaints against the government or its servants
opt for	vb.	to choose, show preference for
opulent	adj.	wealthy, plentiful
overtly	adv.	openly; deliberately

P

painstaking	adv.	extremely careful
palliative	n.	something that relieves or alleviates without curing, such as a sedative drug
panorama	n.	extensive view, comprehensive survey
paradox	n.	self-contradictory proposition, contradiction
parasite	n.	a person who habitually lives at the expense of others
parody	n.	a musical, literary, or other composition that mimics the style of another composer, author, etc., in a humorous or satirical way
participate	vb.	to take part
pathological	adj.	relating to mental illness
PC	n.	personal computer
peculiar	adj.	strange, odd
pejorative	adj.	(of words etc.) having an unpleasant or disparaging association
peregrine	adj.	wandering
perpetrate	vb.	to be responsible for or perform
perpetuate	vb.	to cause to continue
persecute	vb.	to oppress, harass, or maltreat, esp. because of race, religion, etc.
perspective	n.	way of regarding situations, facts etc.
pervasive	adj.	extensive, widespread
pessimism	n.	the tendency to expect the worst and see the worst in all things
phenomena	n.	occurences or facts (singular: phenomenon)
philanthropic	adj.	showing concern for humanity, esp. by performing charitable actions
pinpoint	vb.	to identify, define
plastic surgery	n.	the branch of surgery concerned with the repair of missing, injured, or malformed tissues or parts
platitude	n.	trite, dull or obvious remark
plethora	n.	excess, overabundance
pompous	adj.	self-important
potential	adj.	possible but not actual
precarious	adj.	insecure
precipitate	vb.	to cause to happen sooner than expected
prejudice	n.	1) intolerance of or dislike for people of a specific race, religion 2) an opinion formed beforehand
preoccupied	adj.	busy, absorbed in something
prerogative	n.	exclusive privilege or right
prescriptive	adj.	making or giving rules
pressing	adj.	demanding immediate attention
presupposition	n.	something that is taken for granted or implied
pretext	n.	fictitious reason given in order to conceal the real one

prevalent	adj.	widespread or current
primarily	adv.	principally or chiefly
primary	adj.	relating to the education of children up to the age of 11
profile	n.	a short biographical sketch of a subject
prohibition	n.	the act of forbidding something
prolong	vb.	to lengthen or extend
propensity	n.	natural tendency
proportional representation	n.	representation of parties in an elective body in proportion to the votes they win
proposal	n.	suggestion
protection	n.	the imposition of duties or quotas on imports designed for protection of domestic industries against overseas competition
put together in the same basket	vb.	to consider of equal value

Q

quatrain	n.	a stanza or poem of four lines
quest	n.	a search, the act of looking for
quintessential	adj.	perfect; typical

R

rabble	n.	the common people (contemptuous)
racked	adj.	tortured
ramp	n.	a sloping floor or path, etc. that joins two surfaces at different levels
rank	n.	a line or row of people or things
rapprochement	n.	a resumption of friendly relations, esp. between two countries
rate	n.	pace e.g. *the rate of inflation*
reach	n.	number of listeners
ream	n.	a large quantity esp. of written matter
reap	vb.	to gain or get (something) as a reward for or result of some action
reckless	adj.	showing no regard for danger or consequences, thoughtless
reconcile	vb.	to make compatible, or harmonise
recoup	vb.	to regain or make good a loss
recruit	vb.	to obtain members; enlist
redundancy	n.	the condition of being dismissed from one's job or job-loss e.g. *mass redundancies are in the pipeline* 2) repetition of information
reel	vb.	to sway esp. under the shock, to stagger
register	n.	an official or formal list e.g. *unemployment register*
regress	vb.	to move in a backward direction

regulate	vb.	to control
rehabilitate	vb.	to help someone to readapt to society or a new job
relinquish	vb.	to give up, abandon
reluctant	adj.	unwilling, not eager
remedy	n.	anything that serves to put a fault to rights, improve conditions
remuneration	n.	pay
renounce	vb.	to give up (a claim or a right)
reprehensible	adj.	open to criticism; blameworthy
representative	adj.	relating to the political principle of representation of the people e.g. *representative government*
repress	vb.	to restrain or keep under control; to inhibit
reservation	n.	not accepting a complete idea or proposal
resort to	vb.	to use
restrict	vb.	to control or inhibit one's behaviour
retain	vb.	to keep
revel	vb.	to take pleasure or wallow
revert	vb.	to go back to a former practice, to return
revision	n.	rereading or rewriting
riot	n.	a disturbance made by an unruly crowd; tumult or uproar
root	n.	the source or origin
routine	n.	1) a set sequence of dance steps or exercises 2) set of habits
RSI	n.	repetitive strain injury (caused by computers)
rule out	vb.	to dismiss from consideration e.g. *he was ruled out of criminal inquiries*
run-of-the-mill	adj.	ordinary, average
running	n.	the functioning or operation

S

saddle	vb.	to burden, charge e.g. *the banks are saddled with bad debt*
sanction	vb.	to give authority; to permit
sarcasm	n.	a mocking language intended to convey scorn or insult
saturate	vb.	to fill
scapegoat	n.	a person made to bear the blame for others
scornful	adj.	contemptuous
scruple	n.	doubt or hesitation as to what is morally right
scrutiny	n.	close examination
sectarian	adj.	limited; restricted to a particular group
select	adj.	limited as to membership or entry e.g. *a select gathering*
self-determination	n.	the right of a nation or people to determine its own form of government without influence from outside

self-regulatory	adj.	controlling oneself from within an organisation, making sure something conforms to rules
sell-by date	n.	a stamped date on a food product
seminal	adj.	very important
senile	adj.	mentally or physically weak on account of old age
sequel	n.	a novel, play etc. that continues a previously related story
shareholder	n.	the owner of one or more shares in a company
short-lived	adj.	lasting only for a short time
short-sighted	adj.	lacking foresight
shortcoming	n.	weakness, defect
shrink	vb.	to withdraw or stop back; to feel great reluctance
shun	vb.	to avoid deliberately; keep away from
simper	vb.	to smile in a silly self-conscious way
simplistic	adj.	naive
skein	n.	a length of yarn etc. wound in a long coil
sketch	n.	a brief, informal piece of writing
slavish	adj.	unoriginal, imitative
slovenliness	n.	neglect of personal appearance
sluggish	adj.	slow-moving, inactive
slump	adj.	an economic depression
slumped	adj.	collapsed
smirk	n.	smile expressing scorn
smutty	adj.	obscene, dirty, rude
soap	n.	1) erialised drama usually dealing with domestic themes and characterized by sentimentality broadcast on radio or television 2) a substance used for washing
sole	adj.	only
sonnet	n.	a verse form consisting of fourteen lines, usually three quatrains and a couplet
sound	adj.	complete, thorough
sovereignty	n.	an independent state
spark	vb.	to trigger, start or excite
spectrum	n.	any range or scale, as of capabilities, emotions, or moods
spoonerism	n.	the transposition of the initial consonants or consonant clusters or a pair of words, often resulting in an amusing meaning, e.g. *'hush my brat' for 'brush my hat'*
stagger	vb.	to place in alternating time period (to prevent confusion or congestion)
stagnant	adj.	not growing or developing e.g. *a stagnant economy*
staid	adj.	of a settled, sedate and steady character
stalwart	adj.	dependable, solid

stance	n.	a general, emotional or intellectual attitude e.g. *he adopted a neutral stance*
standard	adj.	normal, generally accepted
standardize	vb.	to make everything on the same pattern
stanza	n.	a verse of a poem
staple	adj.	principle, main
stem from	vb.	to originate
stifle	vb.	to smother or suppress; crush or stamp out
stilted	adj.	unnatural, pedantic
stingy	adj.	unwilling to spend or give
stop at nothing	vb.	to do anything (without any scruples)
stop-gap	n.	a temporary substitute for something else
streamline	vb.	to make more efficient esp. by simplifying
strive	vb.	to fight, contend
suffuse	vb.	to spread over or flood over, to pervade
suit	vb.	to be fit or appropriate for
summation	n.	the act of determining a sum
supply	n.	1) an amount available for use; stock 2) food, equipment, etc. needed for a campaign or trip
support	n.	the means of maintenance of a family, person etc.
support	vb.	to provide the necessities of life for (a family, person, etc.)
supposition	n.	a supposed theory
supremacy	n.	supreme or highest power; domination
swallow	vb.	to believe innocently, to be taken in
swell the ranks	vb.	to increase the numbers
synchronise	vb.	to occur at the same time or in unison
synonymous	adj.	similar, equivalent

T

taboo	adj.	forbidden or disapproved of
tactful	adj.	careful, diplomatic, skilful
tag along	vb.	to follow, trail behind
take into account	vb.	to take into consideration, allow for
tax burden	n.	the amount of taxes to be paid
technocracy	n.	a theory or system of society according to which government is controlled by scientists, engineers, and other experts
temping agency	n.	an agency that provides temporary employment
tendencious	adj.	showing a bias
tender	n.	a formal offer to supply specified goods or services at a stated cost or rate
tercet	n.	a group of three lines of verse

testament	n.	1) proof 2) will
testimony	n.	evidence or a declaration of truth
third-rate	adj.	mediocre or inferior
thrive	vb.	to do well, prosper
tight-lipped	adj.	reticent, secretive or taciturn
tighten one's belt	adj.	to economize
tomboy	n.	a girl who acts or dresses in a boyish way, liking rough outdoor activities
totalitarian state	n.	a dictatorial one-party state that regulates every realm of life
trafficker	n.	a person who engages in illegal trade
transaction	n.	a business deal or negotiation
transcendence	n.	state of being free from limitations of consciousness
transformation	n.	a change
transgress	vb.	to go beyond or overstep (a limit)
transition	n.	a passage from one state to another
trauma	n.	a powerful shock that may have long-lasting effects
trepidation	n.	fear or anxiety
tress	n.	a lock of hair
trimming	n.	an extra piece used to decorate or complete
trot	vb.	to go at a steady, brisk pace
trundle	vb.	to move heavily
turbulent	adj.	wild
turn of phrase	n.	1) a saying 2) a distinctive form or style
turpitude	n.	corruption, evil; depravity
U		
underclass	n.	the poor and disadvantaged
underestimate	vb.	to fail to appreciate
undervalue	vb.	to value at too low a level or price
underwrite	vb.	to support (in a financial deal)
uneasy	adj.	disturbing, disquieting
unequivocal	adj.	absolutely clear, not ambiguous
uneven	adj.	1) not level or flat; 2) not fairly matched; 3) variable
unmask	vb.	to appear or cause to appear in true character
unravel	vb.	to untie
untainted	adj.	not affected or not contaminated
untenable	adj.	incapable of being defended or maintained
update	vb.	to bring up to date
upheaval	n.	a sudden disturbance
urge	vb.	to plead, press

Utopian	adj.	relating to a perfect or ideal existence

V

vacancy	n.	an unoccupied post or office
venture	vb.	to dare
validity	n.	the truth
veneer	n.	a superficial appearance esp. one that is pleasing e.g. *a veneer of scientific truth*
vested interest	n.	a strong personal concern in a state of affairs, etc., usually resulting in private gain
vice	n.	a failing, defect
violation	n.	the mistreatment, abuse
virtuosity	n.	exceptional skill
visualise	vb.	to form a mental image of something
vivisection	n.	the practice of performing experiments on living animals, involving cutting into or dissecting the body
void	n.	an empty space or area

W

wane	vb.	to decrease or weaken
waste	n.	garbage, rubbish
well-being	n.	the condition of being contented or healthy
Wellington	n.	1) Duke (Arthur 1769-1852) 2) Aeroplace of World War II 3) Wellingtons (plural) rubber boots
white-collar	adj.	relating to non-manual and usually salaried workers employed in professional and clerical occupations
will power	n.	the ability to control oneself and determine one's actions
win	vb.	to gain or procure e.g. *to win new markets*
witness	vb.	to experience directly
woo	vb.	to gain the support of someone or to convince
wreak havoc	vb.	to cause chaos

X

xenophobia	n.	a hatred or fear of foreigners or strangers or of their politics or culture

Y

yen	n.	the standard monetary unit of Japan (formerly) divided into 100 sen
yoga	n.	exercises and postures designed to promote physical and spiritual well-being

Z

zeal	n.	enthusiastic devotion
zest	n.	keen excitement or enjoyment e.g.: *a zest for living*

Bibliography

All the books listed are paperbacks available in most bookshops.

Should you wish to order any of these books direct from the publishers, *you will find the relevant address at the end of this bibliography.*

Although some books cover several fields of interest we have classified them under the following headings:

POLITICS, ECONOMICS, SOCIETY, PHILOSOPHY, CULTURE, THE MEDIA, ASPECTS OF ENGLISH POLITICS AND SOCIETY.

We hope that this selection of books will enable you to acquire facts and information, and assist you in becoming more familiar with certain issues and topics, the art of debate, and successful essay writing.

POLITICS

Attfield, R. and Wilkins, B., eds., *International Justice and the Third World*, Routledge, 1992

Cammack, P. Pool, D. and Tordoff, W., *Third World Politics. A Comparative Introduction*, Macmillan, 1988

Lively, J. and Reeve, A., eds., *Modern Political Theory from Hobbes to Marx: Key Debates*, Routledge, 1988

Macridis, R., *Contemporary Political Ideologies,* Harper Collins, 1992

Marcuse, H., *One-Dimensional Man*, Routledge, 1991

Nicoll, W. and Salmon, T., *Understanding the European Communities*, Philip Allan, 1990

Randall, V., *Women and Politics: An International Perspective,* Macmillan, 1991

Smith, G., *Politics in Western Europe*, Gower, 1990

Waldron, J., *The Law*, Routledge, 1990

Weale, A., *The New Politics of Pollution*, Manchester University Press, 1992

ECONOMICS

Allen, M., *The Times Guide to International Finance*, Times Books, 1991

Brett, E.A., *The World Economy Since the War: The Politics of Uneven Development*, Macmillan, 1986

Dunnett, A., *Understanding the Economy*, Longman, 1992

George, S., *The Debt Boomerang*, Pluto Press, 1992

Swann, D., *The Economics of the Common Market*, Penguin, 1992

Vickerman, R.W., *The Single European Market*, Harvester Wheatsheaf, 1992

Whitehead, G., *Economics*, "Made Simple Books", Butterworth-Heinemann, 1992

SOCIETY

Blackburn, C., *Poverty and Health*, Open University Press, 1991

Bryson, L., *Welfare and the State*, Macmillan, 1992

Clover, J., *Causing Death and Saving Lives*, Penguin, 1990

Clutterbuck, R., *Terrorism, Drugs and Crimes in Europe after 1992*, Routledge, 1990

Donnelly, J., *Universal Human Rights in Theory and Practice*, Cornell University Press, 1989

Fitzpatrick, P., *The Mythology of Modern Law*, Routledge, 1992

Heidensohn, F., *Crime and Society*, Macmillan, 1989

Jackson B., *Poverty and the Planet*, Penguin, 1990

Jean, F., *Populations in Danger - Médecins Sans Frontières*, John Libbey, 1992

Miles, R., *Racism*, Open University Press, 1991

Morris, A and Nott, S., *Working Women and The Law: Equality and Discrimination in Theory and Practice*, Routledge, 1991

Williams, R., *Keywords. A Vocabulary of Culture and Society*, Fontana Press, 1988

PHILOSOPHY

Castoriadis, C., *Philosophy, Politics, Autonomy,* Oxford University Press, 1991

Freeden, M., *Rights,* Open University Press, 1991

Hollis, M., *Invitation to Philosophy,* Basil Blackwell, 1992

Kearney, R., *Modern Movements in European Philosophy: Phenomenology, Critical Theory, Structuralism*, Manchester University Press, 1987

Raphael, D. D., *Moral Philosophy*, Oxford University Press, 1990

Sayers, S. and Osborne, P., eds., *Socialism, Feminism and Philosophy*, Routledge, 1990

Schrödinger, E., *What is Life?*, Cambridge University Press, 1992

Skinner, Q., ed., *The Return of Grand Theory in the Human Sciences*, Cambridge University Press, 1990

CULTURE

Barthes, R., *Camera Lucida*, (translated by Richard Howard) Flamingo, 1984

Barthes, R., *Image, Music, Text* (translated by Stephen Heath) Fontana Press, 1977

Barthes, R., *The Pleasure of the Text*, (translated by Richard Miller) Basil Blackwell, 1975

Belsey, C., *Critical Practice*, Routledge, 1980

Bourdieu, P., *The Field of Cultural Production* (Edited and introduced by Randal Johnson) , Polity Press, 1993

Bowlby, R., *Still Crazy After all these Years: Women, Writing and Psychoanalysis*, Routledge, 1992

Branigan, E., *Narrative Comprehension and Film*, Routledge, 1992

Cohen, S. and Shires, L., *Telling Stories: A Theoretical Analysis of Narrative Fiction*, Routledge, 1988

Con Davis, R. and Schleifer R., *Criticism and Culture*, Longman, 1991

Connor, S., *Postmodernist Culture: An Introduction to Theories of the Contemporary*, Basil Blackwell, 1992

De Beauvoir, S., *The Second Sex*, (translated by H M Parsley) Picador, 1988

Doane, M., *Femmes Fatales: Feminism, Film Studies and Psychoanalysis*, Routledge, 1992

Eagleton, T., *The Ideology of the Aesthetic*, Blackwell, 1990

Marvick, A., *Culture in Britain since 1945*, Basil Blackwell, 1991

Sartre, J-P., *What is Literature?* (translated by Bernard Frechtman), Methuen, 1986

Tagg, J., *Grounds of Dispute, Art History, Cultural Politics and the Discursive Field*, Macmillan, 1992

Thompson, M., Ellis, R., Wildavsky, A., *Cultural Theory*, Westview Press, 1990

Williams, R., *Culture and Society*, The Hogarth Press, 1992

Williams, R., *The Politics of Modernism. Against the New Conformists*, Verso, 1993

THE MEDIA

Cook, G., *Discourse of Advertising*, Routledge, 1992

Curran, J. and Curewitch, M., *Mass Media and Society*, Edward Arnold, 1991

Fowler, R., *Language in the News: Discourse and Ideology in the Press*, Routledge, 1991

Gunter, B. and McAleer, J., *Children and Television: The One Eyed Monster?*, Routledge, 1990

McCracken, E., *Decoding Women's Magazines: From Mademoiselle to Ms*, Macmillan, 1992

Skovmand, M. and Schroder, K., eds., *Media Cultures: Reappraising Transnational Cultures*, Routledge, 1992

Taylor, P., *War and the Media: Propaganda and Persuasion in the Gulf War*, Manchester University Press, 1992

Van Dijk, T., *Racism and the Press*, Routledge, 1991

ASPECTS OF ENGLISH POLITICS AND SOCIETY

Holmes, C., *A Tolerant Country? Immigrants, Refugees and Minorities in Britain*, Colin Holmes (Faber & Faber), 1991

Jones, B., (ed.) *Politics UK*, Philip Allan, 1991

McIlroy, J., *Trade Unions in Britain Today*, Manchester University Press, 1988

Oakland, J., *British Civilization: An Introduction*, Routledge, 1991

Rosher, B. and Teff, H., *Law and Society in England*, Routledge, 1980

List of Publishers

Basil Blackwell Ltd
108 Cowley Road
Oxford   OX4 1JF

Butterworth-Heinemann
Linacre House
Jordan Hill
Oxford   OX2 8DP

Cambridge University Press
The Edinburgh Building
Cambridge   CB2 2RU

Cornell University Press
124 Roberts Place
Ithaca
NY 14850
USA

Edward Arnold a division of
Hodder and Stoughton
Mill Road
Dunton Green
Sevenoaks
Kent TN13 2YA

Faber & Faber Ltd
3 Queen Square
London   WC1N 3AU

Flamingo an Imprint of
Harper Collins Publishers
77 - 85 Fulham Palace Road
London W6 8JB

Fontana Press
Harper Collins
77 - 85 Fulham Palace Road
London   W6 8JB

Harvester Wheatsheaf
Campus 400
Maylands Avenue
Hemel Hempstead
Hertfordshire HP2 7EZ

John Libbey
13 Smiths Yard
Summerley Street
London   SW18 4HR

Longman
Longman House
Burnt Mill
Harlow, Essex CM19 5AA

Macmillan Distribution Ltd
Houndmills
Basingstoke
Hants, RG21 2XS

Manchester University Press
Oxford Road
Manchester   M13 9PL

Methuen and Co. Ltd
11 New Fetter Lane
London EC4P 4EE

Open University Press
Celtic Court
22 Ballmoor
Buckinghamshire
MK18 1XW

Oxford University Press
Walton Street
Oxford   OX2 6DP

Penguin
27 Wrights Lane
London   WE8 5TZ

Philip Allan
66 Wood Lane End
Hemel Hempstead
Hertfordshire   HP2 4RG

Picador
Pan Books Ltd
Cavaye Place
London   SW10 9PG

Pluto Press
345 Archway Road
London   N6 5AA

Polity Press
65 Bridge Street
Cambridge   CB2 1UR

Routledge   ITPS
Cheriton House
North Way
Andover
Hants   SP10 5BE

The Hogarth Press
an   Imprint   of   Chatto   and
Windus
20 Vauxhall Bridge Road
London   SW1V 2SA

Verso
6 Meard Street
London   W1V 3HR

Westview Press Inc.
5500 Central Avenue
Boulder Colorado 80301 USA

Index

A

Aborigines 30
accuracy 5,11-5,23,200-2
acrostic poem.................... 125
advanced societies 175
adventure........................ 279
advertisements 9-11,15-7
advertising 11,23,187-90
aesthetics 102
Africa 44-5,271-2
aggression....................... 14
Aids 35,91,253-4
animal rights 146
Apple Macintosh............... 125
architecture 31
Aristotle........................ 240
art.......49-50,51-2,53-4,94,104,
        107-9,125-6,133,172-4,
        250-1,275-6
articles ON

see also exercises ON, vocabulary and
topics

    Aborigines 30
    advertising 23
    Aids 35,253,254
    animal rights................ 146
    art............ 49-50,51-2,53-4,
    125-6,159-61,275-6,279-80,
                            281-2
    Bellow, S.................. 281-2
    business........41-2,43,117-8,
                    265-6,269,270
    Carey, J. 49-50
    cars 39,259
    censorship....................256
    Church............... 145,147-8
    cinema 159-61,279-80
    community care 20-1
    computers ..27-8,122-3,125-6
    democracy................. 271-2

depression 17
disabled, the................. 46
discrimination 24,145,
                    147-8,265-5
ecology 19
economy................120,124
education............ 117-8,143
environment 19,48,122-3,259
ethnic minorities.....22,267-8
Europe.............. 114,117-8,
                    170-2,275-6
family........................ 162
fund-raising.................. 47
government 27-8
health 26,32,263
heritage....................... 31
holidays 166-7
homelessness 20-1
homosexuals................ 145
housework 261-2
human rights ... 27-8,143,145
imperialism 19
inequality 267-8
industry 120,122-3,263,
                            269
Jehovah's Witnesses 144
justice............... 33-4,273-4
language............ 41-2,147-8
literature ... 49-50,51-2,53-4,
            125-6,275-6,281-2
marketing 265-6
media 22,114,256,257
modernism................49-50
Morrison T 53-4
music 191
naturalism 51-2
poetry.......................125-6
privatisation 260
racism 22,30,53-4,258
religion 146,147-8
royal family 39

sexual habits 40
single mothers 264-5
soaps 22
supermarkets 265-6
technology 122-3
television 22,113-4,257
theatre...............51-2,275-6
theology 147-8
Third World 19,271-2
Third World Debt,the ... 44-5
underclass 37-8
unemployment........... 163-4
urban violence....... 37-8,258
women 24,261-2,264-5,
273-4,277-8
work 24,261-2,263
yoga 32
Asians........................ 267-8
autonomy........................ 198
assessment, essay.................5

B

Bach, J.B....................... 174
banks...................44-5,176-7
battered women 273
beliefs........................... 228
Bellow, S...................... 281-2
Berkoff, S...................... 51-2
blacks 22,37
black children 267-8
body of principles 224
books........................... 196
book characteristics 2
book objectives 2,3,7-8
boredom 150
broking firms.................. 269
bureaucracy.................... 175
business 17,41-2,43,70,95,
117-9,265-6,269
buttoned fly-jeans............... 23

C

Carey, J. 49-50
cars............................ 39,259
censorship 187-90,256
childcare 278
Church 145-8
cinema............. 157-61,279-80
code of practice................ 256
Coleridge, S.T................... 82
communication skills 5
communication, social........ 220
communicative skills 2
community care........... 20-1,33
competition 180-188
computers.... 13-27,122-3,125-6
conciliatory................139,141
conclusion 237,240-1
conflict 186
constructions 4
consumers 264-5
consumer art 172
consumption.................... 173
contemporary literature 51-4,
125-6,208-9,275-6,281-2
context........................... 57
corruption..................... 272
courage...................... 127
Coward R. 277
credit cards 270
credulity....................... 186
crime................. 37-8,154,257
culture.................9,172-4,248

D

De Quincey...................... 82
debate.............................3,6
debating
see also under essay writing strategies
and techniques
debt, the Third World...... 44-5,
176-7

democracy 271-2
depression....................... 17
destabilisation 260
disabled, the.................... 46
discrimination 25,145,147-8,253
discussing

see under exercises ON, exercises IN, topics ON

divine rights 232
doctrinaire 225
doctrines..................... 223-7
dogma........................... 224
domestic violence.............. 273
dreams 104-5
drugs........................... 82-5

E

ecology 19,112-3
economy................... 120,124
education........89-91,117-8,143
electoral systems............ 182-3
employment................. 163-5
Empson, W. 209
English, proficiency in 191
Enlightenment................. 186
environment 19,29,48,95,
                              122-3,259
essay assessment............... 5-6
essay titles 56,59,60,92,
                         94-110,172
essay titles ON
    art........................ 250-1
    culture 248
    language and literature249-50
    mass communication ... 248-9
    society 245-7
essay titles, interpreting...... 222
essay titles, types of 102

essay writing strategies
    & techniques 6-8,55-6,
    60-2,76,92-4,96,98-9,103-4,
    109-10,111-2,137-8,139,157,
    178,215-6,219-20,221-3,
    236-7,242-3,244,251-52
    agreeing/disagreeing 63,11-3,
                         127-8, 134-6, 140
    analysing essay titles
        as messages........... 98-102
    assessing attitudes.... 139-40,
                              146,172-4
    drawing up a
        questionnaire 133-4
    distinguishing private
        and public statements .57-60
    finding a solution to
        a problem 74-5
    identifying varieties of . 57-9,
                              209,210-12
    speech/registers.......... 212-5
    interpreting charts....... 191-6
    memorising words 206-8
    picking up ideas from 210-12,
                                 212-5
    an oral text raising
        questions on essay
        titles........ 94-8,105,128-31
    rating key social issues.....76
    reaching a compromise 141-2,
                                 139-40
    saying the opposite... 3,202-3
    selecting useful turns
        of phrase 215-9
    translating into your
        mother tongue..........59-60
    using data 242
    writing accurately in
        English 201-2,203-5
    writing a conclusion .. 237-41
    writing an introduction.221-9
    writing meaningful
        sentences 203

Exercises ON

see also under articles, topics

advertising 11,23,187-90
aggression.................... 14
Aids 35,91
animal rights................ 146
art...............50,52,54,104,
107-9,126,172-4
banks..................... 176-7
business.......... 17,42,43,119
Church............ 144,145,148
cinema 158,159
communication 57-60
community care 21,33
computers 13-4,123,126
courage 127
culture 172-4
depression................... 18
disabled, the 46
discrimination 23,25,35
drug abuse 82-5
economy... 20,121,124,176-7
education 89-91,119,143
employment.............. 164-5
environment 20,29,48
ethnic issues 12-3,23,30
Europe..... 115,119,169,172,
204-5
family 162-3
fashion 65-7
freedom..................... 149
fund-raising.................. 47
government 28,151
health 26,32,123
heritage..................... 31
holidays................... 166-9
homelessness 21
human rights......... 28,143-5
humour 212-5
industry............ 26,119,121
inherited wealth........... 63-4
international terrorism..... 91
justice................... 34,228

language 148
leisure 200
literature 50,52,54,104,
126,133,205-9,241-2
literature and society 209
living and telling 132
malice....................... 152
media 23,115-6,193,197
modernism...................50
music 60,191,193
nationalism 198
nuclear power............. 87-9
poetry................ 126,201-2
pollution...................20,29
poverty 38,45,112-3
privacy 28
racism 23,30
radio 191-3
reading 129-31
reading habits 197
royal family 39
social equality............77-80
society today 70-2,172-5
sport 67-8
strikes......................235-6
television................ 23,115
theatre 52
thinking 177-8
Third World, the...........45
Third World debt, the 176-77
theology 148
tourism 72-4
trade unions 175,210-12,
235-6
town and country.....199-200
tragedy 199
underclass....................38
unemployment 80-2,178-9
urban violence 38,85-7
virtue 128-9
women.................25,68-70
work 25
world hunger................91

324

world stability 136-7
existentialism 209

F

fairy-tale 23,279
families, one-parent 162-3
fashion 65-7
feminist 277
femininity 279
finding arguments 54
flexibility 9,139-40
foreign languages 95
free trade 180-1
freedom 149,179
freedom of information 181-2
frescos 186
fund-raising 47

G

gadget 174
gastronomy 174
general essay 5
generous people 94
gingham 279
God 147
Goldsmith, O. 34
government 27-8,151
graded objectives 1

H

happiness 241
have-nots 37,175
Hawkins, S. 240
health 26,32,263
Heimat 2 160
heritage 31
Herriot, E. 223
history 186-7
HIV 253
holidays 166-7

homelessness 20-1,264
homosexuals 145
housework 261-2
housing 264
human nature 152-6
human rights . 27-8,143,145,235
Hume, D. 153
humour 212-5
hunting 146
Huxley, J. 240
hyperpoem 125-6

I

ideas 4-5,221-2,224-5
imbroglio 176
immigrants 267-8
immortal soul 146
imperialism 19
imports 181
income statistics 268
indifference 103
industry 120,263,269
inequality 178,267-8
inherited wealth* 63-4
insider traders 269
integration 204
international financial
    system 176
international monetary
    system 183,185
international terrorism 129
interpreting essay titles 222
introduction 221
introduction, examples of .. 233-4
introduction, purpose of 231
investment 180
Irish, the 213-4
issues 76,230

J

Japanese disease 263

jargon 229
Jehovah's Witnesses 144
job-centres 165
jokes 213-4
justice 33-4,96,228-34,273-4

K

Kafka, F. 182
Karoshi 263
key issues 230,238
keywords, ...223-4,226,230-1
King, Martin Luther 79

L

Landowski, E. 241-2
language 41-2,147-8
language and literature ...249-50
law 228-30
legal aid 229
leisure............................ 200
literature............... 49-54,105,
          125-6,133,249-50, 275-6
living and storytelling 132
Lodge, D. 136,186
Lowry, M. 218

M

Maastricht treaty....... 170-1,204
macho........................ 23,261
magazines 195
malice............................ 152
Mamet, D. 161
market economy 173
market forces.................. 179
marketing 265-6
Marx, K. 151
masculinity..................... 279
media 22-3,114-6,192-3,
          240-1,248-9,256,257
men and housework........... 262

message 98-110
metaphor 209
metonymy....................... 209
middle classes................172-4
Mill, J.S. 232
modernism....................49-50
money 176-7
Morrison, T. 53-4
motherhood...................277-8
multinational companies 184
multiracial societies.......... 12-3
music 60-2,191

N

naivety........................... 128
national identity 198
nationalism 198
naturalism...................... 51-2
negative attitudes................35
neo-Nazi 258
New History, the.............. 187
New Man, the................. 261
New Novel, the................ 187
North-Sea divide, the.......237-8
novel, the 186-7
nuclear power................. 87-9
naturalism..................... 51-2

O

obsolete 184
offices 122-3
one-parent families..........162-3
optimism 208
ordinary girl.................... 280
ordinary people................ 186
organising thoughts 137
organising your ideas......... 157
Orwell, G. 182
Oz, land of 279
Oz, Wizard of 279-80

P

painters 188
pandemic 253
parody 208
part-time work 179
personality 138
pessimism 208
philosopher 152
plan.............. 137,157,227,230
playrights 275-6
playschool...................... 261
poetry 125-6,201-2
police 37-8
politics...................... 94,151
popular capitalism............. 175
popular culture................. 173
popular novel.................. 186
post-yuppy 275
posters 188
poverty 44-5,95,112-3
press 256
privacy.................... 27-8,256
privatisation 175,260
privileges...................... 173
products 188
proficiency in English 191
proletariat..................... 174
proportional representation .. 183
public and private
   statements 57-8
pupil's charter................. 143
purpose of an introduction... 231

Q

questionnaire 63,133
quintessential 279

R

racism........ 12-3,22-3,53-4,258
radio 192-3
random thoughts....... 222,238-9
reading 129-31,194,197
recession 37-8
recycling 259
redundant 188
Reitz, E. 160
religion.... 128-9,144,146,147-8
rents........................... 264
representative democracy.... 182
responsibility.................. 179
right to strike, the...........235-6
right to work, the 179
riots 37-8
role-playing......... 2,4-5,7,8,62,
   64,82,87-8,93,98,112-5,128-9,
   139,140,143,146,149,158,
   169,172,212,215
rouble area.................... 184
royal family 39

S

sexual bias.................... 147
sexual habits....................40
science......................... 241
Scots, the 214
shareholders 175
Shaw, G.B..................... 216
simple statements............. 136
single majority ballot......... 182
single mothers 264-5
smoking 255
soaps...........................22
social communications 220
social inequality ... 77-80,97,189
society 70-2,103,172-5,
   177-8,245-7
Socrates ... see mission statement
sport 67-8
stability....................... 136
stereotyped roles 189
stock market.................. 124
stress..........................122-3

strikes........................ 235-6
style............................ 111
supermarkets 265-6
superstition 151
surveillance.................... 265
syntax........................... 220

T

Tavernier, B.................... 161
taxation...................... 179-80
techniques
see under essay writing strategies and techniques
technology 122-3
television............22,113-6,257
temping agencies 165
temporary workers 165
terrorism 91
text, use of................... 251-2
theatre 51-2,275-6
theology 147-8,186
thinking...................... 106-7
Third World, the ... 19-20,271-2
Third World debt, the 44-5
thought and action.. 107-8,177-8
thoughts, organising 137
time 187
topics ON
see also exercises ON, articles ON and vocabulary
    advertising 187-90
    aggression.................... 14
    art.......... 94,104,107-9,133,
                 172-4,250-1
    art and science 240
    banks..................... 176-7
    boredom.................... 150
    business...................... 95
    censorship............... 187-90
    cinema 157-9
    contemporary
        literature................ 208-9

courage..................... 127
culture............... 172-4,248
doctrines 223-7
dollar 183-4
dream and action 104-5
drugs....................... 82-5
ecology....................112-3
economy...........176-7,183-4
education..................89-91
electoral systems 182-3
employment 163-5
equality before
    the law.................. 228-34
essay writing 242-3
fashion...................... 65-7
free trade................ 180-81
freedom 149
freedom of
    information 181-2
foreign languages............95
generosity....................94
government.................. 151
happiness.................... 241
human nature.............152-6
humour 212-5
indifference...............103-4
inherited wealth........... 63-4
language................. 249-50
language and
    literature 249-50
literature 105,133,206-9,
             241-2,249-50
living and telling 132
multiracial societies...... 12-3
music 60-2
naivety..................... 128
North sea divide,the 237-8
novel and history........186-7
nuclear power............. 87-9
our age 70-2
poetry....................184-6
politics........................94
pollution.....................95

poverty 95,112-3
proportional
    representation 183
reading........... 129-31,241-2
reading habits 194-7
religion 128-9
right to strike............ 235-6
science 241
social inequality..... 77-80,97
society 70-2,177-8,245-7
sport........................ 67-8
strikes.................... 235-6
taxation 179-80
Third World debt, the . 176-7
thought and action..... 106-7,
                         177-8
tourism 72-4,95
town and country 199-200
trade unions.....210-12,235-6
unemployment........... 178-9
urban violence............. 85-7
virtue.................... 128-9
wealth.................... 112-3
women in society 68-70
world hunger 112-3
world today............. 112-3
world stability........... 136-7
tourism 72-4,96
town and country 199-200
trade unions......143,175,210-12
tragedy........................199
transmission 253-4
truth 186
Turner, W. M................. 174
turns of phrase, useful..... 215-9
types of essay titles 103

useful expressions................ 5
useful turns of phrase 215-9
Utrillo, M.......................82

vacancies...................... 164
vaccine 253
violence 37-8
virtue 128-9
vocabulary............8,111-2,220
vocabulary ON

    see also under articles, topics and
exercises ON

    aggression 14
    art 206-7
    computers.................. 13-4
    history.....................206-7
    justice.....................206-7
    literature 206-7,208
    marketing 206-7
    modern societies.......... 12-3
    nationalism 198
    politics....................206-7
    racism 12-3
    tragedy 199
    virtue 128-9
voting patterns 182
vulnerability................... 253

wages 24-5
wealth 112-3
women in society............68-70
workaholic...................... 263
working hours 263
world hunger.................112-3
world today...................112-3
world stability 136-7
writing an essay

    see also under essay writing strategies &
techniques, exercises IN and vocabulary ON

U

underclass...................... 38
unemployment........80-2,163-5,
                        178-9
urban violence.....37-8,85-7,258

V

W

drawing up a plan 157, 164-5,167,169-90,226,227-8

finding ideas 5-6,8,76,92, 94,152,222,224-5,251-2

organising your ideas .. 5,6,7, 60-2,63,64-75,111-138, 139-42,152-6,187-90, 223,226,228,241-3,252

students' reactions to 4-5, 152-6

understanding the titles .. 3,6, 56-60,92,94-110,222-4, 228,236,244

useful expressions and turns of phrase 191, 197-8,215-9

writing a conclusion 237-41,243

writing an introduction....... 221,233-4

X

xenophobic attacks 258

Y

yellow brick road 280

yen 185

yoga.............................32

Young, J. 38

yuppy 275